Dedicated to children

and young people everywhere.

You are the future of the human race;

take it further.

The Laughter of God

Selected Writings of John Roland Stahl

The Evanescent Press

Leggett, California

WWW.TREE.ORG

SECOND EDITION

reprinted MMXVIII

ISBN: 978-0-945303-24-4

Contents

The Emerald Tablet

by Hermes Trismegistus

As Above,

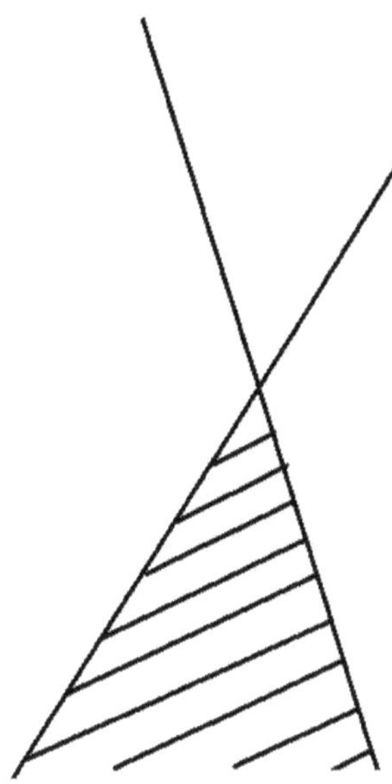

So Below.

Introduction

The *Emerald Tablet* of Hermes is the original source of Hermetic Philosophy and Alchemy. According to one legend, the text was originally carved by Hermes on tablets of emerald and placed in the King's Chamber of the Great Pyramid of Cheops. While such stories are probably apocryphal, the document has been well known to scholars and occult philosophers since at least the 10th century.

Although the language of the original version is in doubt, it is through the Latin version reproduced here (along with our own English translation), that the Emerald Tablet rose to pre-eminent fame as a Key to the primary Mysteries of Nature.

Outwardly a recipe for the preparation of the Philosopher's Stone which may be used for the transmutation of the baser metals into Gold (the Sun refers to Gold in Alchemical terminology), it has always been clear to the Masters of the Alchemical Art that the process described was of far more universal application ~ in fact, it is nothing less than the Process of Change itself through which (in the words of Aristotle):

Nature strives towards Perfection.

SOLVE ET COAGVLA

Tabvla Smaragdina

Vervm, ſine Mendacio, certvm et veriſſimvm:

Qvod eſt Inferivs eſt ſicvt qvod eſt Svperivs, et qvod eſt Svperivs eſt ſicvt qvod eſt Inferivs, ad perpetranda Miracvla Rei Vnivs. Et ſicvt res omnes fvervnt ab Vno, meditatione vnivs, ſic Omnes Res natæ ab hac vna Re, adaptatione.

Pater eivs eſt Sol. Mater eivs eſt Lvna. Portavit illvd Ventvs in Ventre ſvo. Nvtrix eivs Terra eſt. Pater omnis Teleſmi totivs Mvndi eſt hic. Virtvs eivs integra eſt ſi verſa fverit in Terram. Separabis Terram ab Igne, ſvbtile ab ſpiſſo, ſvaviter, magno cvm ingenio.

Aſcendit a Terra in Cœlvm, itervmqve deſcendit in Terram, et recipit Vim ſvperiorvm et inferiorvm. Sic habebis Gloriam totivs Mvndi. Ideo fvgiet a te omnis Obſcvritas. Hæc eſt totivs Fortitvdinis Fortitvdo fortis, qvia vincet Omnem rem ſvbtilem, Omnemqve Solidam penetrabit.

Sic Mvndvs creatvs eſt. Hinc ervnt Adaptationes Mirabiles, qvarvm Modvs eſt hic. Itaqve vocatvs ſvm Hermes Triſmegiſtvs, habens tres partes Philoſophiæ totivs Mvndi.

Completvm eſt qvod dixi de Operatione Solis.

The Emerald Tablet

Truly, without Deceit, certainly and abſolutely ~

That which is Below correſponds to that which is Above, and that which is Above correſponds to that which is Below, in the accompliſhment of the Miracle of One Thing. And juſt as all things have come from One, through the Mediation of One, ſo all things follow from this One Thing in the ſame way.

Its Father is the Sun. Its Mother is the Moon. The Wind has carried it in his Belly. Its Nouriſhment is the Earth. It is the Father of every completed Thing in the whole World. Its Strength is intact if it is turned towards the Earth. Separate the Earth by Fire: the fine from the groſs, gently, and with great ſkill.

It riſes from Earth to Heaven, and then it deſcends again to the Earth, and receives Power from Above and from Below. Thus you will have the Glory of the whole World. All Obſcurity will be clear to you. This is the ſtrong Power of all Power becauſe it overcomes everything fine and penetrates everything ſolid.

In this way was the World created. From this there will be amazing Applications, becauſe this is the Pattern. Therefore am I called Thrice Greateſt Hermes, having the three parts of the Wiſdom of the whole World.

Herein have I completely explained the Operation of the Sun.

Hermetic Alchemy

by John Roland Stahl

The writings of the Hermetic Alchemists have exercised a fascination upon the imaginations of scholars and casual seekers alike for centuries. On the one hand, the Hermetic writings have a well deserved reputation for being among the most obscure writings ever penned. But on the other hand, they have also managed to retain their status as some of the most authoritative original sources of ancient wisdom.

Hermetic Alchemy was one of the first branches of esoteric knowledge that I studied in my youth, drawn thither by my studies of Carl Jung, whose researches on Alchemy absorbed his attention throughout most of his later years. Something about the Alchemical symbols spoke to me very powerfully; I understood Jung's thesis that throughout the history of Alchemy, these symbols have welled up from the souls of sensitive people all over the earth, taken from the same ultimate source ~ the "collective unconscious" in the words of Jung.

Alchemy is Change. The Process of Change is the ultimate "Atom" of the ancient Greeks, the original building block of the Cosmos. All of the symbols of Alchemy emphasize the aspect of Change: the transmutation of the baser metals into Gold through a process of *Solve et Coagula,*

Separatio et Coniunctio ("disintegrate" and "unite;" "separate" and "join"). Alchemy is the "spagyric art," from Greek words meaning "to tear apart" and "to bring together."

Whenever I run across some path for personal growth that seems to suggest that the seeker need only sit on a shelf, meditate on his navel, and suddenly find himself rising ever upward on a linear path towards perfect clarity or Nirvana, I feel all the more strongly how much more power there is in the Alchemical symbols. (I should suggest here an appropriate way to study alchemical texts or any expressed idea of philosophy ~ rather than reading with your blue pencil, deciding what is right or wrong, it is better to try to figure out what true idea the author is trying to convey with his sometimes limited or misleading words. In the case of an exclusive emphasis on the journey inward, for example, the student must supply for himself the complementary ideas which are necessary for the true illumination of wisdom.)

Since the earliest times, Alchemists have been interested in applying their Hermetic wisdom towards the perfecting of the body and soul of Man ~ the quest for Gold being left to the "puffers." For the Alchemist, the first stage of the *Great Work* is the *Nigredo*, the stage of Blackness, disintegration, chaos, where the material (metal, the soul of Man, or what have you) is reduced to the *prima materia* or formless original stuff, before it can proceed to the second stage, the *Albedo* (whiteness), where the material may be unified once again. The Alchemical process is circular, alternating between *Solve* and *Coagula* on its path towards perfection.

Originally, "Alexandrian Alchemy" had as its purpose the transmutation of the baser metals into Gold. Although this goal was quickly superseded by the loftier notions of the Alchemical Adepts, it is instructive to review the original understanding of the old *Masters of Fire.* Aristotle laid the groundwork with his famous dictum: *Nature strives towards Perfection.* This was an article of faith that defined for proponents of the ancient wisdom the source of the whole underlying pattern of order in the cosmos.

Next, it is necessary to understand that metals were considered to be alive in some sense, and already undergoing a very slow process of gradual evolutionary growth towards perfection. That is, the most primitive form of metal was considered to be Lead (Saturn). If left in the earth on its own, it would eventually evolve its way towards Tin (Jupiter). Centuries later it would grow to become Iron (Mars), followed by Copper (Venus), Quicksilver (Mercury), Silver (the Moon), and finally, at the end of a very long road, it would achieve the ultimate realization of Perfection: Gold (the Sun). This was already happening on its own; nothing at all needed to be done ~ if you had sufficient patience. Now the Alchemist comes along and decides to speed up the natural process: the Art of the Alchemist replaces the Time of Nature.

So Alchemy is not black magic. The Alchemist thought that, by diligent searching into the ways of Nature, he might be able to imitate the natural process in his laboratories in order to realize the perfection of gold in his own lifetime, instead of waiting centuries for the same thing to happen more slowly. So, from the point of view of Hermetic philosophy, it is a matter of no consequence that the ancients were laboring under mistaken ideas about the nature of metals.

The Four Elements of Fire, Water, Air, and Earth (established by Aristotle) illustrate the four cardinal points of change, of which the four Seasons are the most common analogy. Since the process is circular, we can not really speak of first, but, to start with a new beginning, we start with Fire ("Young Yang" to students of the *I Ching*), corresponding to Spring. This is the stage of "Active Concentration." At a pivotal point, the energy suddenly changes to "Active Expansion," Air, Summer ("Old Yang"): COAGULA. The next change is very gradual, as both the activity and the expansion peter out, being followed by "Passive Contraction," Water, Autumn ("Young Yin"). This accelerates until there is a sudden change at the point where the energy turns to "Passive Expansion," Earth, Winter ("Old Yin"): SOLVE. The next change is very gradual, as the active yang energy re-asserts itself in a fresh "Active Concentration."

The most famous theory of the composition of the metals held that all metals were some sort of compound ("marriage") of Sulphur and Mercury (the King and the Queen, the Sun and the Moon, the Fixed and the Volatile, the Tiger and the Dragon, etc.). Then, along about the sixteenth century, Paracelsus, a famous Swiss Alchemist and Physician (the real father of holistic medicine) introduced Salt as a third essential ingredient in the work. Paracelsus was one of the most stunning Alchemical writers of all time. His ideas must have been rubbed fresh from the "collective unconscious" because they were immediately absorbed into the dogma of orthodox Alchemy.

The esoteric significance of the number three has impressed occult philosophers since time immemorial. The Sulphur and Mercury theory expressed the polarity of Yang and Yin, but the introduction of Salt elevated the theory to the heights of classic occult metaphysics.

The same fundamental ideas keep turning up in one's readings, but it is not all the same idea. There are many expressions for the most primary ideas of occult philosophy, but the numbers of mathematics suggest the most logical catalog of primary mysteries. According to this idea (dating from Pythagoras), the number "One" expresses the highest mystery, about which nothing more can be said. (Wittgenstein: "Whatever can be said at all can be said clearly; whereof one cannot speak, thereon must one be silent.") The number "Two" represents a mystery that can be spoken of: it is the Distinction between undifferentiated primal Unity expressed as Yang and Yin, Expansion and Contraction, Solve et Coagula, etc. But it is the number "Three" which suggests the point of perspective which separates the two complimentary illusions that are the consequence of every distinction.

Does this make any sense yet? Let me present one of my favorite analogies to occult metaphysics: the origin of the Cosmos *ex nihilo* as a consequence of God laughing at His original Joke: the Distinction between Zero and Infinity. First, I quote from the beginning of the *Tao Te Ching* by Lao Tzu (D. C. Lau translation):

"The Way that can be spoken of is not the constant Way; the Name that can be named is not the constant Name. The nameless was the beginning of Heaven and Earth; the named was the mother of the myriad creatures. Hence always rid yourself of desires in order to observe its Secrets, but always allow yourself to have desires in order to observe its Manifestations. These two are the same, but diverge in Name as they issue forth. Being the same, they are called Mysteries. Mystery upon Mystery, the gateway of the manifold secrets."

In order to understand how the Universe was created, it is necessary to have an understanding of the fundamental nature of Reality. We start with the Perfection of God, at rest, at a Point at the Center. The whole concept is meaningless, of course, until it is contrasted with the concept of Error, or movement away from the Center. This corresponds with old notions of the Devil as distance from God, moving away from the Perfection at the Center. Now, in order to maintain the existence of any deviation from the Center of Perfection, an alternate and complimentary deviation in another direction must be simultaneously sustained. There it is in a nutshell, the whole secret to the existence of the Manifest Cosmos as a Knot in the Æther composed of an intricate Field of Vibration of opposing concepts which, taken altogether suggests the illusion of our visible world. All of the energy of the Cosmos taken together adds up to Zero (or Infinity).

Zero and *Infinity* are examples of a Distinction created out of an undifferentiated sameness through the process of applying divergent names. Zero and Infinity both represent absolute states which can not even be imagined precisely, since they are beyond the consciousness of finite man. They seem to represent two different concepts only because we can only conceive of them at all by means of a process of movement between them. We can imagine a very large sphere which we expand mentally until our impoverished imagination fails us; likewise, we can imagine a dot vanishing towards nothing. But at the approach to the limit in each case, the last to go is nothing but location: the point where the dot is vanishing, or the center of the sphere which is trying to become all-encompassing. So there is the Joke:

you establish two Names which are really the same thing at the Limit, but then by alternating between them you set up a Field of Vibration which presents the Illusion of finite Manifestation ("the Gateway of the manifold Secrets")! Hilarious. So when God made this Joke, the vibration alternating between *Zero* and *Infinity* was the *Laughter of God* which created the finite Universe.

The most famous original source of Hermetic Alchemy is the *Emerald Tablet* of Hermes Trismegistus. While there are lots of writings attributed to "Hermes," there is little agreement about the actual authorship of any of these writings. However, the author of the *Emerald Tablet*, whoever he may have been, is the Hermes who has given his name to "Hermetic Philosophy." The basic Hermetic axiom is expressed there: *As Above, So Below.* This line has more than one meaning. In the first place, it suggests that the laws of the Cosmos may be found mirrored in Man: as the Macrocosm, so the Microcosm. But many other ideas are linked by the doctrine of correspondence. For example, there is a plane of pure energy, magnetism, or electrical field "above" that corresponds to the physical body of Man "below." Even Plato voiced a similar idea: the Form of the Good (for example) exists "above" in correspondence to some physical reality of some good thing "below." We might go on: Astrology posits the movements of the Heavenly bodies to exert corresponding influences on earthly events.

Likewise, Sympathetic Magic is the art of establishing associative correspondence between objects not demonstrably connected (as in Tarot cards or Voodoo dolls).

"Alchemy" is usually understood as the Western Alchemical tradition which may have come from the Arabs of the Middle East and reached its highest development in the famous European Alchemists, but it is very interesting to notice that a parallel alchemical tradition has flourished in China with no perceivable connection to the Western Alchemical tradition, but which has symbols that are strikingly familiar. In *The Secret of the Golden Flower*, for example, there is described a process of evolution towards perfection featuring a "circulation of the light" that is practically a translation of the Emerald Tablet (from the Emerald Tablet: "It rises from Earth to Heaven, and then it descends again to the Earth, and receives Power from Above and from Below.") But this is, finally, not really surprising. I quote from another Chinese philosopher, Ko Ch'ang:

> *. . . it may be objected that this method (Taoist Yoga) is practically the same as that of the Zen Buddhists. To this I reply that under Heaven there are no two ways, and the wise are ever of the same heart.*

§

Patterns of Illusion and Change

by

John Roland Stahl

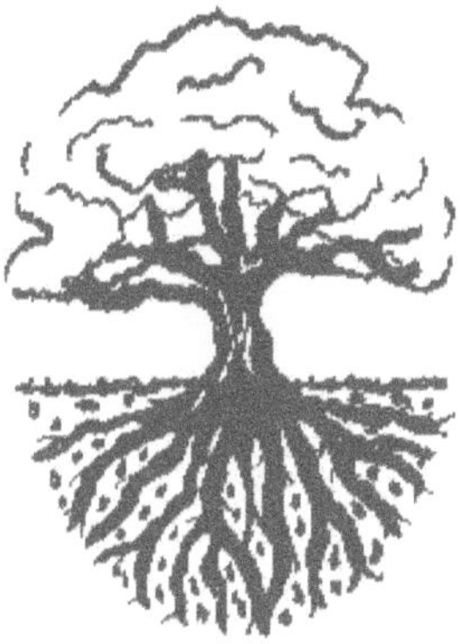

First published in 1984
THE EVANESCENT PRESS
Laytonville, California

Second Edition

THE EVANESCENT PRESS
Leggett, California

www.tree.org
tree@tree.org

Ever ſince the earlieſt times, philoſophers have been ſearching for the underlying patterns of order that ſuſtain our world. Theſe efforts have reſulted in a great many ſyſtems of ſymbolic expreſſion purporting to illuminate the various myſteries of reality and life. Careful inſpection of theſe different ſyſtems reveals that many of them are baſed on remarkably ſimilar fundamentals. The numbers of mathematics, for example, have been almoſt univerſally regarded as indiſpenſable keys to an underſtanding of the primary myſteries.

The Tree of Life *from the Hebrew* Kabbalah *and the* I Ching *of Chineſe philoſophy are two of the moſt remarkable ſyſtems of analogy baſed upon numbers. A clear underſtanding of theſe ſyſtems will provide a powerful calculus whereby all of the complexities of contemporary life may be clearly underſtood by analogy. Symbols from Hermetic alchemy, aſtrology, and other ſources are uſed throughout for the purpoſes of compariſon becauſe of their colorful effect and ingenious application. They provide a vivid contraſt to the ſtarkly abſtract ſyſtems of the* I Ching *and the* Tree of Life.

Once the viſion has begun to clarify, the next ſtep is to participate in the unfolding of the infinite univerſe by a more conſcious awareneſs of the conſequences of our actions. The ſame calculus which allows us paſſively to underſtand the intricate patterns of the movement of life allows us as well to influence the evolution of thoſe ſame fields of energy at any level through the agency of the Philoſophers' Stone at any one of the Points of Change. Once the fundamentals are underſtood, the benefits of application and analogy will quickly follow.

We preſent an arrangement of the Tree of Life *which divides it into four parts, correſponding to the* Tetragrammaton, *the Hebrew name of God* (Yod-He-Vau-He). YHVH, *the four letters of the name of God, have long been conſidered to conceal Keys to the higheſt underſtanding of the ultimate myſteries of the coſmos, ſhowing the evolutionary progreſſion from God to Man, although the knowledge of their meaning is ſaid to have been loſt. The firſt letter* (Yod; Kether *on the* Tree of Life) *repreſents the* First Arcanum, *or Myſtery. Since this* arcanum *refers to the moſt primary myſtery, efforts to define it are inevitably eluſive. It has to do with Original Infinity (or Zero). The beſt way to underſtand this point is by contraſt with all that follows.*

> The way that can be spoken of
> Is not the constant way;
> The name that can be named
> Is not the constant name.
> The nameless was the beginning of Heaven and Earth;
> The named was the mother of the myriad creatures.
> Hence always rid yourselves of desires
> In order to observe its secrets;
> But always allow yourself to have desires
> In order to observe its manifestations.
> These two are the same
> But diverge in name as they issue forth.
> Being the same they are called mysteries,
> Mystery upon mystery ~
> The gateway of the manifold secrets.
>
> ~ *Lao Tzu*, Tao Te Ching
> *(D. C. Lau tranſlation)*

The Second Arcanum *repreſents the primordial Diſtinction which cauſes the previouſly undifferentiated Coſmos to ſplit apart and come into being. This manifeſtation of a viſible Coſmos is the Field of Vibration which has come into being as a conſequence of the Diſtinction. The operation of this myſtery provides the creative aſpect for every idea or microcoſm. Common ſymbols for this myſtery are Heaven and Earth, Light and Dark, Creative and Receptive, Active and Paſſive, Order and Chaos, Life and Death.*

In the I Ching, *the energy which causes this Diſtinction* (SOLVE *in the ſymboliſm of Hermetic Alchemy) is called* Yang (—). *This* Yang *may alſo be viewed on another level as being itſelf compoſed of the diſtinction between the Creative and the Receptive. On the* Tree of Life, *this level of* yang *is* Chokmah *(the Sun) while* yin *is* Binah *(the Moon). Together they form the ſecond part of the name of God:* He.

The Third Arcanum *(the letter* Vau *of the name of God;* COAGULA; Yin - -) *contains the unifying principle of the initial* arcanum (Yod; *the Original) added to the Diſtinction of the* Second Arcanum *to create a field of perſpective unifying the oppoſite elements together. The rhythm of the vibration ſet up between them flows through the Philoſophers' Stone as the focus of attention between Subject and Object through the preſent Moment, the infinite turning point of the proceſs of change.*

On the Tree of Life, Chesed *and* Geburah *are balanced by* Tiphereth. *(We include the Indian terms* Rajas, Tamas, *and* Satva *for compariſon.)*

The Fourth Arcanum *(the fourth letter of the name of God: the ſecond* He) *moves beyond the pure abſtraction of the firſt three* arcana *into the Illuſions of Manifeſtation. The four ſpheres on the Tree of Life which apply to this poſition* (Netzach, Hod, Yesod, *and* Malkuth) *repreſent the four elements ~ Fire, Water, Air, and Earth ~ of Hermetic Alchemy. Theſe four cardinal points repreſent the whole realm of Manifeſtation and Illuſion. In the* I Ching, *theſe four elements are called (in the ſame ſequence and with the ſame meaning)* Young Yang (⚎), Young Yin (⚍), Old Yang (⚌), *and* Old Yin (⚏).

To further clarify this progreſſion of primary ideas, compare the analogies of Pythagoras to the firſt four numbers: One: a point; Two: a line; Three: a plane (triangle); and Four: a ſolid (pyramid). In terms of the dimenſions of phyſics, the point is dimenſion zero. A line extends as the firſt dimenſion. A plane triangle has two dimenſions, and a ſolid has three dimenſions. The fourth dimenſion of phyſics, time, is what we call Arcanum Five: *Change. This progreſſion of ideas continues out at different levels of perſpective towards infinity. However, it is very uſeful to ſee the ſimilarity in character of each of the odd numbered myſteries in contraſt with another kind of idea for the even numbers. The terms which beſt expreſs this contraſt are* Coagula *for the odd numbers, and* Solve *for the even numbers.*

§

•

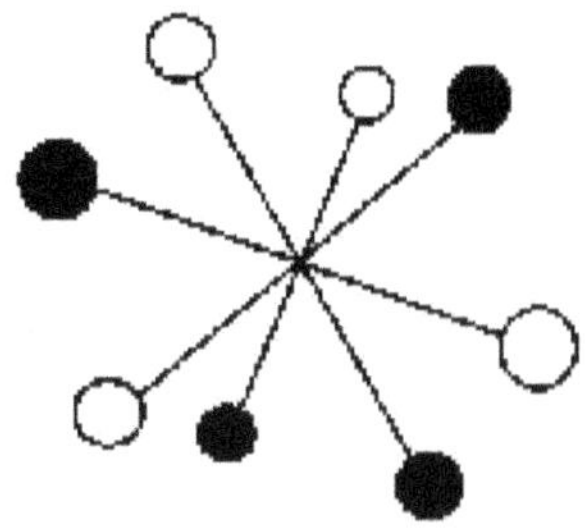

— —	——
Yin	Yang
Passive	Active
Contraction	Expansion
Apollo	Dionysus
Reality	Illusion
Inertia	Novelty
Clarity	Confusion
COAGULA	SOLVE

COAGULA

Yin

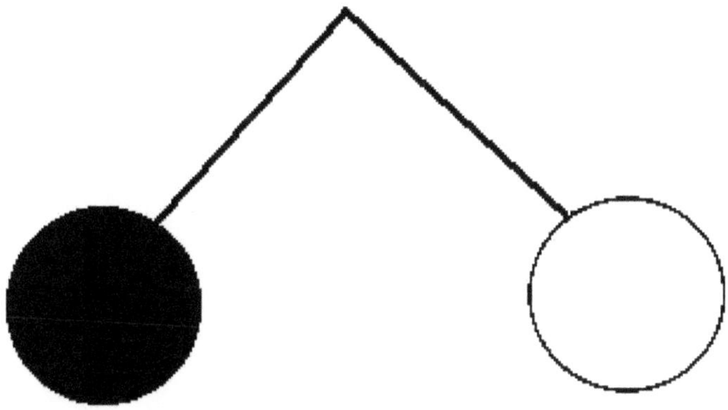

Yang

SOLVE

"From Tao there comes One.

From One there come Two.

From Two there comes Three.

From Three there come all things."

~ *Lao Tzu*

Yesod ↓
Wands
Air ↑
Old Yang

———
———

Hod ↓
Cups
Water ↓
Young Yin

———
— —

Netzach ↑
Swords
Fire ↑
Young Yang

— —
———

Malkuth ↑
Pentacles
Earth ↓
Old Yin

— —
— —

Yod **Arcanum I.**

He **Arcanum II.**

SOLVE

Vau **Arcanum III.**

COAGULA

He **Arcanum IV.**

Manifestation

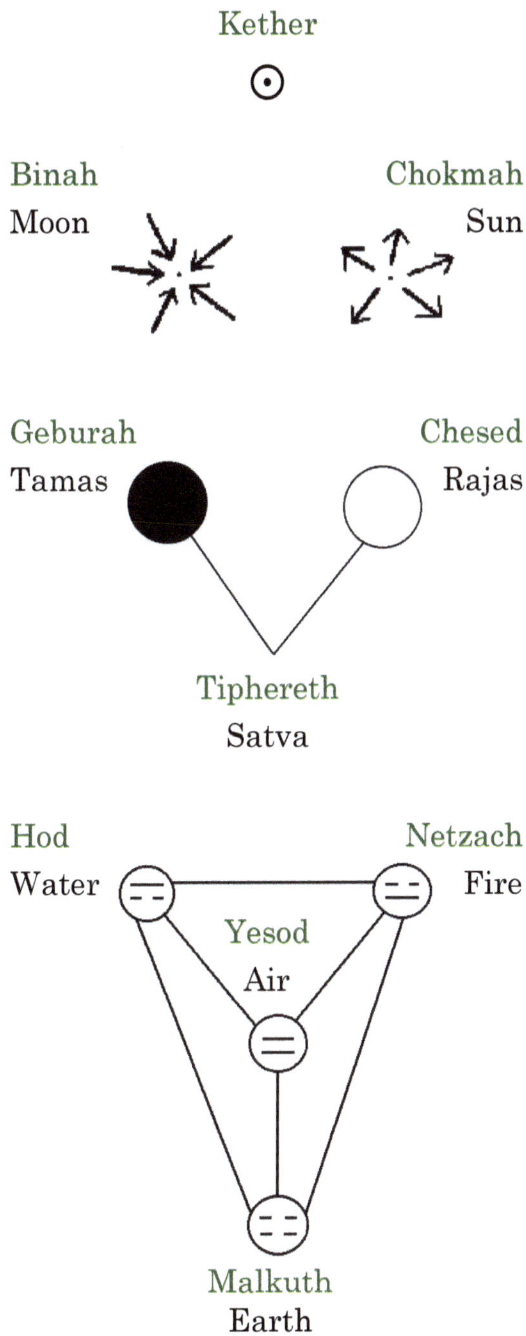

As Above,

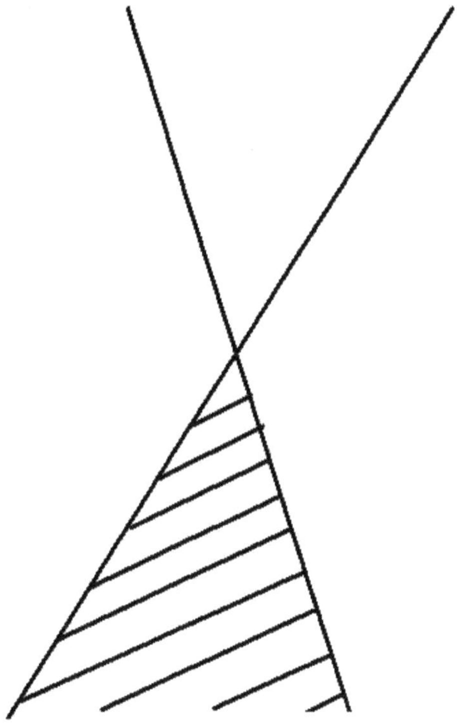

So Below.

Arcanum V.

Change

Passive
Copper
Venus
Gentle
Wind, Wood
Sun

Coagula
Gold
Sun
Creative
Heaven
Ch'ien

Peace
Silver
Moon
Abysmal
Water
K'an

Light
Tin
Jupiter
Joyous
Lake
Tui

Conflict
Quicksilver
Mercury
Clinging
Fire
Li

Heavy
Lead
Saturn
Keeping still
Mountain
Kên

Active
Iron
Mars
Arousing
Thunder
Chên

Solve
Prima Materia
Earth
Receptive
Earth
K'un

The colored diagram illustrates every arcanum. *The point in the center represents the* First Arcanum, *the Point of Origin. The same point, from a different level of perspective, represents each of the odd numbered* arcana (COAGULA)*: Three ~ the Point of Balance; Five ~ the Point of Change, etc. The rest of the diagram represents the even numbered* arcana (SOLVE)*: Two, the original Distinction, is clearly seen above and below the central point of balance (Light and Dark, Creative and Receptive, Heaven and Earth, etc.).*

The four elements of the Fourth Arcanum *are also clear:* Young Yang *(Fire, Spring, Active Contraction) begins out of the Chaos of Black* (K'un, ☷) *with the aggressive Red energy of new life* (Chên, ☳). *This continues, intensifying and concentrating its energy in Orange* (Li, ☲). *Suddenly a Change takes place and the energy "turns inside out" and begins to expand* (Old Yang, *Air, Summer, Active Expansion) upward through Yellow* (Tui, ☱)*, and finally to White* (Ch'ien, ☰)*, the height of integration and order. At this point, another Change takes place and the energy begins to contract again* (Young Yin, *Water, Autumn, Passive Contraction). This energy falls through Green* (Sun, ☴) *to Blue* (K'an, ☵). *At this point, another Change occurs as the energy falls through the balance point again on its way down to* Old Yin *(Earth, Winter, Passive Expansion), through Violet* (Kên, ☶) *and back again to Black* (K'un, ☷).

The eight Primary Trigrams of the I Ching *may be more particularly defined by assigning a precise meaning to each of the lines. The specific interpretation of each Trigram (or Hexagram ~ the traditional six lines) is a very creative matter which depends upon the particular purpoſes of each analogy. The following abſtract patterns may be more creatively interpreted whenever they are uſed to repreſent real ſituations.*

According to traditional uſage, the bottom line of each Trigram repreſents the Subject and the top line repreſents the Object of the analogy. Yang *lines may be defined as Active,* Yin *lines as Paſſive. The center line may be taken to indicate the value of the conjunction, with* Yang *taken as poſitive, and* Yin *as negative. The directions of energy of each line may be variouſly interpreted due to the principle of* enantiodromia *where each energy reverſes to it's oppoſite at each extreme poſition. However, any conſiſtent uſage will reveal the ſame patterns. From theſe definitions, it is an eaſy matter to prepare a ſimple catalog of the eight Primary Trigrams:*

The firſt Trigram of the ſequence is Chên, ☳, *Thunder, the Arouſing. Here, the Subject is the ſource of an energy of diſtinction from the paſſive Object. This repreſents the birth of a new idea or microcoſm: an Ego diſtinct from the whole. It is active and aggreſſive. Baſically, it is the aſſertion of diſtinction and independence from the paſſive Earth* (K'un, ☷) *which produced it. It is repreſented in other ſymbols by the color Red, the planet Mars, and the metal Iron.*

The ſecond Trigram is Li, ☲, *Fire, the Clinging. Here, the Subject is in conflict with an Object. The interpretations of this arrangement range from warfare, where each tries to overcome the other, to tenſion, energy, games, or ſocial activity. The color is Orange, the planet Mercury, and the metal Quickſilver.*

The next Trigram is Tui, ☱, *the Lake, the Joyous. The ſolid center line indicates a change of ſtate where the energy of the Subject ſeeks union with the paſſive Object. The color is Yellow, the planet Jupiter, and the metal Tin.*

At the extremity of the Subject's Yang *energy is the Trigram* Ch'ien, ☰, *Heaven, the Creative. It repreſents the attainment and perfection of balance and order which completes the ſyntheſis into unity,* COAGULA. *It is the White light (the union of all light), and it is the Sun and Gold.*

The following Trigram, Sun, ☴, *Wind, Wood, the Gentle, repreſents the beginning of the path of the paſſive Subject as the* Yin *phaſe of the cycle begins the downward movement towards* SOLVE. *In this caſe, it is the activity of the Object which maintains the integration with the paſſive Subject. The color is Green, the planet Venus, and the metal Copper.*

The next Trigram, K'an, ☵, *Water, the Abyſmal, repreſents the laſt ſtage of harmony. Both ſubject and Object are paſſive, and the integration of the two is maintained by inertia alone. The color is Blue, the planet the Moon, and the metal Silver.*

The next Trigram is Kên, ☶, *the Mountain, Keeping Still. The broken center line indicates that the ſeparation has been made, the Object rejecting the Subject. The color is Violet, the planet Saturn, and the metal Lead.*

At the end of the cycle is the point of complete liberation of finite Manifeſtation into Eternity repreſented by the Trigram K'un, ☷, *Earth, the Receptive. This is the empty blackneſs of infinite night, cold, quiet, and ſtill: the chaos of randomneſs, the complete* SOLVE *where not one ſtone is left upon another. The abſence of light is Black; the planet is the Earth, and the metal is the* Prima Materia *of the Alchemiſts to which it was conſidered neceſſary to reduce all metals before they could be improved or perfected (tranſmuted).*

Of courſe the proceſs is endleſs, as it is preciſely the infinite potential of the Solve *from which a new point of* Coagula *may make an appearance into Manifeſtation.*

If the eight primary Trigrams offer a view of eight poſſible arrangements of primary energy (Fixed Field Illuſions), the ſixty-four Hexagrams ſuggeſt all poſſible conjunctions of thoſe eight patterns. There are a great variety of poſſible ways to correlate the lines of the I Ching *to analogous ſituations in the outer world, but according to traditional uſage, the upper Trigram refers to that which is "above, without, or in front," and the lower Trigram refers to that which is "below, within, or behind." For example, the analogy may be made that the upper Trigram refer to the external or viſible aſpect of a ſituation, while the lower Trigram refer to an internal (occult) aſpect of the ſame ſituation.*

Changing lines modify each Hexagram according to the ſignificance of their poſition. A changing line (Old Yang *or* Old Yin) *is conſidered to be unſtable and liable to reverſe its direction. Every time a line reaches its Limit, a Change occurs and the Wheel of Manifeſtation rolls on to a new poſition. (Both poſſibilities of every changing line ſhould be conſidered when preparing an* I Ching *analogy.)*

Complex as they are, the ſixty-four Hexagrams of the I Ching *ſtill compriſe a ſtarkly limited world, yet it is a true microcoſm, repreſenting all of the patterns with equal clarity. There are many other repreſentations of theſe primary patterns of energy, ſuch as the game of Cheſs which beautifully illuminates the Trigram* Li, *Conflict. Starting with the Separation into Black and White, each game of cheſs is a claſſic battle of* Yang *and* Yin *~ the Irreſiſtible Force (White, with the firſt move, ſhould always be able to win) againſt the Immovable Object (Black, which reſponds, and ſhould always be able to force a Draw, or better, if White ſhould make a miſtake).*

But ſince the Macrocoſm is infinite, and the unchanging Tao ineffable, particular perſpectives are only poſſible at the expenſe of perfect clarity. That is, we may ſee "Reality" as a ſucceſſion of Fixed Field Illuſions ~ a ſequence of ſtatic arrangements like the ſtill frames of a "motion picture," whoſe motion or change only becomes apparent by the rapid ſucceſſion of thoſe ſtill frames. (Here, too, the game of cheſs is an excellent analogy to this idea.) Or, on the other hand, we may ſee reality as a ſucceſſion of changes. Of courſe, the only way we can view reality at all through either perſpective is by means of the other. The ſucceſſion of Fixed Field Illuſions forms one perſpective of reality, and the ſucceſſion of Points of Change forms a complimentary perſpective as a parallel univerſe.

The importance of retaining both perſpectives ſimultaneouſly is illuſtrated by the dilemma of the phyſiciſts who can not agree on whether a photon of light is a point or a field. Of courſe it is both at once, and neither the one nor the other! It requires a larger viſion of conſciouſneſs to perceive the ultimate balance where the entire Macrocoſm finally becomes equivalent ſimultaneouſly to Zero and Infinity, only apparently exiſting as a field of manifeſtation between them by means of the diſtinction imagined to exiſt between infinite moments of eternity.

Postscriptvm

As I prepare the ſecond edition of Patterns of Illusion and Change, *twenty years after its firſt publication, I ſee that ſome of the moſt important concluſions are not explicitly drawn. Of courſe, I have always conſidered this text to repreſent juſt the working notes to a ſeries of claſſes which I would teach, expounding the principle points in greater detail, but I wanted to draw a few concluſions here, juſt to ſhow the direction in which it can go, as well as to introduce ſome of my lateſt ſpeculations on the nature of conſciouſneſs and its relationſhip with God.*

The moſt glaring omiſſion in the original text, it ſeems to me, is any mention of Love. I have tried to make the caſe that both directions of energy are eſſential and good, both the Going In as well as the Going Out. The alchemical ſymbols have always made this point very clear. It is not "God and the Devil", but two different aſpects of God. (Of courſe the meanings of words muſt be freſhly defined for every uſage in order to avoid miſunderſtanding. Many apparent contradictions are reſolved by diſcovering a diſcrepancy of definition.) On the other hand, the relationſhip between the two directions is not a random one at all ~ that would belie the underlying order which informs it all. No, it is the Movement In which defines the center line of the path of the inertia of God. To make it ſimple, let us ſay that the Movement In goes towards a theoretical point of Perfection at the very Center, at which point all "good" things converge. For example, if a perſon's life is out of balance, out into realms of confuſion, if not to chaos, then there will be numerous problems all along the line. Everything will be out of adjuſtment. You will fight with your wife, ſhout at your children, and your buſineſs and perſonal affairs will come apart. But when your life is going towards that point of balance, then everything begins to get better. Things come into focus and clarity; your health will improve; your conſciouſneſs will improve; and your financial and perſonal affairs will proſper. Inſtead of finding yourſelf running faſter and faſter and barely being able to keep from ſlipping backwards (or, in fact, ſliding backwards rapidly) you will find things eaſier all the time with leſs effort until, as Lao Tzu ſays, you will reach a point where "you do nothing at all, and yet there is nothing that is undone."

But that is juſt to define the point and the line, ſo that a pattern of perſpective that encompaſſes the clarity of the coſmos may be ſeen. However, if that were all, the proceſs would quickly achieve the identity of Zero or Infinity, and the manifeſtation of a particular coſmos, apart from the non-differentiated ſtate of Perfection or Nonbeing, would not be poſſible. So now we come to this movement away from the point ~ that is eaſily ſeen and underſtood as the ſpark of Life, which is an important aſpect of God. As I wrote in one of my earlieſt books, Jokes, *"God is Perfect, but the Devil is looking for another way."*

But now we come to the SOLVE ET COAGULA. *This movement away from the center is only uſeful from the reference point of the center line. Movement away from the center line ſtarts firſt with novelty, then moves towards a ſtate of greater complexity, then to ſtates of confuſion, and finally to ſtates of chaos. So in order for* SOLVE *away from the center to be uſeful, it muſt be followed by* COAGULA *back to the center. This movement away may be varioſly viewed as Don Juan's "controlled folly," or art, or muſic, or literature, or even ornament. Deviations and variations around a point eventually modify the direction, and contribute to the refining of the center line itſelf. A good way to elucidate that thought is from another quotation from the ſame book of* Jokes: *" ~ But not very often. (Sometimes the Devil has a good idea.)"*

An amuſing idea I have had lately is that "a good meaſure of a perſon's ſpiritual growth is the degree to which they love everyone." What is funny about this is that everyone is welcome to play the game of "more ſpiritual than thou." This notion could ſave the world if it were widely underſtood. What happens, of courſe, is that as you approach the heights of ſpiritual growth, and all things ſtart to converge into clarity and unity, then you will ſee God, and you will love everyone.

Now, what is actually going on in this convergence? It is really the preſence of God. I ſtarted out in life as very much a ſkeptic. At the age of ſix I had a theological criſis becauſe I couldn't underſtand the nature of God. I thought the concept of God were puerile and uſeleſs. (This was brought early to a head by my father's career as a Methodiſt miniſter.) I ſet out to diſcover for myſelf what was the nature of the univerſe, and how it had come into being. When I firſt ſtarted uſing the term "God" in my writings, I thought I were being clever and funny ~ it ſeemed to fit ſo perfectly, but, of courſe, I thought my own peculiar definition of "God" were my own unique underſtanding. I gradually learned, however, that the fit was not coincidental. However, I continued to aſſume that my "God" were at leaſt a metaphyſical concept that bore no relationſhip at all to the old man in the ſky. However, I have to anticipate my lateſt thoughts on the ſubject by ſaying that my current underſtanding of "God" is about as perſonal as any old man in the ſky you could imagine.

How is this poſſible? Let me back up juſt a bit to tackle another ſerious and complicated theological paradox, uſually called "the Problem of Evil." ~ How can we believe in an all powerful and merciful God, who is good, and juſt, and loving, in the face of the manifeſt evil that is preſent in the world? When we ſee innocent children mangled by accident or deliberate attack, when the good die young and villains proſper, when awful diſeaſes waſte away the bodies and lives of the niceſt people (I don't even mention moſquitoes) ~ how, then, can we believe in this all powerful God who is merciful and loving? Either God is not all powerful, or God is not all that good, frankly! So which is it?

That's the problem; I didn't juſt make it up. And what is the answer? ~ No, God is not all powerful. What made you ſuppoſe that God were all powerful? We are juſt doing the beſt that we can. How? To be ſure, this is going to involve a ſomewhat different concept about the nature of God. What? God is evolving, along with His univerſe, as we ſpeak? What hope is there for us if God be not, finally, all powerful? I think the notion that God is all powerful is ſuppoſed to give us comfort, but it only makes me nervous. If God be all powerful, what is going on in our world? I take *greater comfort in the hope that the power of God be increaſing, ſo that we may hope that the world may become a better place.*

If you read the Old Testament Bible, *it ſounds like God actually ſtarted out on a very primitive level, but more recent conceptions of God are far more progreſſive. But to explain what I mean by all of this, let me drop that thread for the moment and take up a new one ~ the growth of conſciouſneſs. I remember being dazzled and amazed (at that firſt theological criſis at the age of ſix) by the whole idea of conſciouſneſs. What I couldn't figure out was how come I happened to be "me" inſtead of anybody elſe? What was this "conſciouſneſs" all about? It baffled me then, and only begins to make ſenſe to me now. I have looked at the evolution of conſciouſneſs. I conſider animals, and wonder to myſelf how much conſciouſneſs they have. It ſeems to be apparent that dogs and cats have more conſciouſneſs than chickens, for example. Does my amazing and wonderful cat Meander Polydactyl really have as much conſciouſneſs as he ſeems to have? ~ or am I juſt projecting this? To ſummarize my ſpeculations, I poſtulate a continuum in which conſciouſneſs may range from "ſub conſcious" beginnings, through to ordinary human conſciouſneſs, and on to ſubſtantial and wide-ranging coſmic conſciouſneſs. There may eaſily be ſpecies overlap. I am quite ſure, for example, that Meander's conſciouſneſs, while perhaps rudimentary, is nonetheleſs conſiderably more advanced than that of the average American Preſident. (Waſn't it Mark Twain who propoſed replacing kings with cats?) (And, as Joan Baez once ſaid, "You ſhould hear the verſes I left out!")*

So, here is where it gets intereſting ~ if, in general, the conſciouſneſs of an organiſm is in direct correlation (more or leſs) with the complexity of the organiſm, then the more complex the organiſm, the loftier the conſciouſneſs. A human body is made up of many living parts, yet the perſon as a whole has a ſingle conſciouſneſs. Now I conſider group conſciouſneſs. There is a group conſciouſneſs about a beehive or an anthill. I have no trouble at all imagining a "real" conſciouſneſs pertaining to a beehive or an anthill. I do not think that each ant has ſo much conſciouſneſs, but I do credit the hive or hill as a whole with having a "real" conſciouſneſs, that is not ſo much different in kind from my own, or Meander's.

Then there are the 100 monkeys. Briefly, the obſerved phenomenon was that when a certain number of monkeys on an iſland learned a new trick, then ſuddenly it entered the group conſciouſneſs and all the monkeys knew it, even the monkeys on the other ſide of the iſland who had no contact with the monkeys who originated the new trick. Obviouſly, it is a clear caſe of ſhared conſciouſneſs.

By extenſion, I poſtulate a group conſciouſneſs at every level ~ there is a group conſciouſneſs to every family, town, ſchool, city, ſtate, nation, race, tribe, or ſub-group. This conſciouſneſs is made up of the individual conſciouſneſs of the members of the group, but then it goes beyond to evolve a unique and ſingle conſciouſneſs that, again, is not ſo very much different in kind from my own or Meander's. This conſcious being would be the "god" of that group.

But juſt as we can break up the human race into as many different countries, races, religions, languages, or any of the other ways in which people differentiate themſelves (ſo that they can go to war with each other), we can alſo go the other way and poſtulate a ſingle, planetary human conſciouſneſs. But why ſtop there? This conſcious Being of our planet muſt include the conſciouſneſs of animals as well as all of the trees and plants, too. This is the Gaia hypotheſis ~ that the entire field of life energy on the planet Earth is a ſingle living organiſm. ~ and, of courſe, it is fully conſcious (which is juſt another way of ſaying the ſame thing, much like "being in the preſence of God" is the ſame thing as "loving everyone.")

It is this Conſciouſneſs of Gaia that I want to look at here. Since we are talking about levels of conſciouſneſs far above our own, that ſhould mean that the nature of that conſciouſneſs ſhould be more advanced than our own. That is, not only do I poſtulate the conſciouſneſs of Gaia to be a "real" conſcious conſciouſneſs, but I ſuggeſt that it exiſts on a more fully developed level than our own. Mother Earth is very much aware, thank you, and ſtruggling to ſtay alive.

Clearly all of the life energy of the entire Coſmos is co-extenſive with the Mind of God, a fully conſcious Being. But I think it is appropriate, at this point in time and ſpace, to limit our preſent horizon to the planet Earth. Relevant to our ſituation, Gaia is the deity to whom we muſt pray! We muſt evolve the god of our little planet for, perhaps, many more millennia before it will be appropriate to look at a larger ſpiritual reality. For right now, though, Gaia needs all the help we can give her! Everyone who is *alive is partially reſponſible ~ we muſt all evolve our conſciouſneſs together. And when all of life is finally joined together in One Love, the Kingdom of God will come on Earth, and we can all live, once again, in the Garden, Mother Earth growing green again, inſtead of withering.*

I thought that was a good "curtain line," but I'm not done. I want to bring this back full circle to the abſtractions of metaphyſics that my book is all about. In ſpite of my "demotion" of God, there is ſtill a ſenſe that the fundamental nature of God is what created the Univerſe in the firſt place. The final ſolution to "the riddle of life," or however you want to expreſs it, may be contained in the equation:

$$0 = \infty$$

It is the conſtant poſſibility of the alternative or oppoſite to every idea that cauſes our coſmos to come into being in the firſt place, and the dynamic tenſion which keeps it forever going on, evolving God knows where. I'm glad Somebody knows.

Jokes

Edited by

John Roland Stahl

(First published as a miniature book,
hand set letterpress, five point type.)

"The way out is via the door.

Why is it that no one will use this method?"

~ Confucius

God is perfect,

but the Devil is looking for another way.

You can always tell a book by it's cover.

A Joke is separation of Illusion from Reality.

Everything is an over simplification.

[The Inside and the Outside]

To make Order out of Chaos,

begin by throwing away the rubbish.

"Anything that can go wrong will go wrong."

(Murphy's Law)

When the Irresistible force meets the Immovable object,

we learn whether it was the force that wasn't irresistible after all,

or the object that wasn't entirely immovable.

Many are called but few are chosen.

The Majority is always wrong.

The source of Authority is the Power of God.

All Manifestation is Error.

"If they give you ruled paper, write the other way."

~ Juan Ramon Jimenez

The Philosophers' Stone is the Key to the Process of Change.

(The point of balance)

You can only teach a person what he already knows.

Paranoids are people whom everyone persecutes.

The Devil take the hindmost.

The more something happens,

the more it happens again.

The Magician directs the Attention.

The Illusion is more important than the Reality.

Magic Power means Solitude.

What are you doing?

~ but not very often.

(Sometimes the Devil has a good idea.)

Lose at the beginning.

The more it changes, the more it remains the same.

The longer it remains the same, the more it tends to change.

(From Talleyrand)

To win at Roulette:

When you're winning, bet more;

when you're losing, bet less.

"The only way to get rid of a temptation is to yield to it."

~ Oscar Wilde

If you give up trying to live, the world will let you die.

Today is the first day of the rest of my life.

It's all part of a larger plan.

The Focus of Attention is the Philosophers' Stone.

The Illusion depends on the Point of Perspective.

The less you use it, the more powerful it is.

Emphasis

"He who knows does not speak.

He who speaks does not know."

~ Lao Tzu

Positional Chess: maybe it doesn't win,

but there's no way it can lose.

After Man, the Desert.

I've learned two things about people:

the first thing is that everyone's different;

the second thing is that all people are the same.

"Clay does not, of itself, become a pot."

~ Paracelsus

The Truth is not the same for everyone.

Time is the measure of Error.

In General, it is the Same; in Particular it is Different.

The Light rises; the Heavy descends.

~ Yawn ~

The Magician always knows the Joke.

Is it better to hold back, or to let go?

Priority: the importance of Sequence.

"Everything is for the best in this best of all possible worlds."

~ From Leibnitz

Eritis ſicut Deus, ſcientes Bonum et Malum.

"Beware of what you wish for in youth,

because you will get it in middle age."

~ Goethe

"Approach ye ever the Infinite Wisdom,

ever before thee recedes the Goal."

~ Doreal

Go Back.

When you can no longer go back, go forward.

The Secret is the Philosophers' Stone.

New Solutions

to the Problems of the Present Day

by *John Roland Stahl*

A Blueprint for International Prosperity
and World Peace

INTRODUCTION

Thomas Jefferson and his compatriots who so well declared the principle that all authority resides ultimately with the people, rather than with established governments, would be turning over in their graves if they thought that the Constitution which they created in response to the needs of the times were to be worshipped as holy writ forevermore.

In the words of Thomas Jefferson from the Declaration of Independence, ". . . that whenever any Form of Government becomes destructive of these Ends, it is the Right of the People to alter or to abolish it, and to institute new Government, laying its Foundation on such Principles, and organizing its Powers in such Form, as to them shall seem most likely to effect their Safety and Happiness." ". . . it is their Right, it is their Duty, to throw off such Government, and to provide new Guards for their future Security."

It is not only the Right of citizens to form a new government when the existing forms do not meet their needs, but it is their Duty, as patriotic citizens.

The world has changed enormously just over the past few years, with the collapse of Communism in Eastern Europe, movements towards ever more coherent unity in Western Europe, and volatile shifts in economic balances according to the fortunes of oil, water, booming economies in Asia and Western Europe, collapsing economies in Eastern Europe, tottering economies in North America, and the fortunes of war in the Middle East, Iraq, South Africa, Yugoslavia, Georgia, Ireland, Algeria ~ (insert today's news). Considering all the changes which have taken place in the world since the Declaration of Independence was written in 1776, maybe it is time to consider a fresh political arrangement more in keeping with the needs of today's world.

Some of the more ingenious visionaries are finally realizing that economic strength is a far more reliable indicator of national strength than mere military power, however formidable. The price one pays for military strength is economic poverty. One reason for the prosperity of post-war Japan was the absence of a fat military budget.

And we all saw what finally happened to the might of the Soviet Union after the screen fell over: Oz, the Great and Terrible, was just a helpless old man: a humbug, after all, who didn't really know what he was doing, and whose people couldn't even feed themselves. Now the United States is not necessarily so far behind. We are living under a pyramid of debt that has a physical weight of its own, and will not go away any time soon without crushing whatever is underneath.

But, on top of this, so much of the worthwhile production of our labor is lost to hordes of inefficient demons and monsters, overloaded with so much chaos and confusion that it feels like we are laboring in the garden while wearing 400 pound suits of armor (under the hot sun). There is no reason why we can't all enjoy good health and long life in a world of peace and plenty, if only we can simplify our lives, slough off the armor, beat our swords back into plowshares, and live happily ever after, tending our trees and our gardens.

Summary

I have designed an integrated theoretical program of political, economic, and social reform that is designed to be implemented world wide, but most of whose principles can also be implemented by any local government or region.

There are several main areas where I propose new arrangements quite different from our present situation:

- A final end to warfare of all kinds ~ both wars of aggression and/or stupidity, and wars to settle international disputes.

- The evolution of planetary cooperation resulting in a World Court as the final arbiter of international disputes, and a World Guard to hold military assets to enforce the decisions of the World Court, and to safeguard basic human freedom from the tyranny of local despots. (This is emphatically not to be understood as *Pax Americana!*)

- The establishment of a Seminary to produce the Judge of the World Court who would have final responsibility for decisions.

- The dismantling of most local military establishments, with the exception of local police forces as needed to keep the peace.

- A total free market for economic activity, unhindered, untaxed (*i.e.* no tax on business activity, or profit; a resource depletion tax would be the only limitation on economic activity, see below); free market exchange of currencies, no regulation of wages or prices for commodities or services.

- A monumental simplification of taxation: all taxes swept away except for a universal land tax and a resource depletion tax (on trees, oil, water, energy, etc., including any kind of environmental degradation or pollution), collected and disbursed by the World Bank, with the authority of the World Court and local governments.

- The total elimination of transfer payments of any kind: welfare, social security, health care, the works; replaced with direct housing, food, and services to the indigent (Free Farms).

- Elimination of the National Debt by a one time printing of 90,000 one hundred million dollar bank notes (or, perhaps, 9,000,000 one million dollar bank notes, to make them easier to spend). From now on, the budget and the tax base should always come out even, except for extraordinary circumstances. [It is interesting to observe that, when this was first written, in 1992, the debt was a mere $4 trillion.]

Most of my suggestions are based on a fundamental premise: that the present system is so frightfully wasteful of resources that we are squandering the accumulated wealth of the world, sliding down into poverty and despair, tension and warfare, toxic pollution and disease. If the world's resources were more sensibly managed, it is surely possible for everyone on earth to live a comfortable life in peace and joy.

The miracles of endless credit allow for a system to whirl around with a life of its own greatly in excess of its theoretical balance. The pattern, however, is for bills to come due suddenly. One fine day, without warning, you hear from your bank and credit cards that they decline to extend any further credit; please pay the balance due immediately. When your credit cards reach the level of 29.5% annual interest, you may take that as the handwriting on the wall.

Most of what passes for "happening" in the world "happens" to the people who have money. But that doesn't help the others much. Right now there are plenty of people who are broke, without funds, employment, or both. Companies are broke; federal, state, and local governments are broke. A great many individuals, companies, and governments are operating from debt. What this means is that most people and institutions are spending wealth faster than they are creating it. The present economic mess is so inefficient that we are just sliding backwards and downwards into chaos.

I will never forget the amazement I felt when first confronted with the machinations of gross inefficiency masquerading as business as usual: in my youth I was briefly employed to stuff envelopes for a direct mail campaign for funding. Here were all these stacks of slickly printed promotional brochures which I was collating and stuffing into printed envelopes, and sealing. In the course of the job I learned that they did one of these direct mail campaigns twice a year. It cost them about $30,000 each time for all the printing, postage, etc. (including hiring people like me), but then they predictably received about $35,000 with each mailing. That left them with a total of $5,000 each time or $10,000 per year, which funded their activities. Free money! I was appalled. It made me sick to think of all that commotion of waste just so that a tiny film could be skimmed off the surface for their needs.

All the bureaucracies of the federal government resemble the direct mail campaign in all essential particulars. The whole whirlwind of taxation is such a commotion of waste that it just disgusts me. Never mind, for the moment, that once the government gets their hands on our money they waste it in the most foolish or criminal ways imaginable; let's just consider the whole industry of taxation in the first place. What does it cost to regulate and administer all the provisions of the tax codes? How many forests are cut down to produce those stacks and stacks of forms and bulletins and announcements? How many very expensive attorneys are grinding away their services in the toils of the taxation swindle? What is the cost for businesses to comply with all of the endless requirements of forms, busywork, and tax collection, not to mention the payments themselves? Add to all this the ongoing parade of tax tinkering shell games to obscure the facts of where the money actually comes from and where it goes. Then there's the lobbying, the politics, the compromises, the power maneuvering, the gimmicks, the fraud, and the lies. Finally there are the armies of IRS collectors, investigators, and purveyors of confusion. And what is it all for? Does our tax system end up being "fair"? Has anything changed since the *Ancien Regime* in pre-Revolutionary France? It is the poor who always pay taxes, not the rich. The whole thing disgusts me. I propose to sweep it all away.

Most of the activities of government should be simply discontinued altogether; most remaining activities that are found to be useful ought to be parceled out to independent, self sufficient entities. The post office should be self sufficient, for example. All expenses of mail handling should be borne by the users. Discontinue, or greatly reduce the discounts for junk mail, and the Post Office could easily balance its budget without another rate increase, while the rest of us would be spared the tremendous waste of paper that sweeps through our post offices every day.

One time I saw a pie graph of the federal budget and found it very illuminating. It was divided into three main sections plus a fourth tiny sliver.

The three main sections were, in order: the military, welfare, and service on the debt. The remaining sliver represented all other functions of government. I want to slash all three main categories of expenditure to reduce the government's voracious need for money in the first place. There is an economic role for a central government, but it doesn't need such major budgets for such worthless programs.

The problem of military expenditures is of paramount importance, but must be addressed on an international level. Other recommendations presented here may easily be implemented by any sovereign state, but the problems of war and military expenditures can never be solved without involving all the peoples of the Earth in a negotiated solution. This may appear to be a tall order, but, with the recent collapse of Communism, there appears to be some sort of consensus emerging about the role of government. To date, no major departures from the principles of private ownership of property and a free market economy have managed to endure for very long. It may not be unthinkable that some sort of international co-operation might be reached along the lines of the proposals presented here.

Transfer payments for Welfare, Health Care, etc. represent an enormous expense, not only for the payments themselves, but also for the bureaucracies which administer the system and collect taxes to pay for it. But the payments rarely provide any real solutions for the recipients. It is always worth while to feed hungry people, but without some provision for their future welfare, they will just be hungry again in a few hours. One of the principle ideas behind the Free Farm idea, elaborated later on, is that the community of a Free Farm would constitute a kind of melting pot, where people would have an opportunity to change their lives. Where welfare payments simply provide the means to continue a lifestyle that is unproductive, the Free Farm would present opportunities for new social and economic arrangements which might eventually lead to a resumption of life in "the wild world."

The weight of inertia opposes any change (such as going to a free farm), but some such change may be advisable for persons who come into a situation of need. But instead of advocating the immediate cancellation of traditional transfer payments, I would advocate a parallel establishment of Free Farms as an alternative. Whatever the number of people who take advantage of the Free Farm option, it would result in savings for the tax payers. If the Free Farm becomes a popular alternative to the welfare treadmill, it could lead to a gentle transition to a new social and economic alternative for new generations.

The National Debt is nothing short of an outrageous rip-off. Deficit financing is a scheme where governments spend money today by assigning the bills to future taxpayers. That is an unconscionable Ponzi scheme that does nothing productive at all. It is as bad as the direct mail solicitation scam ~ a big inefficient waste of money. Whom do they think they're fooling? Taxpayers are justly resentful of paying taxes when so much of their money is siphoned off by moneylenders. Sure the money goes round and round, but like any machine, the more friction in the system, the more energy is lost. I want to refuse payment; the debts are not mine. Let's unload all the monkeys from our backs, pay the cost once, and be done with it. Of course, actually paying off the national debt by printing up those million dollar bank notes would produce a hilarious situation, but it would be an instant cure; the transfer would be a swift and devastating one-time tax on players of economic musical chairs who are caught holding cash when the music stops. The World Bank would have to require payment in its own currency, and set its own rates for local currency exchange.

TAX REFORM

My solution for the remaining expenses of government that can't be eliminated or covered in any other way is to rely almost exclusively upon a property tax. A property tax would be one of the easiest to administer and enforce, and ultimately the most equitable way of distributing the burden of taxation. There are numerous advantages of this proposal. First, it would be very easy and straight-forward to administer in a uniformly reliable way throughout the world: since the ownership of private property is one of the economic cornerstones for which there now appears to be an international consensus, there will always be records of ownership. A tax based upon the value of land would be the utmost in simplicity.

This is not, of course, a new idea. It is an ancient idea harking back to the very origins of civilization. The actual land of the Earth represents the ultimate source of wealth, after all; it makes sense that it should be the basis of taxation. It becomes a kind of rent payable to the state as the ultimate landlord. In fact, for most of recorded history, some sort of feudal, land-based economy has been the basis of wealth. It is really only in the last hundred years or so that money has been considered a commodity independent of any real attachment. If money were based upon land, there would always be a fundamental reality underpinning the system.

Of course, setting the amount of the tax on property is of the whole importance; the authority for setting these rates would be among the most important functions of the World Court and the Judge, to prevent the very common abuse of power by greedy despots, tyrants, and landlords. (At the local level of rent on private property there would be no regulation; like everything else, the free market rents would work out to a representation of the actual "value" of the land.) The tax could be collected by the World Bank which would disburse funds in accordance with budgets arranged by the States, the World Bank, and the Judge.

In each region someone has to conduct the central affairs of maintaining the roads, schools, free farms, police and fire protection, etc. They would suggest a budget for those costs which would be considered in assessing their tax rate. The World Bank, with the approval of the Judge, would accept or modify these budgets and assess the rate for the property tax. In general, it would be assumed that the cost of local services would match the local tax revenue, but there are times when an impartial, international Judge could make adjustments for special situations. For example, a devastating earthquake might ruin a region's economy for quite a while, but the Judge might temporarily reduce or eliminate the tax assessment while still funding services. The difference involved would be made up by the wealthier nations. This tool must be used sparingly. It would not be necessary or politically popular to try to equalize the wealth of the world overnight by levying a tax ~ the ordinary workings of free market economics should eventually raise the living standards of the poor countries, as long as their labor be cheaper. This is already happening ~ it may not be too much longer before products are manufactured in the United States once again, to take advantage of cheap labor.

In general, this economic plan would not have to interfere with the ways in which each separate State or Country manages its ordinary affairs, except to safeguard freedom and prevent the abuses of power.

While the universal land tax would be the fundamental source of tax revenue, additional taxes might be levied by the same authority to modify the free market cost of resources. This means that a tax could be placed upon the extraction of resources (oil, trees, water, etc.) to reach whatever level of conservation and renewal were required. Further taxation would be imposed upon destructive activity of any kind: producers of pollution would be taxed at progressively higher rates until essential targets of pollution abatement were reached. The point is that the taxation would not be used primarily to generate revenue, but to regulate destructive activity and promote an evolution towards sustainable and non-destructive lifestyles. At some point, the distinction between "destructive activity" taxation and financial judgments from the criminal/legal system might become moot.

The role of limiting special taxation to discourage activity harmful to the earth is the basis of my proposal to liberate economic activity from all of the burdens which have been placed upon it over the years. If all these burdens were lifted, just think what an enormous boost it would be to commercial productivity in every way. Leaving all economic activity wide open to the action of free markets would eventually solve all economic problems, and do so pretty quickly.

Obviously, there would entail some changes in the relative balance of economic realities, but ultimately, when the dust settled, a fair and simple system would evolve that would benefit everyone. Initially, it may appear that landowners would be forced to bear a much larger burden than they currently do, since all other taxes (other than resource depletion and pollution taxes) would be eliminated, and the government would balance its budget solely with revenues from landowners. But rents would be raised to cover any additional cost of owning land. The cost of food production as well as all manufactured goods would be affected in the same way. The net effect on the economy as a whole would be the savings accomplished by simplifying the whole system. That is, any increase in land tax or rents would be more than offset by the elimination of all other taxes. Since the primary idea is to greatly reduce the total amount of taxation required in the first place, landowners would surely join in the feeling of general relief from the burden and waste of our present irresponsible tax-and-spend fiasco.

The only persons not joining in the celebration would be those involved in industries found to be harmful to the environment in some way. The resource depletion and pollution taxes would have effects ranging from minor changes in industrial activity with small loss of profits, to being totally wiped out by an unacceptable tax liability (e.g. the tobacco industry or the nuclear power industry ~ once the full cost of nuclear power be realized and accepted, all other forms of energy generation would be found to be much more cost-effective; any alternative would be cheaper than the true cost of nuclear power: one might cultivate oak trees to feed acorns to squirrels running on treadmills, for example.)

It may be argued that one consequence of eliminating taxes on profit or income would be to allow the few to become very wealthy at the expense of the many. But any economic activity that was making its promoters rich would be quickly copied. Competition would bring prices down to reasonable levels. Of course, many individuals and companies would become very rich when their businesses prospered, but that is the incentive for the activity! If these policies were adopted world wide (and no one else could compete who had to operate under the burdens of restriction or taxation) then all economic imbalances would eventually work themselves out.

Since most wealth really does eventually come down to the land as its ultimate source of value, the real holders of wealth, the land owners, would end up paying the tax. Renters would pay the tax at second hand, so there would remain the incentive to own the land. Businesses usually have a land base of some sort that would be taxed, but for the rest of it, let them keep their business profits! This is a considered policy. If businesses were allowed to retain their profits, without any taxation or paperwork, whether of payroll or profits or income or capital gain or anything else, then the energy and ingenuity of the liberated human spirit would galvanize the economy back into high gear really quickly. [2018 review ~ perhaps some tax on wealth will be inevitable, to put some limit on endlessly expanding wealth.]

If this policy were to be adopted in the United States, there would be no further problem about competing with Japan or China! In fact, it would quickly become imperative for every country to follow suit or else get left behind. Inevitably there would be some winners and losers whenever such major changes are made to the financial system, but I am sure that when the system adjusts to the changes and finds a new equilibrium almost everyone would feel that a great weight had been lifted.

Free Farms

For a long time now I have been having ideas about freedom. I keep thinking how central Freedom is to the solutions to all of the problems of the world. I keep thinking of what a radical idea it is to be Free!

I am not only thinking of political freedom here. Of course I believe in the importance of real freedom in every sense of the word, but I keep thinking about the possibilities of what it means to be Free, even when applied to the concept of money. What if everything were Free?

Of course you are thinking that this is useless. It is such an axiom of fundamental truth that everything must be measured by money. "Of course, if everything were free, then no one would do anything and everything would fall apart."

Well, perhaps that may be true. The spirit of Freedom has raised its head time and time again, only to be beaten back by the grim face of reality. The enthusiasm of the Diggers, who wanted everything to be Free, struck a resonant chord that many of us have felt. I am an original hippie, and I am old enough to have seen the disillusion as one fragile vessel after another was cracked by the inertial entropy of the real world.

But I still believe in Freedom, and I believe that it is possible to extend the range of freedom so that more and more things can be free. Giving something away for free is a very radical act. It is as radical as loving everyone, which is another holdover 60's myth. But as a matter of fact, loving everyone and giving everything away for free are related ideas.

There are two trends in physics: sharpening and leveling. You can call it Yang and Yin. The sharpener wants to get more for himself and less for his neighbor, and accumulate the advantage for himself. The leveler wants to nourish all life and cultivate the garden. The Sharpener wants to emphasize distinctions and select the best for himself, while the leveler emphasizes the unity and wants to share the wealth.

I think it is very liberating to give things away for free. The world is so heavily cemented into the bonds of the financial imperative that Freedom almost doesn't fit into the equation. Yet if enough of us start giving things away for free, then the market will eventually collapse. We see it on the Internet. So many people are trying to figure out ways to make money on the Internet and they are constantly frustrated because there are so many other people offering services for free. You can't sell software anymore, because there is so much of it everywhere that is entirely free. You can't charge for services anymore because there is someone else offering it for free. I remember when promoters thought that people would pay something for every visit to their site! The wealth of information and services offered for free staggers the imagination. I have published some of my books on the Internet, and what do I care if no one needs to buy my bound copies? I wasn't publishing them to make money in the first place, and I should be (and am) delighted to save myself the trouble and expense (and waste of the earth's resources) of actually manufacturing a physical book and sending it to someone by the Post. So there is no need to go to a site where you need to pay any money!

I want to give away food and housing. Once a Free Farm is set up, it ought to be self-supporting enough so that at least there will be enough food so that everyone can eat, whether or not they contribute anything to the operation of the farm. If there are enough people willing to work in the house and garden, then perhaps life will go on.

One of the major problems of our present economic system is that you really have to be part of it in order to survive. Everyone needs to have money, therefore everyone needs to have a job. Recently I heard some politician-without-portfolio (and no constructive ideas at all, simply negative ones) shouting that the Solution (to any or all of the problems of the world) was Jobs. To which I immediately came up with the response: Jobs are not the Solution; Jobs are the Problem! The way the world is evolving right now, there just aren't enough "jobs" to go around. The necessity for everyone to have a Job, or some source of income, not only drives the fringes into robbery, murder, drug trafficking and the like, but also sets up the situation for a great many people to involve themselves in useless (or worse than useless) activity just to come up with useless products which they can advertise and promote in order to generate profit for themselves, without producing anything worthwhile. The paradox is that the very successes of the industrial and technological revolutions have created a situation in which the insufficiency of available jobs is causing the collapse of the economic system! But if non working members of society were allowed to live the simple life in peace on the Free Farm, and the remaining economic establishment were free and untaxed, the whole of civilization could enjoy a Renaissance of creative flowering.

A major chunk of government spending goes for welfare payments of one sort or another. This whole system is a failure and a fabulous waste of money. So much money gets drained off into payments that go nowhere. In fact, few of the problems for which the payments are offered are ameliorated at all by the funds. The poor and hungry and sick and unemployed remain poor, hungry, sick, and unemployed.

There are a great many reasons for poverty and financial distress: accidents, ill health, bad luck, bad judgment, changing economic climate, advancing age, or even the burden of raising a child without financial support. For a great many people, there just aren't any jobs available. For all of these persons I would introduce a whole new economic arrangement: the Free Farm where the poor or unemployed always have the option to live at peace in a free community until such time as they wish to re-enter the competitive jungle of the free market.

Many times the stress of poverty is the major problem in a person's life. Living a simple life with no concerns about money may allow these people to relax and become re-centered in their personal lives. Artists, writers, and many others just may not be interested in the pursuit of wealth and comfort, and would rather be free, living the simple life, to express their artistic flowerings at leisure. On the other hand, many people would probably opt for the chance to maintain their own place in the world, at a higher standard than that afforded by the free farm. The proportions would work themselves out exactly: whenever there were useful work to be done that others were willing to pay for, someone would come forward to do it, at the right price.

My conception of a Free Farm is a place in the country where everyone is welcome and everything is free. Absolutely no paperwork of any kind should be required of anyone at any time. Wander in, wander out, eat, sleep, or just lie in the sun. You may think too many lazy people would be seeking refuge at the Farm, but I don't think so. At first there may be a lot of people checking them out, but I think most people would prefer to live by their own enterprise if they could. The facilities of the Farms would of course be very basic: dormitories, cafeterias, recycled used clothing, essential medical care only, etc. Eventually the lure of the "great wild world" might inspire someone to check into one of the available slots back in the working world.

Why should someone who is unemployed occupy expensive space in a city? And why would anyone want to live in a city anyway, unless he were tied to some employment? I think operating Free Farms would be vastly cheaper than the whole bureaucracy of welfare payments and paperwork. If the whole thing were totally free, how simple it would all be.

The farms would actually function as working farms, although they may have any other additional economic base. Anyone who is able to work may volunteer to do anything useful: planting trees (my own priority), gardening, construction, maintenance, cooking, or participation in commercial activity. All proceeds from commercial activity would go to the general fund for farm expenses.

The theory is that anyone who would remain in residence at a free farm indefinitely without doing any work at all must be just totally helpless. I think that, sooner or later, most people would want to do something useful, and later on many would prefer to move on and take a paying job outside (the farms would be natural centers for employment agencies).

On the other hand, there has never been any shortage of the totally helpless, but it would be better and certainly vastly cheaper even in the short run, and certainly in the long run, to let them live their lives in peace, than for the rest of us to be subjected to the social problems of theft, violence, madness, and despair.

In order to provide some incentive for participation, an organized core of farm members (who would make all the decisions) would be distinguished from non-member residents. Better lodgings and other benefits would provide the incentive for a resident to participate at a level that would allow for his possible election as a member after some minimum time of residence.

Since the farms would be non-profit, they would not be taxed at all. Once they were totally set up, it is possible that they might operate with little or no additional funding. In fact, well run communities, with, perhaps, a product to sell to independent individuals or companies, might do very well. Their expenses would be minimal; much of their food would be grown on the spot; labor would be volunteer. It is entirely possible that residents of prosperous communities might enjoy their lives better than they ever dreamed possible. Liberation from the stress of constant worry and hassle over money could lead to a great relaxation of tension.

In many ways this idea of the free farm is a very old socialist idea. The significant difference of my idea is that a well rounded economic and social system requires both opportunities: an untaxed free enterprise system which allows for the flowering of commercial activity for those persons who wish to obtain personal wealth, and alternative economic and social communities for those who don't.

The communities which would form around the various avenues of arrival to the free farms might enjoy considerable advantages compared with the present system. For example, single mothers, for whom raising their children is full time work (in the case of infants, of course, it is full time work for three, doing eight hour shifts), may greatly prefer to live in a free, rural environment with other mothers and children than to live on welfare in the city. The advantages of shared childcare, free local schools, and the sharing of domestic chores, might be an ideal situation. And free communities of the retired elderly might find their needs served so well that they may prefer to live on the farm even when they are not at all indigent.

If work really were voluntary, then I think there are a lot of people who would do very little work. There will be many people who will not go to the trouble to learn how to play a Baroque oboe, either. It is their loss. If they are allowed to live their lives as they wish, and the work will be done entirely by those people whose love of the earth and its people, plants, and animals impels them to contribute their part, it just may be that there will still be enough for life to continue.

Of course I know very well that this is not for everyone. The majority of the earth's population is composed of sharpeners, after all, and they would have no interest in any of this. The sharpeners will go on living in the Big House, and will be very satisfied with their share of life's blessings, but I want to encourage the levelers in any way that I can, and help to set up communities where they can live in freedom and in love, cultivating the earth's resources rather than exploiting them.

The Source of Authority

Along with Teilhard de Chardin, Albert Einstein, Bertrand Russell, H. G. Wells, and many others, I believe that no further evolutionary progress can be made until all life on Earth is united into a single political organism. In order to cultivate the garden of the Earth to its greatest potential, it is necessary to recognize the source of authority as the center of perspective which integrates the whole. The Source of Authority is obviously a theological postulate: there must be an attempt to link the final Authority with the Way, or the path of God, or that pursuit of perfection at rest in the center, as opposed to the field of confusion humming around it. In order to bring this about, a planetary consciousness must replace parochial consciousness, whether of family, state, nation, race, species, or religion. There will have to be an international language and currency, although local languages and currencies would continue in use as long as they were useful.

The agenda of a world government would be to cultivate the Earth as a garden. As a direct analogy to the individual life of a person, the life of the planet must strive first to survive, then to flourish. One thing this means is that warfare has to be considered an unacceptable way of settling disputes. All hostilities must cease forthwith. International disputes must be settled through a legal process as an ecologically friendly alternative to warfare. If the disputes of the world were resolved by a World Court with final international authority, and the peace retained by international guards, it would only be necessary to maintain very small military establishments other than local police, saving an enormous world-wide expense on so many levels.

[As I review these ideas about sixteen years after they were first written, it occurs to me that the weak link in the argument is that it is useless to suppose that powerful nations will voluntarily give up control of their military assets to any international body. On the other hand, if the World Court were established in its authority, it may be possible, in most cases, to accomplish the same objectives without requiring sovereign nations to give up control of their own military assets.]

While there are plenty of regions on the planet with obvious and uncontested boundaries, there are many spots around the world where borders and land use are hotly disputed. It may take many years to evolve solutions for some of the most troublesome spots, *e.g.*, the Middle East, but if the legal framework of formal consideration is set in place as the Theater of Change, military confrontations would no longer be tolerated or useful. Violent demonstrations would simply impact badly upon the case of those responsible. Disputing parties would devote their efforts towards presenting their case as effectively as possible before the scrutiny of the international World Court, rather than squandering their resources and credibility in bloodshed and violence.

The international "peace dividend" that would result from a new world order based upon a final authority, would be so enormous that it would independently ensure a period of unprecedented global prosperity.

Historically, the usual way of creating political units was through conflict and conquest: "authority" was merely a variation of "power." The history of the human race is largely the record of the abuse of power and the recurring failures of cohesion, but it is important to remember that many governments, cultivating their patch of the garden as best they could, have managed to provide, at least for brief periods, relatively favorable conditions for life to flourish.

Within comparatively recent times (the last 200 years), an experiment in democracy has been going on in the United States. In spite of the discounts which must be considered for exceptional starting advantages (the opportunity of making a fresh start with a wealth of natural resources and fertile soil), it is clear that the infant nation that followed from the designs of the founding fathers was healthy, and robust with vitality. However, as the nation begins to show signs of age, two main faults have been growing in significance: a sharpening of the inequalities of power and advantage, and an inadequate flexibility to deal with the rapidly changing requirements of contemporary problems. "The Government" is alive, and, like any living thing, it wants to grow as much as it can. Big Government has now grown so big, fat, and ponderous, feeding upon the vitality of the nation, that the people underneath it all are suffocating.

Deal the cards out however you will, the longer the game goes on, the more the gap measuring variations in relative advantage will widen and solidify. The favored group is "The Establishment" and it has always happened this way and always will happen, regardless of the political system or varieties of control. In fact, the realization of the inevitability of this pattern prompted Thomas Jefferson to suggest that a fresh revolution were necessary every twenty-seven years (the average age of a generation).

Hierarchies of wealth, power, and privilege are inevitable, but they may be flexible and moderate rather than rigid and sharp. Everyone wants to make his own life as agreeable as possible. There is also commonly a desire in good times to spread wealth to one's family and friends, and, in times of prosperity, to the rest of the world.

The best arrangement of society is one which follows all of the basic natural laws, but which is responsive and flexible. There are two principle functions in the equation of distinction: there is the degree of difference between the extremes, and the rate of change. In many parts of the world there are small civilizations of very wealthy elites in the midst of large populations of downtrodden poor (there are no old cars in Manila ~ there are shiny new BMWs, and pedal rickshaws ~ nothing in between). Other civilizations are more equally distributed. Some of these regimes are stable, others are highly volatile. Sharpening describes the process of widening the gap; leveling describes the narrowing. A certain amount of sharpening is valuable for the pursuit of excellence, but excessive sharpening leads to instability, loss of balance, and confusion. On the other hand, the rate of change in any microcosm follows a similar pattern: more rapid change is dynamic and interesting, but if change be too rapid, confusion and chaos may follow.

In the abstract pattern of this process, there are four cardinal points of varieties of distinction: sharp and slow, sharp and fast, level and slow, level and fast. As a civilization fluctuates between these variations we see a correlation to the relative prosperity of the civilization as a whole. That is, in times of dwindling prosperity, distinctions of advantage tend to sharpen. In times of improving prosperity, distinctions tend to be less severe. Usually, it is the poorest countries that have the sharpest distinction between rich and poor. As the United States approaches the close of the second millennium, we are not surprised to discover that the gap between rich and poor is widening ~ it is a prime symptom of the underlying reality of a general decline in the overall prosperity of the country, both in comparison with the rest of the world, and also with its own recent history.

From time to time, capable leaders come to power one way or another and for a period of years of peace and prosperity civilization seems to fulfill its promise. Then, with the passing of the particular hero or statesman, the old confusion supervenes. The American experiment attempts to ameliorate that problem by a practice of rapid turnover of national leaders, to prevent anyone from taking advantage of a position of power for very long. Unfortunately, that has come to mean a succession of confused and blundering presidents whose vision is just too shallow and too short to measure up to the challenge of their office.

The greatest problem with the democratic process is its tendency to produce a breed of professional politicians. What it comes down to is that the qualities necessary to be an accomplished and effective politician are entirely different from the qualities required of a competent national leader. The political presence is so close to the surface that political authority fluctuates like a daily stock quotation. At a time when it is absolutely essential for any national leader to consider as large a context of time as possible, we have a situation where every president spends half of his term of office campaigning for re-election (and his second term in total disregard of the opinions of the American people; when it was pointed out to a recent Vice President of the United States that the vast majority of citizens of the country were overwhelmingly opposed to the policies of the Administration, his reply was, "So?"). When it is necessary to have a detached, objective viewpoint to conceive coherent long term designs involving the whole Earth, we have politicians dependent on the whims of every special interest of the moment backed by money or influence. What this means is that we do not have a government with sufficient integrity and authority to correct the abuses of advantage which the greedy and ruthless have been quietly accumulating over the years.

When the American constitution was written, its authors could not possibly have foreseen the circumstances which exist in the world today. Thomas Jefferson may have been overzealous with his revolution every twenty-seven years, but it certainly seems to me to be time to design a new system of social, economic, and political order encompassing not only the entire family of the human race, but also the entire life force of the Biosphere of the whole planet.

The Seminary

Plato suggested long ago that national leaders should be selected in advance and given the most careful training from their earliest youth. The kind of perspective required for exercising primary responsibility for the welfare of a large state is a very specialized one. The only way to ensure that a national leader would be prepared to handle the requirements of his office is to provide specialized training and education beginning as early as possible.

All of the various functions of government should be performed by trained professionals; the function I have in mind for the Seminary is to produce the keystone of the arch, the final Judge, who must develop a total world view which would include every aspect relevant to life on Earth. I see a need for someone who can rise above the level of personal interest, and identify himself not only with the fate of the whole of humanity, but also with the entire field of life energy on Earth.

In order to cultivate this attitude, which is clearly theological, I imagine a kind of Seminary as a training ground for all the qualities most essential for world leaders. This would be a small school, perhaps one or two hundred students at the most ~ possibly much smaller. Admission to this school would be by invitation of the current Judge, with the effort made to achieve wide international representation. Students might be admitted at any age, but the younger the better. The school would be generously funded, but students would not be allowed to accumulate personal wealth. There may perhaps be a trial period of a year or so during which time the Judge might expel a student, but after that trial period, each student would acquire a tenure that guarantees his status, independent of any political pressure.

The Seminary may convene at any time and elect one of their number as the Judge, according to some formula. For example, the new Judge may be elected by a simple majority (after a death or recall), but three-quarters might be required to recall his authority. It would be expected that all students would know each other well, and would make the right choice. It may be advisable to elect a line of succession at some time in advance, to guarantee a smooth transition to the chair of authority.

Some of the remaining members of the Seminary might arrange themselves into various advisory committees, while others may become instructors for the new students who would be entering the college in an ongoing cycle. A University of International Studies would grow up around the Seminary, and form the basis for preparing the decisions of the Judge. After a few generations, this specialized environment may attain more and more of an objective world view and become a powerful institution independent from and above parochial interests. The location of the school might be a secluded mountain top somewhere, although every advanced student would take frequent sabbaticals to live in some location of the real world in order to experience as wide a range of life as possible.

§

This whole program of reform may sound like a pipe dream, but we have seen how quickly events in the world can make yesterday's news seem like last year's snow. This is a time of turmoil and uncertainty. All over the world we are seeing small ethnic groups trying to forge their own political identity independent of the accidents of History. These are actually just the right conditions to favor a new ultimate unity. The alternations of *Solve et Coagula* (separation and union) represent very powerful natural laws. (The convergence of the forces of life on Earth into a planetary union is one example of the Omega Point described by Pierre Teilhard de Chardin.)

While the present ideas are designed as a whole package to reform the political, economic, and social arrangements of the world, it is possible to implement many of the ideas on a local, or at least national, basis. For example, in any country, some of the economic reforms suggested here could dramatically improve the present situation. If they revitalize the local economy, other countries may follow suit, and the visionary goals of world union may not seem so far away.

The Church of the Living Tree

We believe that the most important Manifestation of the Living God on Earth is to be found in the Trees. The greatest Folly of the Human Race has been the Destruction of the Trees of the Ancient Forest, with no Regard to their true Value. Living Trees are worth more than dead ones.

The Church of the Living Tree

Articles of Organization

The Church of the Living Tree
P.O. Box 64
Leggett, CA 95585

July 8, 1992

Articles of Organization

I. Name:

These Articles are to define and organize a Church, the name of which shall be The Church of the Living Tree ('The Church').

II. Founder's Statement:

The Church of the Living Tree worships the Tree as the image of God. We understand God as all of Life. We do not postulate any role as the Creator of the Universe, nor do we concern ourselves with teleological questions ~ these matters being considered outside the scope of our knowledge or concern.

It is all of Life which we worship as God (specifically, but not necessarily limited to, the entire field of life energy on Earth, including plants and animals as well as all human beings), and choose to represent it in the image of a Tree, not only to express our humility that there is more to

God than man, but also to express our reverence for the role which the Tree has played during most of Life's career, and its critical importance right now, and for the future of Life.

We regard Trees as primary and indispensable pillars of the life force on this planet, and any regard to the health of that life force must begin with the cultivation of Trees. The loss of the Trees represents the greatest single mistake the human race has made in its entire history. The burning off of millions of years' worth of fossil fuels in the last century, for example, pales in comparison with the loss of the Trees. For thousands of years the human race has asserted its dominance over the rest of life by destroying its environment, and, both directly and indirectly, killing off other species of plants and animals, not realizing that when all of the birds and fish and Trees are gone, the human race can not long survive. The biological health of the planet has been declining so rapidly that nothing short of an immediate turn around in planetary consciousness can reverse the slide towards the extinction of life.

Our primate ancestors were vegetarian, living in Trees and eating fruits and nuts. The change to a diet of animal flesh, and the resulting changes in lifestyle, have not only caused an increase in disease, a decline in general health, and an increase in aggressive behavior and warfare, but the destruction of the biological resources of life itself.

The pattern of destruction starts with cutting down the Trees, and then raising animals who graze away what's left, keeping the land under constant biological stress until the last of the land's life force is consumed. Most of the topsoil the world over has now been lost, and the thin membrane of the biosphere which covers the globe is being stretched thinner every day. The biological health of the planet is plunging rapidly towards the bleakness of toxic deserts, which will sooner or later become unable to support life.

Trees literally hold the Earth together, their roots extending many feet into the Earth's crust, pulling up minerals, nutrients, and water from below, as well as sheltering the ground surface from above, so that animals and smaller plants and even people can enjoy a habitat supported by Trees. It is not surprising to me that northern California, for example, is beginning to dry up; when the Trees are gone, the earth can no longer hold onto the water ~ the winter rains simply erode the topsoil, and the springs dry up under the heat of the summer sun.

Therefore, the particular goal and purpose of the Church of the Living Tree is to defend and protect the Trees which still remain on this Earth, to plant more Trees by the millions of acres all over the Earth, and to evolve patterns of human lifestyles that will support Trees rather than exploit and destroy them.

Half of all trees harvested are chipped up for the pulp mills; half of all landfills are composed of paper products. One of the first projects of the Church of the Living Tree will be to set up the Alternative Fiber Paper Mill to begin producing paper with no wood content at all, so that the trees that remain to us may be relieved of their greatest oppressor. Timber companies want you to think that they are felling Trees to build houses and fine furniture, but the sad truth is that ever greater percentages of timber harvests are just being chipped up for the pulp mills so that our mailboxes can be stuffed full of junk mail. A paper mill to a tree is like a glue factory to a horse.

Some plants can be cultivated for the fiber as a primary crop, as in fiber hemp, Cannabis sativa, and kenaf, Hibiscus cannabinum. Both of these are fast growing annuals that produce enormous quantities of high quality fiber in a single season. Other fiber may be recycled from agricultural by-products, such as rice straw, or from scraps from the garment industry, or rags and discards from other sources.

While the health of the Trees represents our primary concern, we understand the necessity of modifying human patterns of interaction with the Earth in order to evolve a sustainable lifestyle in which all forms of life can live in harmony. Some evolutionary trends that we want to promote include voluntary simplicity leading to a low impact lifestyle, and local, decentralized political and economic communities which will manage their own affairs: services, schools, health care, social assistance, and environmental consciousness. Simplicity should be the watchword of tax reform also: The entire whirlwind of tax lawyers, forms, loopholes, and endless paperwork for individuals and businesses should be replaced with a uniform land tax for revenue, supplemented by taxes on resource depletion for environmental control.

The problems of maintaining international peace and stability can never be resolved until some sort of international judicial body be established to arbitrate disputes and safeguard environmental integrity. In order for this to be effective, it must be related to a holding company for military equipment. Eventually, once this transition has taken place, inter-state warfare would be history; all disputes would be settled by the arbitration of this world court and enforced by its own military holdings. Separate States would eventually maintain no more than local police forces to deal with local problems, while the international military establishment would gradually subside into a very modest presence that would rarely be used. The benefits of this evolution are obvious: in the first place, the devastations of warfare (including the present potential to destroy all life overnight ~ the nuclear component of which may well be destroying all life slowly in any case) would be eliminated, but, in addition, the savings involved by reducing the military establishments of every sovereign state would be enormous, leading to an immediate and very real "peace dividend."

On the other hand, there is a problem with the idea of international authority: how to empower such an authority and how to prevent the abuse of that power. Our conclusion is that the issue is really one of the most important roles for religion. The Church of the Living Tree suggests the founding of a Seminary to cultivate a consciousness in which the concerns of the human race are subordinated to the concerns of the Biosphere as a whole, symbolized by our reverence for the Tree as the most important and most endangered support of the Biosphere. This Seminary will be designed to maintain the final judicial authority protecting the environment of life.

All of these ideas and projects are related, directly or indirectly, to our central purpose: support for the health of the Biosphere as a whole, starting with the Trees, and including animals and human beings. To further this goal, we are looking for donations of land all over the world, permanently dedicated to the Trees, particularly land whose life force has been depleted through misuse of one sort or another. We will establish volunteer communities of people who share our commitment to re-planting the Trees and restoring the land to fertility. We are interested in evolving alternative, low-impact lifestyles based upon a new paradigm: non-profit communities whose members live simple lives on permanent land trusts without the hassles of economic transactions, or paper work of any kind.

Projects of restoration may take many years and several phases. Preliminary work may involve the cleaning up of any toxic debris, and the care and maintenance of water systems. The next step would be to establish primary anchor Trees and shelter belts. Eventually we will attempt to introduce a variety of valuable Trees, according to the potential of the land. At the same time, complimentary programs of inter-cropping while the Trees are young, and other integrated land use (sustainable and organic) may be employed to accompany and augment the restoration of the Trees, and serve the communities that care for them.

Cultivating annual crops to feed to animals, and then eating the animals, has been shown to be a very inefficient and unhealthy lifestyle; we will expect to provide most of our food from Tree crops, supplemented by our own gardens. Once the land has been restored to fertility, it will support life comfortably, providing an alternative social environment where people can live a simple life on the land, free of the whole complex burden of survival which characterizes life for most residents of the modern jungle.

It may be possible for a large part of the world's population to live on these "free farms," free of economic competition and stress. Of course, this lifestyle would not be for everyone; the present structure of free market economics must be free to continue world wide without other interference than taxation on resource depletion (carefully scaled to attain targets of control). However, the free farm alternative will allow people to opt for a simple life rather than forcing them into unproductive or counter-productive economic activity just to survive (e.g., theft, drug dealing, swindles, manufacture and promotion of useless products, the industries of confusion, the inefficiencies of insurance scams, and countless other parasites on a healthy economy).

If you are concerned that the land you have lived on and worked so hard for might be sold, logged, liquidated, partitioned, developed, or otherwise exploited by some future heir or purchaser, you might want to consider dedicating it to the Trees as a permanent trust under the care of The Church of the Living Tree. If you have no land of your own, plant Trees, and otherwise support the local ecology wherever you are. Or, alternatively, volunteer your services personally as a member of a free farm community to restore Tree cover and fertility to the lands in our care. Families are welcome, including children of all ages. Volunteers are not paid, but all expenses, including housing and food, will be provided as our resources permit.

The Church of the Living Tree has little formal structure and makes no demands upon its members. All Tree-spirits everywhere who share our goals and interests are encouraged to work with us, or to pursue the same goals independently, according to their inclination. No particular forms of religious activity are required of members, but we might suggest at least that spiritual gatherings take place in a grove of living Trees rather than in enclosed buildings of wood or stone. Whenever we wish to feel close to

God, we want to go into the forest, close to the comforting shelter of the Trees, especially the oldest and the largest, with the deepest roots and the highest crowns. We do not want to hear sermons or even music ~ silence feels more appropriate to us while we sit, passive and receptive, that we might be able to hear the messages which God might have for us, and not be drowning them out with our own noise, full of our own importance.

And if you wish to celebrate a holiday at Christmas time, please do not kill any Trees; perhaps you will choose a living Tree to decorate and honor with your celebrations. If no other Trees are available to you, and there is no place for you to plant a Tree, you might cultivate a living Tree in a pot, in order to receive spiritual inspiration from it.

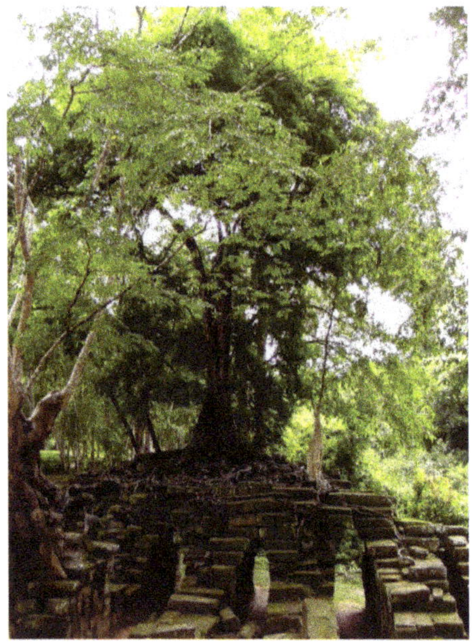

John R. Stahl, Founder,
THE CHURCH OF THE LIVING TREE
tree@tree.org

III. Purpose:

The purpose of the Church of the Living Tree is to defend and protect the Trees which still remain on this Earth, to plant more Trees by the millions of acres all over the earth, and to evolve patterns of human lifestyles that will support Trees rather than exploit and destroy them. In pursuance of these primary purposes, the Church may undertake additional Tree support projects such as finding and promoting alternatives for low grade utilization of forest material ~ specifically, to promote tree-free sources of pulp for paper products. All of these goals have the same end in view: an increase in the population, range, and health of Trees, which we revere as God.

IV. Organization:

The principle unit of organization is the Restoration Project Community. Every piece of land acquired by the Church as a project for the restoration of Trees will be independently managed by the community of volunteers living and planting Trees on the property. The authority for all decisions regarding the operation of the project shall be vested in the Stewards in residence at the project. The first Stewards of a project will be appointed by the Board of Directors of the Church at the commencement of restoration activity. In addition to the Stewards, there may be any number of Volunteers, temporary or resident, who may participate in the work of restoration under the direction of the Stewards. From time to time, Volunteers who wish to make a longer commitment may become Stewards, at the invitation of the current Stewards.

The Church may organize communities for purposes other than a restoration project; for example, there may be a community formed for the purpose of managing a newsletter, or acting as a center of information and outreach to new members. For purposes of organization, each of these communities will be equivalent to restoration project communities, including both Stewards and Volunteers, and a seat on the Board of Directors.

V. The Board of Directors:

The supervision of restoration projects as well as the management of Church affairs shall be conducted by the Board of Directors. Each restoration project community will elect one of the Stewards to serve on the Board of Directors.

VI. The Trustees:

The final authority and responsibility for any and all decisions regarding the activity or operation of the Church of the Living Tree, including matters of finance, policy, activity, and direction, shall be held initially by the Trustees of the Church. The Trustees may over-ride any decisions of the Board of Directors.

As soon as the Seminary of the Church of the Living Tree elects one of their number as the Advocate for the Tree, the authority held by the Trustees shall pass permanently to the Advocate and his or her successors.

The initial Trustees will sign this organizing document; subsequent Trustees will be added by unanimous written approval of the existing Trustees. Documents approving additional Trustees will be attached as addenda to each original copy of these Articles of Organization.

VII. The Seminary:

The Seminary of the Church of the Living Tree will be set up as an independent and self governing body designed as an educational and social environment to produce the spiritual head of the Church, the Advocate for the Tree. Whenever necessary, adult members of the Seminary (sixteen years old or more) may elect one of their number to the role of Advocate for the Tree. The Advocate may be elected by a simple majority, but if the Seminary desires to recall their selection, at least three quarters of the members must vote for recall in order to elect an alternative candidate.

Initially, the members of the Seminary will be selected by the Trustees of the Church at such times and in such numbers as will seem best. Once the members of the Seminary select the first Advocate for the Tree (no time frame is stipulated ~ the members of the Seminary will be expected to select the appropriate time), the Advocate will assume all of the authority of the Trustees, including selection of new members of the Seminary.

The Advocate for the Tree will be responsible for improvements or modifications in the design or functioning of the Seminary; the following ideas from the founder's vision are only a starting suggestion to indicate the idea:

The optimum age for enrolling new members to the Seminary will be found with experience; the founder suggests starting with children of age five to ten. All members of the Seminary will have all their needs provided by the Church, but will not be paid, or allowed to accumulate personal wealth. The school would start small, enlarging to whatever size seems best suited to achieve the intended result. The Seminary would be deliberately selected to represent as wide a range of the peoples and cultures of the Earth as possible (new members must be unrelated to any other members, present or past). Once admitted to the Seminary, members would be encouraged to let go of their temporal attachments to family, culture, or nation, and grow into their role as stewards of the whole Earth and protectors of the Trees. The Advocate may wish to form advisory committees to help with the enrollment of new members, with the appointment of instructors and specialists to form the educational environment, and with the management of any other matters pertaining to the Seminary. The curriculum would encompass the perspective of the entire Biosphere of the planet, with emphasis on the role of Trees. Of necessity, human concerns ~ social, economic, and political ~ will form a major aspect of study. To emphasize their co-dependence with the earth, the Seminary members would spend a considerable part of their time working directly on the land, cultivating the Seminary's lands as an arboretum and garden.

VIII. The Advocate for the Tree:

The Advocate for the Tree is designed to be the spiritual authority of the Church, and the voice for the Trees. The model is the Dalai Lama of Tibet: at the death of the Dalai Lama, the Buddhist priests of Tibet search for the new incarnation of their spiritual leader. Found as a child, the new Dalai Lama is trained for his role for most of his life, encouraging the flowering of a deeply rooted spiritual perspective. The selection of the Advocate for the Tree is similar, but we take a hint from the honey bees and raise a small group of candidates on the royal jelly to create a reservoir of spiritual energy, instead of relying on a single individual. In a manner similar to beliefs of Tibetan Buddhists, we are expecting the chosen Advocate to be the incarnation of the Tree in human form, to speak with the voice of the Trees, and to promote the survival and optimum flourishing of all life on the planet.

IX. Finances:

The activities of the Church of the Living Tree will be financed by donations and grants, supplemented by sales of Tree products or other farm material cultivated on a restoration project, and possible business activity directly related to the interests of the church (for example, pilot projects manufacturing paper from tree-free pulp sources, either selling the paper produced to cover the cost of the operations, or perhaps selling material cultivated as a source for the pulp. These activities will serve the purposes of the Church not only by directly relieving Trees from the pressure of demands for pulp, but will also serve as a vehicle for education and inspiration for other businesses to manufacture tree-free paper on a commercial scale).

No money received by the Church of the Living Tree will inure to the benefit of any private parties, individuals, or organizations. Restoration projects will only be carried out on lands donated to (or purchased by) the Church, or on lands permanently dedicated for public or charitable use. None of the assets of the Church will be used for projects not directly related to its stated goals and purposes, as expressed in these articles.

From time to time, the Church may employ persons with required specialized skills, and will pay whatever wages are necessary. However, residents of Church communities, Stewards, Volunteers, and general members, will not receive payment for their services. As an alternative, community members will have all of their needs provided directly, or paid for by the community. An expense account may be provided for special occasions when essential activity will be carried on off the properties of the Church.

X. Dissolution:

In the event that this organization is dissolved for any reason, the Advocate for the Tree (or the Trustees of the Church, in the event dissolution is effected before the election of the first Advocate) shall distribute all remaining assets of the Church to his, her, or their choice of non-profit organizations which, in the opinion of the Advocate (or Trustees), will most effectively carry on the goals and purposes of the Church of the Living Tree. However, no such dissolution procedures may be carried out that would result in members of the Church being required (without their consent) to alter their status with regard to lands entrusted to them as Stewards.

XI. Initial Trustees:

The names and addresses of the persons who are the initial Trustees of the Church are as follows:

John Stahl
Jeffrey Conant
Etienne Conod

In witness whereof, we have hereunto subscribed our names and date:

{signatures} July 8, 1992

The Church of the Living Tree
P.O. Box 64
Leggett, CA 95585

October 1, 1993

Text of Proposed Amendment

Articles of Organization:

1. Article III. Purpose is amended by the addition of a second paragraph, as follows:

'The purposes of The Church of the Living Tree are limited to those enumerated in these Articles of Organization. None of the members of the Church (while acting in the name of the Church) will engage in any activities not directly related to the purposes of the Church or in any activities not permitted under section 501 (c) (3) of the Internal Revenue Code. None of the assets of the Church will be used for any activities not directly related to the purposes of the Church or for any activities not permitted under section 501 (c) (3) of the Internal Revenue Code.'

2. Article X. Dissolution is amended to read as follows:

'In the event that this organization is dissolved for any reason, the Advocate for the Tree (or the Trustees of the Church, in the event dissolution is effected before the election of the first Advocate) shall distribute all remaining assets of the Church to his, her, or their choice of non-profit organizations which would qualify and would be exempt within the meaning of section 501 (c) (3) of the Internal Revenue Code, and which, in the opinion of the Advocate (or Trustees), will most effectively carry on the goals and purposes of the Church of the Living Tree.'

3. The amendments proposed herein will become effective upon approval of a majority of the Trustees of the Church.

Approved by:

John Stahl
Jeffrey Conant
Etienne Conod

S

Free Farms

The basic concept of the Free Farm is that it is an alternative and a refuge from the complex web of financial entanglements that comprises the daily reality for most individuals at the present time. At the Free Farm, one's account is expected to be kept current and in balance ~ everyone contributes as they can, and everyone's needs are met. Like the kibbutz in Israel, it is the Community that defines the financial unit, not the individual. This pattern allows for a much more efficient arrangement of resources, as advantages of scale are realized quickly, even by very small communities.

This is not a new idea, and communities have formed along these lines from time to time, but they frequently fail, and one of the main reasons for their failure is an inadequate consideration for the operation of the principle of authority. There may be a desire to dispense with the services of any authority, but it is not possible to eliminate the problem of authority by fiat. To set up a community with no other recourse to authority but the consensus of the current members is to abdicate the responsibility of leadership and leave the community vulnerable to dissension.

Our solution to this problem at the Church of the Living Tree is to make a distinction between the Stewards, who share the responsibility for the land, and the Volunteers, who do not. The Stewards are the core group who have a long term commitment to the land, while the volunteers come as guests, and may or may not have more than a temporary interest in the land. After some period of time and demonstration of commitment a volunteer may be invited to become a Steward.

Projects of the Church of the Living Tree are operated by Stewards and volunteers who do not pay rent or receive wages. At the present time we only have a couple of locations with limited facilities for volunteers, but we hope to increase the number and capacity of locations where volunteers can come and work for the Trees.

In the meantime, we are trying to assist placement of interested persons in free farm situations by operating a Free Farm Bulletin Board as a clearinghouse for persons offering or seeking a free farm situation. The Church of the Living Tree can not be responsible for any consequences of contacts made through this service. Please check out offerings thoroughly before making any commitment. (www.tree.org/a3.htm)

Please Note: The limited stipulations for the use of this service are that all situations, whether offered or sought, must be on the basis of free exchange. Situations requiring payment, or persons seeking paid employment will be deleted when found. It should be further assumed, unless otherwise clarified, that a person invited to a Free Farm through the use of this service will have the status of Volunteer, as discussed above, without any tenure to the land, unless it is so arranged by the hosts.

The Metaphysics of Sex

by *John Roland Stahl*

(This article is a previously unpublished analogy drawn from the Author's more abstract text *Patterns of Illusion and Change*)

§

What is this strange entanglement of living energies that we call sexual congress?

One reason there are many answers to this question is that what we usually think of as "sex" is just one of eight possible patterns of the cosmic superimposition of life forms. Why eight, exactly? Well, since this is to be primarily an essay on sex, I will try not to dwell too extensively on theoretical metaphysics, but I must briefly introduce the subject:

The numbers of mathematics are the clearest and most wonderful symbols for the principle mysteries of the cosmos. This was realized by Pythagoras, and represents his most important contribution to the history of ideas. To illustrate the idea very simply, I supply the mathematical images suggested by Pythagoras: the number one: a point; the number two: a line; the number three: a plane (triangle); the number four: a solid (pyramid). To these four, I add the number five: movement (time). The idea is that these symbols and images are keys to the primary mysteries of nature.

One: the undivided whole; two: the distinction between subject and object; three: a point of perspective between subject and object that establishes a field of energy; four: the emergence into manifest reality (Spring, Summer, Fall, and Winter); five: the process of change.

For the present discussion, I pass over the first three Arcana (primary mysteries of philosophy), and move right along to the set of four patterns produced by the conjunction of two distinctions of yang and yin (expressed in the *I Ching*, a binary system, as: young yang: ⚎, old yang: ⚌, young yin: ⚍, old yin: ⚏). (Anyone who is interested in the first three Arcana should refer to my more formal presentation of metaphysics, *Patterns of Illusion and Change.*)

I could begin the discussion of sex here, but I prefer to use the more entertaining patterns that form when a third line is introduced. Three lines produce eight trigrams, and produce a set of patterns at a level of complexity most suitable to an analysis of the possible patterns of sexual relationship. The first and third line may represent the Subject and Object of an encounter, and the third line in the middle introduces the value of the charge: positive or negative.

Passive
Copper
Venus
Gentle
Wind, Wood
Sun

Coagula
Gold
Sun
Creative
Heaven
Ch'ien

Peace
Silver
Moon
Abysmal
Water
K'an

Light
Tin
Jupiter
Joyous
Lake
Tui

Conflict
Quicksilver
Mercury
Clinging
Fire
Li

Heavy
Lead
Saturn
Keeping still
Mountain
Kên

Active
Iron
Mars
Arousing
Thunder
Chên

Solve
Prima Materia
Earth
Receptive
Earth
K'un

Sex begins here:

The first pattern (Chên ☳ Thunder, Red) is an active subject attacking or pursuing a passive, defending, or fleeing object. Sexually, this is aggression or sadism; as a perversion it is when the infliction of pain or suffering is perceived as pleasurable.

The second pattern (Li ☲ Fire, Orange) is an active subject in conflict with an active object. Sexually, this is simply fighting. Ever notice the similarity between wrestling and sex? Because of the warped nature of our society, a great many people are conditioned to obtain their sexual gratification from some form of fighting.

The third pattern (Tui ☱ Joyous, Yellow) is an active subject offering loving service to a passive or retreating object (boy chases girl, who runs away). Sexually, this is simply love that is not returned, although it may be accepted. If it were not accepted, the pattern would more resemble the first pattern, above.

The fourth pattern (Ch'ien ☰ Creative, White) may be the only one easily recognizable as sex: both subject and object actively expressing love for each other. This is the creative act, which can result in the creation of new life.

The fifth pattern (Sun ☴ Gentle, Green) is similar to the third, with positions reversed: the subject is passive, receiving the loving attentions of the devoted object.

The sixth pattern (K'an ☵ Water, Blue) is characteristic of the latter stages of the life cycle of a field of energy: there is a bond of "love" between subject and object, but neither one is actively expressing any energy.

The seventh pattern (Kên ☶ Mountain, Purple) is the opposite of the first: it is the passive subject that is subjected to the negative energy of the active object. Sexually, this is masochism, where the subject obtains pleasure being the object of negative attention.

The eighth pattern (K'un ☷ Receptive, Black) is not, strictly speaking, a variation of sexual possibility at all: it is the absence of sex; there is no contact at all between subject and object.

§

Obviously this catalog is greatly oversimplified; however, it provides a framework by which we can discuss the merits of any particular sexual activity. We can make a distinction, for example, between the actual forms, and projections of those forms in fantasy. Consensual role playing between sadists and masochists can be a harmless way to experience an unusual source of sexual excitement (so that, hopefully, they can progress beyond it); actually deriving pleasure from inflicting real pain or suffering upon another life is a criminal act. A game such as football or chess is a harmless ventilation of aggressive energy. Actual warfare is a regrettable lapse into barbarity, above which civilization strives to ascend.

We take the position that love is wonderful stuff, and that we can all use as much of it as we can get. All alliances based on expressions of love will have positive effects, regardless of the forms, the genders, or the ages of the love makers. Expressions of hostility in any form or for whatever reason can have problematic consequences, and anyone caught up in a web of hostility should try to evolve towards a transcendence of that web of darkness into the light of love.

The colors of the Aura associated with these eight forms can be used to determine the level of life energy expressed. The darker colors below the center point in the illustration above (on either end of the spectrum of light) indicate lower levels of life energy and vitality. The brighter colors higher up indicate much richer levels of life energy and greater overall health.

Advice to Youth

by *John Roland Stahl*

1997

I'm sure I'm not the first adult who has wished that he had the opportunity of reliving another lifetime with the benefit of all the wisdom he has learned since the first one. If only I could do it all over again! I have made some mistakes.

The difficulty faced by youth is very similar to the problem faced by a reader at the library: certainly there are plenty of wonderful books, but there are so many stupid and boring ones, too, that it is hard to find the wheat amongst all that chaff. I don't understand why someone hasn't compiled an extensive hierarchical index of the world's greatest books. Certainly there are "Great Books" lists, but I'm interested in something much more extensive, arranged by categories, and comprising a real map to the treasures in books. I have read many thousands of books since my earliest youth, and I really could have used such a guide. When I think of all the stupid, useless, and boring books I have read in my life, it makes me wish I had another lifetime to live over again during which time I could read only the best and most amazing of the literary creations which have surfaced since writing began.

I have a whole lot of ideas here, and I direct them to young people. Older people don't seem to be interested much in new ideas, which is one of the main reasons why most adults are so boring. A young person with a fresh and open mind and a new life to lead can do anything, and anything can happen. But people end up taking different paths, and not all of them lead to happiness. Many people are finally unhappy, no matter how hard they try to live their lives well. Some of it seems so random sometimes ~ or is it all very carefully under control as so many people seem to believe?

It was entirely by chance that I discovered *The Autobiography of Benvenuto Cellini.* I could hardly believe that such an amazing original window onto the high times of life so long ago should have escaped my attention for so long. Why didn't somebody tell me? Well, here follows some of the ideas I wish someone had told me when I was younger:

Life

If there is any point to religion or God at all, it has to refer to Life. Life is so amazing that it must be reverenced as God. Those of us who are still alive ~ trees, people, animals ~ we are God. Every individual living being is an emanation from the one light.

The purpose of the individual ego is to maintain that distinction by which it separates itself from the rest of the cosmos. Whatever is alive wants to survive, first, and then to grow, as its own independent twinkle of light. This is such an obvious idea, and yet it is sometimes overlooked by young people who are growing so fast in so many directions at once that survival doesn't really seem to be important or relevant to them. But the truth is that everybody dies when their body wears out in one way or another. Some people die young, and some people live forever.

So take care of your body as well as you take care of the house that you live in. A lot is known about health these days. So much of it is negative news: so many familiar things seem to be harmful to life. But suppose you knew ahead of time what your life were to be like? Suppose your life were like a "chose your own plot" adventure book: you could look over the endings first and decide which way you wanted the story to go?

If you choose the ending where you live a long and happy life in good health, then you will be happy to make the obvious health choices. You will eat mainly fresh food which you grow yourself, and avoid toxic substances as much as possible (many people would have no idea of what to eat if they had to eliminate the "three main food groups" ~ fat, sugar, and salt). Wherever you live, plant some fruit and nut trees. If you are still young, you can enjoy the trees' maturity yourself; if you are older, you can plant the trees for your children and still live to enjoy some of the reward yourself.

Why do people use drugs ~ coffee, alcohol, sugar, cocaine, and the rest ~ when they know that they are so toxic to life? And is it worthwhile sampling them for yourself to decide if any of them have any value? In a word, no. Marijuana is probably the safest of the social drugs, and it is possible that there may be drugs like LSD that perform their effects without any direct physical damage to the body at all, but, by and large, most drugs operate on one very famous principle: buy now, pay later. Of course, the payments one makes later always greatly exceed any current value. "But," the apologist says with a smirk, "You do get it right away!" That is true; and one is born every minute.

Coffee is a pretty typical example of an insidious drug. I have grown to develop a taste and fondness for the stuff which makes it very hard to keep it permanently out of my diet. But coffee just exhausts my energy. If I drink coffee on a day when I have some important work to do, I just have a harder time getting it done once I start drinking coffee.

About the only time drinking coffee really seems to be an effective strategy is when you have a three hour final exam. Twenty minutes before the exam, you consume your limit of double espressos or a rich Italian roast, or even a moderately roasted Sumatra, brewed black and strong from freshly roasted beans (avoid the over-roasted beans ~ I don't know why they are so fashionable ~ all subtlety of flavor is lost, and much of the caffeine is even roasted out ~ all that remains is the taste of burnt carbon), and then take your seat in the exam hall. Be sure to fasten your seat belt and wear heavy shoes. Of course, as soon as the exam is over, it may take you three days to recover, but you'll have written a memorable exam paper (not necessarily any good). But it may be possible that even this tactic is based upon a mistake; that your best preparation for the exam is simply a good night's sleep, coffee only clouding your mind with confusion. Certainly a good night's sleep ought to provide you with abundant energy for performing whatever it is you have to do, so it might be totally unnecessary to outrage your body with violent poisons just for the sake of a brief exhilaration. You could drink wheat grass juice instead of coffee.

Sex

After life and health, the next concern is sex. Sex refers to the extent and manner of a person's integration with the rest of life; in other words, a person's relationship with God. It may seem like a surprising way of expressing it, but sex is intimately connected to the very center of Life itself, and its importance can hardly be overstated.

The only way to do justice to the concept of sex is to emphasize that it concerns separation, disharmony, and discord, as much as it concerns love and union. Why do you think pain is so erotically charged for so many people? It is the other end of the lever of pleasure.

There is also a kind of social currency that is analogous to money and power, and is, in fact, often related. Some people are young, healthy, intelligent, beautiful, white, male, rich, and powerful, and some are old, sick, stupid, ugly, black, female, poor, and helpless. And then there is everything in between.

Whoever said life was fair? By the way, what advice is there for those on the bottom? Go out and work in the garden, take off your shoes, and rejoice that you are still alive and may feel the sun on your body and the earth beneath your feet; and eat fresh food.

If you are at least young, on the other hand, there is always something you can do to improve your chances of survival and growth.

What is the secret of life? Go towards the Light. God is at the Center, at a point of balance and clarity, the source of radiance and light. Movement away from this light leads to confusion. The more the lines in your life converge towards a center of peace, happiness, clarity, health, and love, the more you will grow stronger. If, on the other hand, elements in your life pull you off center in random clashes of accident, sorrow, confusion, and sickness, you will weaken and decline towards your eventual death.

Love is wonderful stuff, and we can all use as much as we can get. All manifestations of love are good, as long as they are welcome, in whatever forms they take.

Broadly speaking, there are three ways of managing the energy at the core of life: solitude and celibacy; bonded to another life (usually human, although bonding with dogs, other animals, trees, cars, a cigarette, a syringe, a teddy bear, etc. are all very common); or living in a state of dynamic interaction with more than one other partner.

The first pattern is the pattern of youth. While infants are quickly bonded to their mothers (usually), this usually gives way to a period of life in which children are fundamentally alone, emotionally. Even if sexual activity with another partner is discovered, masturbation is usually the sexual activity of choice for children, whose erotic interests usually center in themselves, exclusively.

Among adults, solitude is often a reasonable or inevitable choice for many people. Living with other people in bonded relationships of one sort or another is frequently destructive to certain personalities in some situations, and solitude allows a chance for independent personal growth. Solitude is basically conservative as far as life force is concerned: no new force is created, but the remaining force is conserved.

Personal pair bonding is so well known as the basic medium of sex, that it is hard to find anything new to say about it here. I will merely remark abstractly that some relationships are fairly well balanced in one way or another and result in a stable bond, while others are fundamentally unequal in ways that are not balanced by other factors, resulting in an unstable bond often expressing oppression, hostility, frustration, neurosis, or other hindrance to the free flowing of sexual energy.

The third pattern of social interaction is less clearly perceived as a sexual alternative by most people. It is possible for a complex relationship of more than two people to be both intentional and stable. Sometimes this pattern is represented by a weak bond between two people, one of whom feels unsatisfied, or confined in too small a box, and who is looking for a different connection.

There is something crude about the economy with which these processes of social evolution manage to accomplish their effects. One problem is the plight of those who prefer an unsatisfactory relationship to the loneliness of solitude, perceived as the obvious precedence to a new relationship. But it is possible to arrange an intentional triangle as a creative way of living intimately with others while at the same time avoiding the attachment of exclusive bonds.

I go even further: all of my life I have been attracted to both men and women; there are two genders, and it has never seemed necessary or good to eliminate either one or the other from the considerations of personal and intimate interest. I certainly want both men and women in my life. I guess I realize that a stable triangle of three persons can't really last forever, but it seems to me that it might be possible to go on for quite a while and enjoy a remarkable array of benefits.

In the first place, there is the matter of economy. If two can live as cheaply as one, three can live as cheaply as two. Furthermore, with three people, there is always another person to wash the dishes, take care of the kids, or work in the garden. As much as I desire a sexual intimacy with both a man and a woman, I also need to have time to myself. Obviously, in a triangular relationship, everyone has time to be alone.

There is nothing inherently better about any of these three basic patterns of relationship; any of them may be appropriate at any given time for a particular person. Heterosexual pair bonding may be the inevitably dominant variety of human relationship, but any other variety may be suitable as a temporary or even relatively permanent alternative. Life is far more complex than it was two or three hundred years ago, and there is no reason why new arrangements may not take the place of traditional relationships in some situations.

The utility of rigidly differentiated sex roles has been rapidly declining during the last hundred years to the point where the only important absolute distinctions which can be made between the genders have to do with the biologically differentiated sexual function. For this reason, there is really not too much difference between heterosexual and homosexual relationships other than the obvious limitation of procreation. In terms of the involvement with another person, it's all the same.

As each person's life unfolds, he may find a different set of personal needs, and the only advice I can give is that you try to find someone whose needs are a complement to your own.

Oh, yes; it hardly seems necessary to refer to an idea which is so painfully obvious in these days of AIDS, but if you do want to survive, you will exercise caution and discretion in your physical sexual activity. It may not be quite as much fun with a condom, but at least you will remain alive.

Money

What's next? Some people put money ahead of sex, but I think that is a mistake. Money may be very important, and may be essential for many aspects of survival and growth, but money alone, as everyone knows, is never enough to compensate for the poverty of an empty life.

On the other hand, after sex, money looms as an abstraction that measures so many other aspects central to survival that it must be taken seriously. Basically, it works like this: you have to work out some arrangement about money before you can make any other plans about your life. Whether you like it or not, most people end up spending most of their time working in order to keep a supply of money coming in that can keep up with their needs.

Since you spend a third of your life in bed, you might as well sleep on the most comfortable bed you can find. And since you spend most of the rest of your life working, you might as well find things that you enjoy doing as the vehicles for your financial resources. I do not say that you should find something that makes lots of money, on the theory that money is so useful and necessary. How you make the money in the first place is the overriding consideration since that is what you will spend your life doing.

Goals

So how do you arrange your goals and desires? What is it that you want to put together? Goethe says, "Beware of what you wish for in youth, because you will get it in middle age." My father put it another way: "Be careful when you pray, lest your prayers be answered."

We come down to the real question: What do I do now? You may see goals in terms of the future of life on Earth, or as a personal solution with one or more partners with your own land and your own business. Or your vision might include all the above, or something entirely original.

The question of what to do also includes the question of where to do it, and with whom. Usually this knot has to be untied all at once. You can't decide to live in Kansas and make your living as a sea captain, for instance. Many people run into the dilemma of wanting to live in the country, and yet feeling tied to the economies of the cities.

Best, perhaps, is to work for yourself; perhaps with one or two partners. Working for wages is as much of a dead end as paying rent. In both cases, the institution is set up to benefit the employer and the landlord, not the worker or tenant. In both cases, of course, this is easier said than done. It is hard to set up in business with no money, and pretty hard to buy property without money either. The rich may be able to buy property with no money, but not the poor.

The place where you live is like the bed you sleep in at night: you spend a lot of time there, so it might as well be a nice place. It ought to have some land attached to it, as much as possible. You want to be able to plant some trees, fruits and nuts, as well as an annual garden to provide most of the fresh food you eat.

And you want children. At least I do. I love children so much that it is hard for me to comprehend how anyone could imagine that his life were totally fulfilled without them. If, on the other hand, you are stuck at the infantile level of emotional development in which you really aren't interested in anyone but yourself, you might want to take a look at some of the Author's other writings, which might give you some ideas for further personal evolution. I think the desire for children is often suppressed in people who don't really have the place or means to care for them properly, but if you have arranged the elements of your life so that you have a place to live and some money to live on, then you may find yourself wanting to have children so that life can continue.

The Marihuana Problem

by *John Roland Stahl*

September, 1998

The use of marihuana should be regulated and taxed by the government, whether federal, state or local. That's what governments are for. It is a great mistake to allow the entire industry of marihuana, from beginning to end, to be conducted as a black market, without any control or regulation. It is the role and function of government to regulate the traffic in any material that is deemed to be hazardous in any way, and it is also the role of government to lead the way in the research of hazardous or controversial materials. Education must be the pillar of any policy of control, not legal sanction.

To maintain the position that such a policy is useless, since the use of marihuana is to be stamped out in its entirety, is indefensible, not only because it is a lost cause, but also because it is legally and politically without authority. It is an arbitrary and unprecedented abuse of power to attempt to interfere with the way people want to live their lives.

The absolute depths of stupidity are reached when the response to a controversial material is to forbid any research on the subject. I don't understand. Certainly anyone can see that to forbid research on a controversial subject is just about the stupidest approach imaginable.

Perhaps the data on marihuana is flawed or incomplete or inadequate, but to date the overwhelming consensus of informed opinion regards the dangers of marihuana as vastly overstated, and potential medical benefits possibly considerable. If this is not true, and marihuana really is a dangerous drug, I certainly want to know, and I ask that research not only be allowed, but funded. I want to know more about LSD too, while I am at it. Without any doubt, LSD is a most incredibly amazing and potent material, and I want to know more about it. Since one of the most common reactions to the use of LSD is to report a spiritual experience, or even an experience of the presence of God, I want to know more about it, not to see it stamped out in fear as something too powerful to investigate.

The lessons from the prohibition of alcohol are so obvious: in the first place, when the Government of those days had the happy notion of simply outlawing the use of alcohol, they at least realized that nothing less than an Amendment to the Constitution would be required before they could assume the authority for such an arbitrary act of power affecting people's personal lives. The argument against prohibition is the same for both alcohol and marihuana: leaving the industry in the hands of an outlaw black market, rather than having it taxed and regulated, turns out to be an incredible mistake, with negative social consequences everywhere you turn.

No matter what you think of alcohol, making it a criminal offense to consume it does not represent the enlightened way to deal with the problem. The only politically correct way to approach a problem such as alcohol is to educate the public, perhaps most especially the youth, to a full and clear understanding of the nature, risks, and possible consequences of the use of alcohol.

The use or abuse of alcohol, marihuana, nicotine, caffeine, theobromine, sugar, or any other hazardous substance should be considered a health issue, not a legal issue. It is one of the functions of Government to maintain a Department of Health that will look out for important health-related issues and make sure to publish important information. This policy has worked quite well in the case of cigarettes, and there is no reason why an educated public should not be able to make informed choices about their use of marihuana.

The only way for so many billions of people to live together on this earth in peace and freedom is to maintain a policy of Tolerance of Diversity. Tolerance for Diversity is related to flowering, and is associated with such times as the Renaissance and the "Summer of Love" in 1967. I find the progressive narrowing of social tolerances which has been going on for many years now to be a very chilling social thermometer. Relax, enjoy life, love one another, live in peace, and let everyone else do so too, in their own way.

If the production and sale of marihuana were licensed by government, its use would still be controlled in two ways: first, by a program of research and education, and secondly, by a tax. Theoretically, there is no limit to the amount of control you can exercise by simply adding a tax. The use of gasoline, alcohol, and cigarettes are all severely modified by aggressive taxation, and marihuana could be dealt with in the same way.

So here is the proposal: allow marihuana to be cultivated and sold under license, but collect a tax of $10 per ounce sold, with the tax revenue used for drug research and education. That would set up a simple machine that would become self-regulating. The exact amount of the tax could be modified as needed.

At one stroke, this would stop a "war" on peaceful American citizens who are just trying to live their lives. This whole slice of America's people who spend time in jail for marihuana related offenses would be relieved of this oppression, and an ineffective and very costly military opposition to marihuana cultivators would be laid to rest. All those who want to play war games should be loaded up on space ships and shipped off to the dark side of the moon, taking their armaments with them.

In its place, the Government quietly moves onto the other side of the pay window, and instead of spending billions of taxpayers dollars on a drug war (in which it turns out that about 98% of the takings are industrial hemp with no THC anyway, a crop which Canadian farmers are once again allowed to farm for their profit), the Government starts collecting a tax that could not only fully fund the education and research program mentioned above, but could replace the income tax, and retire the national debt into the bargain; and all of this as a voluntary tax just like the lottery. If you don't buy lottery tickets or smoke marihuana, you can enjoy a free ride, with all expenses paid.

The buses will run for free.

Triangles

Intentional Complex Relationships

by *John Roland Stahl*

March, 2001

Triangles ~ Intentional Complex Relationships ~ explores the possibilities of intentional relationships of three or more persons. The usual idea of a "triangle" is a situation of competition and struggle which will inevitably end up with two persons going one way, and the third going another way. An intentional complex relationship of three or more persons, on the other hand, is established in the expectation, hope, or desire that all three (or more) may continue to stay together, forming a long term bond.

Some persons may be interested in sharing their lives with more than one partner on a sort of community basis, for any of a variety of reasons, and others may enjoy a typical pair bond but just want occasional and/or temporary contacts with a third person.

We are interested in all sorts of creative arrangements, but the real focus here is relationships in which the intention is to form a long term stable bond of three or more partners, all of whom share an intimate social bond together, in any combination of genders, ages, lifestyles, or other variants.

There may be many reasons why people may be attracted to the concept of an intentional complex relationship of three or more persons. They may be attracted to the economy of scale or the convenience of having three people instead of just two to manage a household; they may be interested in the social richness and diversity of three persons living together; they may prefer the very different social dynamics of the interaction of three; or they may be excited by the sexual stimulation of having more than one partner. They may simply be interested in exploring something new and different in their lives, or they may enjoy the feeling of being a little bit more open minded and radical than the majority of their fellow travelers.

If two can live as cheaply as one, three can live as cheaply as two. Furthermore, with three persons, there is one more person to wash the dishes, clean the house, provide income, take care of the children, and on and on. This idea may be extended, of course, to the concept of a whole community of people in which the intention is to share the advantages of social life without necessarily including intimate social and sexual contact. These considerations can be a significant contribution to the desire to live with more than one partner, but our particular interest in this article is relationships in which the social and sexual intimacy of all the partners is comparable to the traditional pair bond with which most people are familiar.

Next, the experience of three or more people can accommodate more variants in personal lifestyle. When there are only two members of a bond, everything must be done by one or the other person. This may work out fine in some cases, and the couple may live happily ever after. But sometimes the compatibility is just too complex for that, and a third person can possibly plug up some of the holes present in a bond of just two. With three persons, the possibilities of dividing up the tasks of life are geometrically increased.

The social dynamics of the interaction of three persons is where it really becomes interesting. I have seen many relationships in which the two parties may start out together, but sooner or later they become polarized in different ways over different issues. ("Jack Sprat would eat no fat; his wife would eat no lean.") I look at this on the level of physical energy dynamics in which the patterns are altogether different. Instead of energy going back and forth like a pendulum, the energies may swirl around in a far more complex pattern. Even the presumed instability inherent in the dynamics of three can be a source of excitement and strength. Ultimately, I believe that it is possible for a well matched bond of three to be far more stable than a simple bond of two. "Well matched" is the operative concept here! Obviously the complications of matching the needs and strengths of three persons is far more complicated than the simple compatibility of any two persons.

Adding a fourth partner exponentially increases the complexity of the relationship. Because of this complexity, it is almost inevitable for a group of four to break down into two simple couples. In this context, a group of five may be more stable than a group of four. However, the energy dynamics of any larger group are really just compound expressions of the basic pattern of three, so we may profitably confine our attention to the special dynamics of the number three.

The number three has always been the number of occult philosophy, magic, and mysticism. In this introductory article it may not be useful to go too far down these paths except to mention that a successful and stable group of three can exhibit enormous strength and power.

All of the social dynamics of three find their expression mirrored in the sexual dynamics of the bond. Because of the far more complex patterns of energy dynamics, the sexual energies involved with three or more partners are enormous and very complex, leading to a vastly augmented potential for sexual interaction. In this context, the significance of the combination of three personal energies is more important than the genders involved. Everything we are discussing here applies equally whether the bond is three men, three women, or two of one gender and one of the other. In every case there is at least some contact between persons of the same gender, so if that is a hurdle for some, it is the first to be crossed.

Complex relationships are not for everyone. The dominant pattern of human interaction has always been the ordinary pair bond, and that will probably not change any time soon. However, given the vast differences between people, there will always be unusual souls who will find that the potential for personal fulfillment can only be met in some more creative combination. Most people try to live as much like their neighbors as possible, not daring to try anything radical or out of the ordinary, but others are interested in exploring new possibilities, and are always looking for some new way to stretch their horizons and discover new ways of doing things.

The obstacles to forming a stable and happy bond of three or more persons are considerable, but for those few who manage to succeed with it, the rewards are even more considerable.

I think many people might have an idea that with three partners there must be conflict between the parties, but I think, on the other hand, that the balance of three can be a way of resolving and avoiding conflict. With two people, everything is grand as long as both parties agree perfectly with every aspect of their lives. In the real world, however, it often happens that the most loving couples may discover some disagreements, which may be easily resolved or may escalate into fights or alienation.

When two people disagree, what happens? Usually it is the more dominant member of the couple who decides what to do, but this can lead to a pattern of power control that may or may not be acceptable in the relationship. With three persons, however, there is always the third person to arbitrate any dispute, or to cast a deciding vote on any issue. Who would ever set up a Board of Directors with only two persons (or any even number)? Having three persons share responsibility allows for a constantly evolving outlook in which each of the members casts a deciding vote, ensuring that whatever happens is accepted as the general policy.

Pythagoras considered that the abstract concepts of the numbers of mathematics constituted the most wonderful pattern to discover the mysteries of nature, because the concepts themselves are all pure *a priori* concepts which require no validation from the real world. That is, you cannot "do away" with the concepts of number by *fiat* any more than you can decide not to observe "time" any more. (By the way, "money" is another example of a universal abstraction which has some very interesting properties, but that is the subject for another article, in another place.)

Pythagoras related the concepts of mathematical number to the mysteries of philosophy and the dimensions of physics. The number One is a point; the number Two is a line; the number Three is a surface (triangle); and the number Four is a solid (pyramid or cube); the number Five is time, or the process of change.

Before there is number, there is seamless void or chaos. The number One is solitary perfection, or God, the Primary Mystery of Philosophy. The number Two is a separation of the un-differentiated unity into polar opposites: yang and yin, light and dark, all and nothing, and so on: the second Mystery. The number Three represents a compound process that extends out into a new dimension. The number Four is the stable foundation stone of civilization.

When these concepts are applied to personal life energy, the analogies are very interesting. Sexually, the number One represents solitude, which is the domain of the Priest or the Magician. In this context, I have always found it interesting that the essential aspect of being a priest has always been his celibacy. A man entirely alone, personally, inevitably achieves a relationship with God. So how they could ever do away with a celibate clergy, I do not understand. Certainly there can be lay teachers and servants of God, but a priest who is not celibate is a contradiction in terms. The wise woman (or "good witch") also has always been a solitary practitioner, and has served a similar function.

The other alternative, it will be suggested, is that a man (or woman) alone might make his relationship with the Devil, the popular idea of the magician or witch (or Dr. Faustus). In a sense, this is a reasonable analogy, because the essential idea of the magician, or wise one, is someone who, through his knowledge and investigations into the mysteries of nature, is able not only to anticipate events, but to influence them in accordance with his own will.

Compare this with the idea that God is the point of perfection at the center, and the Devil is represented as the cloud of confusion of deviations moving away from the point at the center. At the center is clarity, peace, and bliss; and the deviations away represent so many and various ways towards chaos and confusion. Fundamentally, it comes down to the solitary man following the will of God or his own personal will.

Oh, yes, let me not forget the third possible direction of energy for the man (or woman) alone: madness. When the inertia, clarity, and focus of the path of God through the center is not followed, it becomes increasingly difficult to maintain a system in balance; a failure to maintain balance results in chaos or madness. This is one reason why religion has always served as a support against madness for persons who otherwise couldn't cope, having no fixed point to hang on to.

The even numbers of Two and Four are so much simpler than the odd numbers of One, Three, and Five. The typical pair bond of man and woman (or even two of the same gender) results in a more stable and productive relationship than solitude, but it is subject to the continuing inertia towards polarization.

The pattern of the number Three is literally a whole dimension beyond the pair bond of two individuals. The level of complexity of the interaction is greatly magnified beyond the levels of the pair bond, leading to unusual possibilities of creative interaction.

Then when pairs bond together with other pairs, great stable blocks of civilization are built up, but at the cost of fairly rigid stratification. It is the most conservative, and the most resistant to change of any kind.

A relationship of Five brings back all the dynamic magic of the number Three, by spinning the wheels again to unleash an infinitude of expanding possibility. This is the Pentagram, and it represents the most creative expression of personal dynamics. Numbers beyond this are either boring chunks of even numbers, such as eight, or unwieldy and increasingly volatile numbers such as seven or nine or above at which point the intensity of the energy is diluted past the optimum, and the creative potentials of the compounding complexity reach diminishing returns.

Conclusions? Oh, no ~ there are no conclusions here! We simply wanted to broach the possibilities.

Hemp Prohibition ~ Folly or Crime?

by *John Roland Stahl*

May, 2001

I want to make one thing clear right from the start ~ the "crime" mentioned in the title does not refer to anyone's use of hemp; it refers to the intolerably criminal abuse of power which prohibits the use of one of the most useful plants on earth. The folly (to use the more polite expression) is so monumental that I hardly know where to begin with the expression of my astonishment, indignation, and outrage.

I may as well begin with my own work, which is making paper. For nearly thirty years I have been making hand made paper from a great variety of non-wood fiber sources, starting with the classic cotton, and moving on to experiment with flax, hemp, kenaf, mulberry, and numerous weeds and recycled materials. Cotton is very wonderful material for a papermaker: it is both soft and strong and readily available for free as textile scraps. You have to be very careful to avoid synthetic materials and blends, because they do not beat down into pulp suitable for papermaking at all. Paper is composed of cellulose fiber, which breaks down naturally when beaten in water, and is then ready to be formed into a fibrous mat by lifting on screens and then pressing. Polyester, on the other hand, just gobs up into wads of plastic which have no business in any respectable paper. No glues or chemicals of any kind are required for making paper. This miracle which is paper was discovered about 300 BC in China. The very earliest scraps of paper which date from this period have been analyzed as composed of hemp fibers.

In my work with paper, I have discovered that you can make paper out of just about any natural vegetable fiber, as cellulose is widely present in nearly all plants. However, there are great variations in the quantities and qualities of cellulose. Not only do some plants have more or less cellulose than others, but some plants have particularly long and strong cellulose fibers, while other plants have weak, short fibers that are only of very limited use in papermaking ~ perhaps in combination with other stronger fibers.

Cotton, as I have said already, rates very high, being almost pure cellulose from the start, with long fibers and few impurities which need to be cooked out. On the other hand, there are two problems with the use of cotton. In the first place, an enormous amount of pesticides are used on the cotton crops world-wide ~ I read somewhere that as much as 50% of all pesticides used in the world are used in the cultivation of cotton. Secondly, cotton is just too expensive to be used for any large scale commercial use.

Of course, no hand papermaker would have any reason to use such a poor material as wood chips for making paper. Since the cost of a hand made sheet is almost entirely the labor cost, hand papermakers want to use the finest materials available, unless they have some artistic or research interest that over-rides the desire to make a high quality paper. Wood contains practically no cellulose (about 30%), and there is so much lignin in the remainder that enormous amounts of highly toxic processing are required to produce a paper-like substance that will quickly degrade after about 50 years.

So why is wood used at all in the industry? The answer to that question prompts just as much outrage and indignation as the prohibition of hemp! To make a short answer of it, the same government that prohibits the use of hemp for papermaking (or at least its cultivation in the Land of the Free, which amounts to the same thing) subsidizes the logging industry by building roads at public expense and awarding lucrative logging contracts at far below the real cost of the resource extraction; the difference, of course, being picked up not only by current tax payers, but by future generations yet unborn. Furthermore, the same government also tolerates the disposal of waste products into our rivers and streams which are killing us all with dioxin and other toxic chemicals. Certainly there are continuous efforts to mitigate these problems and these levels of toxic disposal ~ the days when you could simply dump your effluent in the river are over (now you have to pay somebody off) ~ but it is way too little and way too late.

But enough about wood. Let me summarize by saying that the net effect of these government policies is to make wood appear to be cheap (although that illusion is quickly fading), but, even at that, the disastrous environmental effect of the destruction of our ancient forest, munching up trees into junk mail and burying most of it as landfill, presents a very steep bill which, once again, will be presented to future generations.

There are a great many alternatives to wood pulp, many of them of very high quality indeed, but in most cases the cost of production makes them unattractive as candidates for any large scale paper manufacture. Back in 1916 the USDA studied the problem, realizing that by the end of the century available forest reserves would be pretty well exhausted, and tried to find an alternative to the use of wood. The answer, published in Bulletin

404, was to use hemp, which they calculated could produce 4.1 times as much pulp, on a sustained yield basis, as wood. Not only was hemp of supremely high quality as a furnish for paper (more than double the cellulose as wood and much longer and stronger fibers), but it was also very economical in its cultivation, as it produced abundant crops year after year without the use of pesticides.

Since that time kenaf has also been proposed as an alternative, and the economics of kenaf rival that of hemp, while capable of producing paper almost as good as hemp. Kenaf is amazing and wonderful stuff; I grow it myself, and use it in my paper, and I have nothing bad to say about it at all, with the possible exception that its cultivation is confined to very temperate or semi- tropical latitudes, whereas hemp can be cultivated on the dark side of the moon (well, almost). Seriously, hemp can be cultivated on what are known as "marginal lands" where little else of commercial value will grow.

I only know of two real objections to the use of hemp for paper making: it is an annual crop, which means that it is harvested all at once and must then be stored and delivered to the mill as needed, in contrast with wood, which is logged, chipped, and delivered to the mills on a daily basis. That problem simply has to be factored into the economic equation of its use. The other objection is that such enormous quantities of wood chips are pulped up into paper every day (about half of all trees harvested are pulped up into paper products) that no one could ever cultivate enough hemp to replace it. That objection is foolish. Even if only 5 or 10% of the world's paper were made from hemp, that would still produce a very significant environmental improvement. The obvious conclusion is to grow as much hemp and kenaf as possible wherever in the world they will grow.

But there is far more to this story than just paper! According to the Popular Mechanics magazine of 1938, there are over 25,000 uses of the hemp plant. The catalog has been paraded so many times that I don't want to reproduce the whole thing in the present essay, but I will briefly outline the main headings: first there is the fiber, which includes textiles as well as paper. Other products may be made from the fiber as well, such as automobile parts and building materials, but paper and textiles are the biggest items. Next comes the seed and the seed oil, which have most of the balance of the 25,000 uses to their credit. Someone has said that "anything you can make with a hydrocarbon you can make with a carbohydrate." This means you can make everything from fuel to paints and varnishes, cosmetics, and a host of other industrial products from the oil of the hemp seed.

But there is also the very important item of food products. Once again, this story is not exactly late breaking news, but in case you haven't heard it yet, the hemp seed is just about the most perfect nutritional food every discovered ~ very high in protein and especially high in essential fatty acids (one hemp seed a day was supposed to have sustained the Buddha on his way to enlightenment).

That is enough of an introduction to move along to the real intention of the present essay (if you want more information about the uses of the hemp plant, any bookstore should carry dozens of books, from *The Emperor Wears No Clothes*, by Jack Herer, which started it all, to any of a numerous crop of more recent hemp books). I am not finished with the catalog of uses of the hemp plant, by the way, but this is enough to get started.

So why, the obvious question comes to mind, does our government see fit to prohibit its cultivation? (If you ever wondered what a "rhetorical question" was, this is a splendid example.) Yes, of course: the hemp plant resembles the dreaded marijuana plant, the scourge of youth, the demon weed, reefer madness. This substance is considered to be so bad that a policy of "zero tolerance" is to be enforced. Otherwise law abiding citizens are to be arrested and incarcerated at levels unheard of in the history of civilization. Not enough room in the prisons to hold all the pot smokers? We'll just build more prisons; no problem. Not content to deal with abuse as it comes up, the government mounts a campaign of seeking out marijuana users by an aggressive campaign of drug tests. When it turns out that eating hemp seeds can produce a false positive on a drug test, our government is fully prepared to outlaw the ingestion of arguably the most nutritious health food ever discovered in order to prevent any possibility of undermining their drug testing agenda!

Before I address the issue of medical marijuana as the continuation of the catalog of beneficial uses of the hemp plant, let me address the issue upon the assumption that marijuana really is as harmful as our government pretends it to be. The analogy with the Prohibition of alcohol has been made many times, but no one (in the government) seems to get it. There is no one of any credibility (say a medical doctor or health professional) who would risk the ridicule of maintaining that marijuana is more harmful than alcohol. Alcohol destroys the liver and also causes great emotional and psychological harm with excessive use. Families are destroyed left and right, and lives are destroyed directly by drunk drivers. Nonetheless, prohibition was rejected as a monumental failure for the following reasons: number one, it didn't work ~ a whole black market industry developed which provided alcohol of dubious quality to anyone who wanted it, which brought on a whole array of social problems far worse than the original problem (compare the current arguments of "harm reduction" which favor regulating marijuana rather than leaving the entire industry in the hands of outlaws). Secondly, the prohibition of alcohol was an unfair infringement on the rights of those who enjoyed its use in moderation. Even alcohol is conceded to be harmless or even beneficial as long as it is used in moderation.

Moderation is the key, here. Having a beer or two at the end of the working day, or enjoying a glass of wine with a meal, is not to be compared with the alcoholic who always has a glass going, all through the day, or who binges on it, destroying his health, getting into fights, losing his job and his family. Both alcohol and marijuana are social drugs; if someone prefers to take a moderate amount of cannabis at the end of the day instead of drinking alcohol, that is a distinct improvement in every way.

So my conclusions are tiered one on top of another. In the first place, there is no justification whatsoever for the Prohibition of marijuana at all, but even if there were, to carry this fanaticism over to the Prohibition of industrial hemp, and finally to even propose the outlawing of hemp as a foodstuff goes way beyond folly; it is criminal.

That conclusion, let me remind you, is based upon the assumption that marijuana really is harmful. But I now want to proceed with my catalog of the beneficial uses of the hemp plant by including the medical benefits. Before I go any further, however, I want to emphasize that I do not recommend smoking it. While I believe in the principle of freedom, and the rights of people to smoke marijuana if they so choose, it is clear that filling your lungs with smoke on a regular basis is very bad for your health. Before marijuana was outlawed in the '30s it was the second most prescribed drug in the pharmacopoeia (first place was held by hashish, a more potent preparation of marijuana). It was produced in many forms: pills, elixirs, etc, so that it could be ingested rather than smoked. Smoking became popular because it was more efficient and more controllable than eating it. But in recent years, the vaporizer technology has been greatly improved to the point where it is no longer necessary for anyone to smoke cannabis in order to experience the benefits. Vaporized marijuana causes far fewer problems than smoked, due to the absence of all the really toxic material in the smoke: carbon monoxide, tar, benzene, etc. This concept is still very new; well, actually, it is not so very new, but early vaporizers were not very well designed and most people were disappointed in the experience. The latest generation of vaporization devices (which generally feature a heat source with a precisely controlled temperature) offer a greatly improved delivery for a much more satisfactory experience all around.

There are a host of medical benefits of marijuana, from the relief of the inter-ocular pressure of glaucoma to the relief from nausea and other side effects of medications for AIDS and cancer, to the relief of pain in many forms, as well as many other benefits, some documented better than others (see, for example, *The New Prescription* by Martin Martinez, for a discussion of the range of medical benefits of cannabis). One of the most common medical uses of cannabis is for relief of pain. It has been used in this way for thousands of years with no known side effects. In contrast with this safety record, pharmaceutical drugs which are prescribed for relief of pain ~ all of them, every single one ~ have been proven to cause very serious and life-threatening side effects, such as a dramatically increased risk of heart attack. One typical finding shows that regular use of one of these pharmaceutical pain relievers will triple the patient's risk of a fatal heart attack. But that is no problem ~ at least the pharmaceutical drug companies are making obscene profits, and that's the main thing. So our government encourages patients to use expensive pharmaceutical drugs, of which it has been proven that regular use will certainly kill them, while any attempt to circumvent the pharmaceutical drug industry by using the much safer and cheaper alternative of cannabis (cheaper if you grow it yourself ~ never mind the high prices which are caused by the "drug war") will be met with arrest and incarceration. But the health care industry has no interest in curing anyone ~ "a patient cured is a customer lost" ~ all they want is your money. When you run out of money, then you can die.

But it is continually objected that the medical benefits are just a smoke screen for the dreaded "recreational uses" of cannabis. I prefer the term "social use" to "recreational use." It is not so much that users simply want to intoxicate themselves for some "recreational" use; marijuana is used as a social catalyst. In some social environments, when guests or friends come to visit, one puts on a pot of coffee or tea. In other cultures, alcoholic drinks are offered. Even tobacco was originally a social drug. I read in an old novel where someone meets a friend on the street and invites him to come up to his rooms "to smoke a cigarette." When I was young, I tried alcohol like everyone else, but I rejected it as unnecessarily toxic. I didn't like the way it smelled; I didn't like the "high"; I didn't like the effects. Where alcohol stupefies the user and dulls all the senses, marijuana intensifies all sensory experiences. Where alcohol makes users aggressive and sloppy, marijuana makes users peaceful and gentle. Where an excess of alcohol can lead to a very unpleasant experience of sickness, drunk driving, and social alienation, an excess of marijuana usually just puts the user into a passive state which will wear off with no ill effects. While I do not recommend driving while under the influence of marijuana, studies have shown that marijuana smokers usually compensate for their moderate impairment by driving especially slowly and carefully, in contrast with drinkers who usually drive faster and more recklessly.

So the principle benefit of using marijuana socially (apart from the direct social benefits, of course!) is the alternative to the use of the really harmful drugs like alcohol and narcotics. I have known lots of people who used to use harmful drugs who now only use cannabis. People who used to use crack cocaine and methedrine and/or alcohol find that they are able to satisfy their social (or "recreational") need with just marijuana. It is a true "gateway drug" after all! Why would young people sniff glue if they could just as easily (and as cheaply) take cannabis with their friends?

But before I end this essay I want to emphasize a few important points: while I believe that moderate amounts of marijuana are relatively harmless and even beneficial, I certainly do not deny that there is a "potential for abuse." Certainly there are persons whose use of marijuana is excessive, but the zero tolerance of Prohibition is not the answer. Education is the answer. The Drug War is the source of all the evils it is ostensibly put forward to correct. I believe that the vast majority of people want to live long, healthy, and happy lives. If government would give up the impoverished policy of Prohibition and rely upon a campaign of education after the very successful model of cigarette smoking, then I believe that most people would end up with a pattern of use for themselves that would provide more benefit than harm.

The Great War of Alcohol against Cannabis

by *John Roland Stahl*

September, 2002

So you think that King George II's war in Iraq is all about Oil and Money, do you? Well, you're all wrong. This is the Great War of Alcohol against Cannabis.

The roots of this conflict go way back. Nearly a thousand years ago, in 1095, Pope Urban II urged the Christian Faithful to embark upon a war to seize control of the Holy Land from the Infidel. All the great Christian nobles thought this was a great idea. Motivated by lust for spoils and plunder, this large drunken host of iron-clad warriors comes riding out of the West, spoiling and plundering their way to Jerusalem, which they finally conquer and in which they install a King of their own selection.

All subsequent campaigns, however, were met with increasingly disappointing returns. Almost all of the many Crusades that followed were routed by the defending Moslems, who considered that they were justly defending the Holy Land from the Infidel. This conflict between the Judeo-Christian tradition of the West and the faithful of Islam in the East only settles in ever more deeply with each passing generation, with no end in sight.

It is fundamentally a very complicated theological conflict instigated by the Catholic Pope of the Christian world of the West against the "heathen" Moslems of the East. If you consider the similarities and differences between Islam and Christianity, what is the most obvious and profound theological difference between them? Right! It is the Islamic ban on alcohol, as exhorted by Allah through his Prophet Mohammed. The Moslems fully understood that alcohol was a very dangerous drug. It can seriously undermine your health; it can impair your judgment; and it makes you belligerent and stupid. On the other hand, there is no record that Allah found any fault with cannabis, so faithful Moslems to this day avoid alcohol, turning to the benefits of cannabis when they wish to alter their mood. This is quite different from Christianity, whose Savior drank wine with his Disciples at the Last Supper. There are many Sects of Christianity, from the Orthodox who drink wine, to the Zealots who drink gin or whisky or vodka, to the Reformed who drink beer, but they all recognize Bacchus as their spiritual father.

What the problem comes down to theologically and metaphysically is the classic problem of "How many Angels can dance on the head of a pin?" Specifically, we want to know whether we can attain the greatest number of Angels dancing on that pin after they have been drinking wine, or after smoking some ganja. The Moslems have always maintained that a great many more dancing Angels are able to fit on that pin when they are using cannabis, and the Christian world has never been able to dispute it (since drunk angels will fall off the pin), so they fall back again and again to "the last argument of kings," which is their cannon. (Never mind the phallic imagery of them shaking that stick in the faces of weaker people.)

(Then the clever idea occurred to me to consider that this theological conflict could be looked upon as the Opposition of Bacchus and Ganesh. But, upon reflection, I had to give it up, because, as everyone knows, the Christian God of the West is not really Bacchus, the God of Wine. It is Mammon, the God of Money. And as for the Moslems, everyone knows just as well that there is no god but Allah, so I had to turn to the Hindu Pantheon to find, in Ganesh, a suitable Cannabis God of the East.)

Now it is clear why those of us who consider that cannabis is far safer and more effective than alcohol, cigarettes, and most pharmaceutical drugs are looked upon as "siding with the enemy" by adopting such a dominant cultural distinction. This same "sympathy with the opposition" can be seen by the numbers of Black Americans who choose to adopt Islam. It is easy for them to feel a cultural affinity for Moslems, once they realize that there isn't much room in the White Man's Heaven for the likes of the dark brother. In fact, while we're at it, not only Blacks, but Hispanics, Asians, Homosexuals, and Pot Smokers (and other riff-raff too numerous and impecunious to mention) needn't trouble themselves with waving any American flags these days. Frankly, "they" would just as soon not see you waving any flags at all ~ certainly not the Red, White, and Blue, but neither the Rasta colors, nor any Rainbows, or Earth Flags. The True Patriots (the ones with the Money) will wrap themselves up in an ever shrinking American Flag, as they try to control and "own" the whole world for their continuing and increasing personal profit. (Non-American Internationals who nonetheless consider themselves part of the same Club may simply wrap themselves in their local currency, which has always been perfectly acceptable attire at any Country Club.)

This is a very, very dangerous game, however, and it is one which has never lasted all that long, historically. Machiavelli made it clear to the Rulers of the world that it were better to be Feared than Loved, but that hasn't made the Hot Seat any safer. And, in today's world, the rule of armed might is getting harder and harder to sustain. The overarching problem is that mankind now has such abundant available firepower that any serious confrontation will quickly mean the end of most life on earth. It will be a question of whether the ants finally take over the earth, or whether they, too, will finally succumb, forcing the spirit of God, which is Life after all (and not really Money, Power, Drugs, or Oil ~ Sex is closer to God than any of the others) to start out all over again from viruses and bacteria.

The other problem is that it is so very much easier to destroy something than to build it. To get a clear perspective of last September, just consider Big Sister who has spent all morning patiently building a tower out of building blocks, and then Little Brother comes running in, laughing, and kicks it all down. Sure, Big Sister can pound Little Brother (Lucy and Linus), but that game has been going on for a million years, and it isn't going to stop any time soon. But someone has already observed that the higher the tower, the greater the fall.

I was going to say something about wondering why nobody wants to destroy or conquer Canada, to see if there is any lesson there, but then I considered that, among plenty of other conspiracy theories going around, the notion is taken as a given that if (when?) Uncle Sam decides it is time to declare Martial Law and take over complete control of the country, Canada and Mexico would be routinely annexed "just to secure the peace." So if there are any lessons here, it is pretty scary to think of what they might be. You have heard that a Crisis is being deliberately manipulated in order to set the stage for a Declaration of Martial Law?

So what do we do? Stop pushing those polar opposites to extreme positions. Let us all drift back towards the center a little bit. Relax, sip a little wine with your cannabis, or try a little cannabis (vaporized, not smoked) to moderate that whiskey binge. Let us understand the inescapable connection between Freedom and Tolerance. You can't have one without the other.

Psychedelic Childhood

by *John Roland Stahl*

May, 2003

As a child, I seemed to experience effects very similar to a psychedelic experience, and I have long wondered how common my experience was. I am interested in the research into the naturally occurring chemicals (or lack of them) in the brain that might be related to this experience, and I would like to suggest some of my own interpretations of the data.

From the time of my earliest memories, which go back at least to the first year of life (verifiable, since we left the town I have memories of when I was about one year old), I have experienced visual and auditory "hallucinations" resembling an LSD experience. Auditory experiences were more noticeable with less background noise, and the visual experiences were most noticeable in dim light. These experiences gradually began to subside as I reached adolescence. As a child, I assumed that everyone experienced these effects, and I attributed them to ordinary imagination. Even now it is impossible accurately to compare my own experience of the world with any normal standard; however, various indications suggest to me that I continue to experience a richer depth of sensory experience than normal.

For example, I have an extremely acute sense of smell, which has advantages and disadvantages. I cultivate and propagate fragrant flowers, especially roses, and these give me a very great pleasure. On the other hand, passing a diesel truck on the highway is always very distressing, especially if I neglect to shut off the air vents in time. As to visual experience, I continue to experience the world as a mild LSD experience, and it is very difficult to tell how my experience compares with the norm. One indication occurred to me a few years ago ~ I am always amazed to see that almost everyone tunes their television sets up to a very florid level of color. I look at a screen which appears so densely saturated with color that I wonder how anyone can watch it. For my own preference, I tune the color levels way down, yet I still experience the colors vividly. I finally had the idea that perhaps I am taking in much more of the color than most people see ~ there is no other way I can understand the nearly universal experience of finding television sets tuned way above any color level that I can watch in comfort.

As a young child, I remember seeing a constant display of swirling patterns of light and color and energy all around me. At night, in the dim light of my bedroom, these colors and patterns always exceeded anything I have ever experienced on any dosage of LSD (and I have taken "heroic doses" of well over 1000 micrograms many times). The only thing that ever came close to the normal experience of my childhood was a particular batch of synthetic psilocybin that I obtained around 1969. This was so good and so amazing that two weeks later I repeated the experience, doubling the dose. On this occasion, it didn't make any difference whether my eyes were open or closed; my vision was saturated with multi-layered pinwheels, flashes, energy forms, pictures, and every manner of explosions of light and color, morphing into fantastic shapes and designs and patterns. Yet, this was my ordinary experience every day of my youth, and especially every night.

I was extremely introverted and "mystical," with a very elaborate internal life. I was a solitary child, reading books while my peers were playing baseball. I have always been extremely sensitive, "tuning in" ideas from the collective unconscious constantly. I was given to metaphysical speculation, having a theological crisis at the age of six, when I couldn't resolve the problem of "where does the sky end," or "who or what created the universe." It simply begs the question to say (as my father did, a Methodist minister) that God created the world. Who created God? I have continued these speculations as the major effort of my life's work, putting my conclusions into a series of books. Motivated to create these books, I make my own hand-made paper, and I set type by hand and print my books by letterpress and bind them by hand.

Auditory sounds were not so much "voices," as simply a constant background noise of which I was constantly aware (thank you, Classical High School, for the archaic grammatical construction). But the visual experiences were very dramatic. They did not appear as a flat screen movie, but as a fully six dimensional chaos of a multi-layered and constantly moving display of colors, lights, patterns of energy, and pictures. There was kind of a matrix of these geometrical patterns swirling around in the background, with a more defined series of pictures dominating over them. The energy forms varied from simple and very common pinwheels, to larger and much more intense and complex energy forms. Out of this matrix appeared pictures of identifiable things, including people, animals, bizarre creatures, and monsters of every description. I distinctly remember the impression that many of these "energy forms" were not just "pictures" but were real, live "entities" of some sort.

Remarkably, I was rarely frightened by any of this. While there was a brief period of my youth in which I experienced nightmares (and I never made any distinction between sleeping nightmares and wakeful experiences of the same sort, displayed all around my bedroom at night), for the most part I simply found these experiences fascinating and entertaining.

I move along to the experience of perceiving some of these energy forms as real entities. This happened constantly. A typical display would include thousands (millions) of swirling patterns of light and color, ranging from blips that appeared and vanished in a twinkling, to elaborate and complex patterns of energy that would evolve and grow, colliding and morphing with other energy forms, etc. Then, over this background matrix, there would be innumerable pictures, usually in constant motion, which included full "movies," with elaborate plots. An interesting feature of these movies was the experience of perceiving a 30 hour movie, complete with elaborate plots and characters, condensed into mere seconds of objective time. (I believe this experience is common in dreams.) Many or most of these pictures seemed to be just that ~ pictures that were not "alive." But over and above all of this (and all going on all at once, in riotous cacophony) there were also "living beings" or "dæmons" which had the appearance of consciousness. Specifically, they related to me as life forms. They would look at me, appear to be aware of me, and even communicate (telepathically) with me. They would hear my (telepathic) responses, and frequent dialogs were a continuing feature of my nightly psychedelic experiences.

These "life forms" varied immensely from little divas and sprites and fairies, to major and intense visitations. I will describe the most intense such experience that happened to me when I was seven years old. Out of the usual matrix of patterns of color and light and all the other images and random "beings" that flitted around in my space, one night there was a very intense visitation that appeared as a very bright white light (sorry for the lack of originality, but there must be something to this "white light" since so many people see it). I was aware of a very intense energy presence that overshadowed everything else. The whole experience took only a brief few seconds (perhaps only the smallest part of a second, but it seemed to be several seconds long), but there were several clear impressions. The first impression was that this being was more surprised than I was at the encounter! I'm not sure whether the being were surprised that I were aware of the being, or whether there were some other source of surprise, but, for my part, "communication with alien beings" was the common experience of every evening for me, although never before with such an intense energy field as this one. The next impression was that the being identified itself (telepathically, as always) by "saying" "I AM GOD." ~ to which I replied, comically enough, with all of the innocence of my seven years, "Oh. I'm John Stahl." (My reply was also telepathic.) That was the end of the interview. The light vanished, and the more usual and more common life forms and swirling patterns of light and color again took over the stage of awareness. I don't know if it were "God" or not, but it certainly seemed to be "somebody big."

What's going on here? Do other people, particularly children, experience these things?

Next, here are my own ideas as to what is actually happening. To begin with, it has been evident to me for many years that everything we experience under the influence of LSD is perfectly real. There are no "hallucinations" going on at all. I make the analogy of television and radio programs that are all around us all the time, but not available to our ordinary perception without a television or radio receiver to isolate and magnify these signals. The signals themselves are all around us. I consider that it is obvious to understand our space to be filled with energy fields of every description, and under the experience of LSD, we simply become aware of what is going on around us all the time. I believe that when a baby is born and opens his eyes, he sees the world exactly as it really is. The problem is that most of what the baby sees is not useful information! The baby's brain very quickly begins to distinguish between data that is useful, concerning tangible reality, and data that may be interesting, but doesn't have any bearing upon the substantial part of his life. So, in the course of about 8 to 10 hours (roughly the length of time it takes to come down from the intense phase of an LSD trip) the baby's brain is able to filter out non-useful information, so that his vision corresponds to the "normal" vision which relates to the kind of useful stuff that everyone else sees.

So when we take LSD (or similar substances), what happens is that all of the filters which our brain has acquired to interpret the sensory data flooding in all the time become wiped out, and we experience everything out there as it "really is." But then I have to add to this the influence of our own energy as it interacts with the energies out there. It is this interaction which accounts for the final experience, as perceived by the tripper. That is, I believe that the matrix of energy forms are "real," and that these interact with our own energy fields to form the visual "hallucinations" common to the LSD experience.

"Free" as the Next Horizon in Radical Philosophy

by *John Roland Stahl*

June, 2004

How can anything be free? Any cynic will tell you that there is no free lunch. No free lunch? The cynic only sees the color of his own money. I remember attending the 30th anniversary of the Summer of Love ~ a free concert in Golden Gate Park in 1997. I had a wonderful time. The sun was shining, and almoﬆ everyone seemed to be as happy as myself. And you didn't even have to wait for the big name bands to come on ~ if you have never heard the Ancient Future band (Matthew Montfort and friends) that played there as an opener, you missed a very good show. I ﬆill can't underﬆand why they are practically unknown ~ they are even Marin county locals.

But any time I passed a particular acquaintance of mine ~ a very talented artiﬆ who was set up with his paintings, trying to sell his artwork ~ he would fuss and fume darkly about how It's All Over Now, Baby Blue ~ "It's all about Money, now! Humbug! No more peace and love! Humbug, Humbug! 'Summer of Love' ! Ha! It's all juﬆ about Money, now! Humbug, Humbug." I thought this was pretty surprising ~ I guess he wasn't selling too many paintings, but what does he mean "it's all about

Money"? He was the one out there just trying to sell his paintings ~ all the rest of us were just out there having fun! The concert was even free, so what was his point? I wandered around the grounds, high on life . . . but every time I entered his space, the sky was dark and gloomy.

Free is very radical, and always has been. There is a famous story of a man standing on a street corner handing out twenty dollar bills (they could have been fives or hundreds, or maybe the story is entirely apocryphal, but it doesn't matter). Sooner or later he was arrested. I don't remember the charge. Disturbing the Peace?

Free is not easy! I was so sad to see all the idealistic youth in the 60's getting trashed and taken advantage of ~ they wanted to be free, and for a brief time we all shared a space where everything was totally free and easy, and we all loved everyone. ~ But then, those who figured that "there was one born every minute," and that they were one of the ones born to take them, converged on the scene and burned all those beautiful souls until everyone figured that "Peace and Love" was all just an illusion.

No, it's not an illusion, but it isn't easy, either. It only really works (at least, as a lifestyle) in communities of like minded individuals. But it is possible to spread the concept further and further, in small ways, here and there. For example, you don't have to be a fully dedicated Sadhu, give away all your possessions, and live a life of pure light. That is not an easy path, but it can be done ~ I have seen it. I will give two examples. I met a young man of radiant light hitch-hiking, and I invited him to stay with us for a while. He had nothing but the clothes on his back, not even shoes. ~ But he was amazing. He was always out and around, and he kept bringing back free food. There are fruit trees everywhere with fruits and nuts just dropping on the ground, rotting away, which he would gather and bring to us (I don't mean the rotten ones!). There were edible foods in forests and in vacant lots which he would bring to share with us. He was so friendly and helpful that he was always welcome. He would come and go, and we were always glad to see him return.

I met another young man at an international rainbow gathering in Slovenia. Once again, he was penniless and barefoot. I was familiar with American "drainbows" who crash every party, eat all the food, smoke all the dope, trash the place, and steal whatever they can as they leave. Not fun. But this man was totally different. I saw him always working ~ cooking, carrying water, building ~ just contributing his energies from a place overflowing with love. He was distinctly welcome everywhere!

But you don't have to have this total commitment in order to savor the joys of Free ~ it is possible to dip your toe in the water in many ways. For instance, some people are cynical about "free concerts." Don't we know how much money it costs to put on a concert? How do we expect musicians to live if we expect them to perform for free? Yet a successful musician can perform at an evening concert hall at regular rates, and still play for free at a Free Concert in the Park. The key is that not everything you do has to be measured in money ~ at least not all the time. You can just give your energy away for free here and there in small doses, and discover the magic and the joy of it. In careful doses, giving your energies away for free can be very rewarding. It can even be a coldly calculated financial gimmick ("they give you this, you pay for that"). But that's not what I'm talking about.

If you start out in small ways, you may find that it is easier and easier to offer your energy and your love, even your possessions, for free. It is a very liberating experience to do this. It is most "liberating" when it is not just a concealed trade. When you give something with the expectation that you will be given something of equal or greater value in return, that is useless. But help someone who is in no position to give anything back, and you will feel yourself growing lighter (no pun intended!) ~ as you grow in spiritual grace, your feet will never touch the ground.

Giving freely is a radical philosophy because it runs counter to the way the dominant world is set up. Once people start giving their love away for free, it exerts a real power for radical change. The internet is a great example. I think it is so funny to see all these sites trying to make money by charging people to visit the site! It just doesn't work because so many people are happy to offer their sites for free! Why pay money when you can get the same service for free?

Once more and more people join the Free bandwagon, then it is possible to contemplate a real surge in spiritual growth world-wide. It is kind of a conspiracy! Are you in? Let go, little by little, and discover the freedom and the joy that comes from just living in freedom and love. Soon more and more people will "get it" and start to do the same thing. Soon there will be plenty of places in the world where you will be welcome "for free." Of course, you will "freely" help out, wherever you are, so everyone benefits. Finally, the Kingdom of God will come on Earth, and everything and everyone will be Free.

How to Measure Spiritual Growth

by *John Roland Stahl*

June, 2004

I remember reading about "Spiritual Materialism," which refers to the pride that comes from spiritual growth and spiritual attainments. After practicing yoga for years, or working on your path of spiritual growth, there is a common tendency to feel a kind of satisfaction in your accomplishment. For some people, it even becomes impossible not to play the game of being "more spiritual than thou." This, of course, is very funny, so I would like to share a true measure of spiritual growth that works magically and inexorably to transcend this problem.

First, I have to prepare the ground with some discussion of a fundamental principle of philosophy. There are basically two directions of energy flow ~ inwards, towards the center, and outwards, away from the center. The typical Western style ("the rat race") is a movement reaching ever outward, grasping towards more and more. The Eastern wisdom, on the other hand, stresses the opposite direction ~ a movement back towards the center, within. It sounds simple enough ~ "Oh, yes, I get it ~ moving outward is bad; moving inward is good." But it is not at all so simple. I am especially fond of the alchemical symbols for personal growth, because they stress a balance between both directions. The basic alchemical dictum which summarizes the whole art is "SOLVE ET COAGULA." This means, literally, "to separate, and to unite." Break apart, and bring together. It is the alternation between these two directions which comprises the "process towards perfection" which the study of alchemy is all about.

Let's start with the movement towards the center. There is a point at the center which is a point of perfect balance, peace, and clarity. Moving away from this point goes towards, in the first place, greater novelty and complexity, but ultimately it leads to confusion and chaos. The movie *Bonnie and Clyde* is a perfect model of this process. Bonnie and Clyde pursue a career of violence and greed which leads to greater and greater confusion and chaos. As the movie progresses, they become crazier and crazier, moving faster and faster, and when they are finally blown apart, literally, in an explosion of chaos, it is inevitable and obvious. Is your life like that (even a little bit)? Then you need to see an Indian guru who will give you a calming mantra and help you to compose yourself and begin the long journey back to the center.

But the lesson of the alchemical symbols is that the fastest way to the center is not to attempt to go there all at once, in one non-stop instant ride (that, of course, is the Western model ~ we want it all NOW, so that we can attain Nirvana before lunch). No, the fastest way to the center is, like breathing, to alternate going in with going out. Both directions are meaningful and valuable.

Some people consider that God is this point of perfection and balance at the center and "the Devil is distance from God" (to use a famous definition). It gets complicated here, because I have to make a small digression, advising the reader always to look very carefully at an idea in order to discover the truth of the idea, which may lie beneath the surface, rather than simply to judge an idea as right or wrong. There are many ways to use words, and the same words may be used in different ways at different times to express the truth. So, that concept may be illuminating (that God is Perfection at the Center, and the Devil is movement away from that point), but I prefer to consider that both directions are aspects of "God." The movement away from the center is the Creative aspect (Yang, if you like), while the movement towards the center is the Receptive aspect (Yin).

A good example of all of this may be found on the chess board. Those of you who play chess may understand the distinction between "Positional Chess" and "Combinational Chess." Positional chess follows the direction towards the center, as the game simplifies towards the inertia inherent in the position, while combinational chess strives to throw the game outward again into chaos and confusion, out of which the player hopes to extract a new inertia favoring the pieces of his color. So the movement away from the center is the road to change, but it is only brought to completion when it returns back to the direction towards the center.

That's enough philosophy ~ it's almost lunch time, after all. So now that we are on this path towards the center, via *Solve et Coagula*, how can we tell which of us is approaching closest to the center? As we get closer and closer to the center, everything converges. The center is a point of clarity, balance, peace, and infinite love. So the closer one is to this point at the center, the more one will feel the spirit of infinite love. This is obvious ~ look at any spiritual teacher you can think of ~ all of the really advanced spiritual teachers radiate an energy of peace and love. You can feel it and you can see it.

Now for the funny part! Everyone is invited to play the game of being "more spiritual than thou" ! Everyone who wants to show how advanced they are spiritually only has to work on radiating infinite love! The funny part is that it actually works. No matter where you are on the spiritual hierarchy, the more you practice infinite love, the closer you will come to perfect clarity. So go ahead; impress your friends; be the first on your block to manifest infinite love, and spread this measure of spiritual growth far and wide. And do it quickly, because this world needs all the peace and love it can get, and it needs it soon.

Memoir of Chogyam Trungpa Rinpoche

by *John Roland Stahl*

December, 2005

Recently I was reading a very entertaining book by Sam Kashner, *When I Was Cool*, a memoir of the author's days as a student of Allen Ginsberg, William Burroughs, and the "School of Disembodied Poetics," which was contemporaneous with the Naropa Institute at Boulder, Colorado, headed by Chogyam Trungpa Rinpoche. Since I had attended a class given by Rinpoche in 1972, I recognized many of the references, and it occurred to me to wonder what had become of that venerable teacher. To my dismay, I found that he had died in 1987. Now I want to add my own recollections of this very interesting man.

I first heard him speak in an interview with CKGM radio station in Montreal, Quebec, probably around 1971. There was a very talented DJ in those days (Doug Pringle, I think his name was) who made that radio station the "hippest" station anywhere. One program I very much enjoyed was his weekly Sunday night interview. Montreal was a large and exciting city, and there were always visiting gurus and holy men of every description, so it was never any problem finding some interesting "guru of the week" to interview of a Sunday night. I listened to these gurus with amusement ~ it seemed to me that most of them were using the interview for their career advancement. Basically, they had the period of a one hour interview, complete with questions from the listening audience, in which to drum up business for their own particular path toward enlightenment, or whatever they were selling.

I should explain that I have always taken a very great interest in this kind of teaching. In fact, I have studied esoteric teachings of every description all of my life, and my major life's work has been to discover the central ideas which are common to just about every path, and to present them in a systematic and logical presentation.

It used to amuse me to hear these gurus sounding like used car salesmen, hawking their wares, speaking loud and fast about meditation and peace! Anyway, comes the turn of Chogyam Trungpa Rinpoche. In most cases, it doesn't take much to get the guru being interviewed to launch into his spiel. The interviewer barely has a chance to get a word in edgewise. Usually, he just introduces the weekly guru, and then turns him loose. Rinpoche, however, had nothing to say. After the usual introductions, he just sat there, smiling. (I could easily hear him smiling, even though it was just a radio program.)

As I have said, the interviewer was very good, and very well versed in all manner of esoteric thought, so he would try to draw him out. "What do you think about the following idea? Would you say that blah, blah, blah, and blah, blah, blah?"

And Rinpoche would answer, "Yes."

The problem, of course, was that the interviewer was too good. "Well, what about this: do you think that blah, blah, blah, and blah, blah, blah?"

"Yes, that's right."

This went on for a while, with Rinpoche saying practically nothing at all. Finally, in despair, the interviewer turned to the telephone lines.

Since the callers were so much less erudite than the interviewer, their questions revealed errors of one sort or another, and I noticed with growing awe that Rinpoche took every question and identified the error in a very few well chosen words, and then reduced the matter to brilliant clarity in a matter of moments. I could still hear him smiling. This continued for the duration of the interview ~ Rinpoche had nothing whatever to say, but if any caller had any question or any confusion, it was quickly and brilliantly reduced to clarity in a very efficient and incisive manner.

I was very impressed. I was so impressed, as a matter of fact, that I packed up my few possessions and went out to Boulder Colorado to attend Rinpoche's class in Tibetan Buddhism.

His class met once a week for three hours. At the appointed time, the class was full. There were regularly enrolled students, along with a large number of un-enrolled persons "auditing" the class without academic credit. I was one of the latter category. However, Rinpoche was not there. He was late. Everyone waited patiently for him to arrive. We waited and waited. Finally, about forty-five minutes late, he arrived. Rinpoche's lateness to his classes is legendary ~ you may be surprised to hear that he was only forty-five minutes late, but this was the first class of the semester. At each succeeding class, he was later and later, finally reaching as much as three hours late.

As soon as Rinpoche arrived, everyone rustled their papers, took out their pens and notebooks and adjusted their seating positions in readiness to begin. Rinpoche took a chair at the front of the class and sat there quietly and smiled at the class. He continued to sit there smiling for about another twenty minutes before beginning to speak.

Finally he began to speak. This was supposed to be a three hour class, but he only spoke for about twenty minutes. Those twenty minutes, however, were clear and brilliant expositions of the tenets of Tibetan Buddhism, and I was not disappointed. Then he allowed questions from the class, and he repeated his Montreal stunt ~ every question was very easily and brilliantly reduced to clarity in a very few well chosen words. This was the pattern of every one of his classes. He arrived later and later to his classes as the semester wore on. What I found surprising was that not one of the students ever missed a class or arrived a moment later than the posted starting time! No one wanted to miss a moment, and everyone seemed perfectly content to wait for two hours or more ~ as long as it might take ~ to hear the great man speak! There was never the slightest indication that anyone were restless or annoyed. Everyone sat in the classroom as patiently as you please, waiting for him to arrive. You might think that Rinpoche were returning from some special event in Denver, or at least he might be researching some point he wanted to make for his class, but this was not the case. It soon became common knowledge that he was simply sitting in some local bar, drinking. Of course, as the semester progressed, he would show up for his classes later and later, and more and more drunk.

Every time he finally arrived at the classroom, he would begin by sitting in his chair and smiling quietly for at least twenty minutes or half an hour before beginning to speak. No one seemed to mind his eccentricities in any way. He was non-attached to his ego to a fault! He seemed to live in a world in which he really didn't care what anyone thought about him.

His basic philosophical position was that there is no problem at all. Everything is clear, and he has nothing to say. But when a student has a problem, he is happy to point out the error and reduce the problem back to serene clarity, where he seemed to reside all the time, smiling, and fully at peace.

At one time I showed him some of my own writings, and I wondered what he would have to say. He looked at my writings very carefully for some minutes with close interest, and finally he said, with obvious surprise, "Yes, this is right!" There could be no higher praise from Chogyam Trungpa Rinpoche than when he has nothing to say.

Is Religion Good or Bad?

by *John Roland Stahl*

June, 2006

Let me start this essay off right at the beginning by telling you my conclusion ~ religion is a primary source of evil in the world! It shouldn't be this way. In fact, I should clarify that by saying that what I mean is that religion, as it is understood and practiced by most of the people of the world, is a primary source of evil.

In some of my other writings (*vide, e.g., Patterns of Illusion and Change*, or *How to Measure Spiritual Growth*), I have explained what any study of religion should do ~ it should lead the student closer to God, closer to that Center of Convergence at which all Good Things come together. It really shouldn't matter in the slightest what outward form your religious beliefs or practices take. As soon as you make any progress along the path of spiritual growth, you should find yourself converging towards that point at the center where "It Is All Good" ~ a realm of Peace and Love.

But this isn't what we find happening! On the contrary, Religion seems to function as a fulcrum by which people are torn apart into Us and Them. It is a very pernicious and aggravating process that only serves to ratchet up the levels of tension in the world, not make anything better. Wherever Religion rears its ugly head and takes hold of a people, they usually use it to wrap their adherents into a close in-group, while declaring everyone else "infidels," who are surely bound for hell.

The world is a big and scary place, and out of the diversity of peoples, languages, cultures, and historical backgrounds, it is not surprising that people want to find smaller groups of people with whom they can more closely associate themselves, while excluding everyone else. In this way, religion seems to serve the same function for its communicants as an inner city gang provides for groups of impoverished and ignorant adolescent boys. And, in perfect conformity with the analogy, the consequences are continual warfare.

Some religions are worse offenders than others on this point, and I am going to speak my mind, no matter how offensive some people may find it. I think most of the religions of the world represent an "adolescent" stage of spiritual growth, and should be supplanted by more evolutionary theological concepts.

Specifically, there are two aspects of religion that I find offensive ~ one is Exclusivity, a religion that is only available to a particular group of people, and the other is Radical Missionary Zeal, in which the adherents are driven to convert the heathen, at the point of a sword, figuratively or literally.

It is no coincidence that the worst offenders for both of these unacceptable aspects of religious belief have been at each other's throats for thousands of years in the Middle East. Yes, I am talking about Judaism and Islam.

I remember an email correspondence I carried on for years with a Moslem gentleman from Egypt. We discussed many things, rarely touching upon religion, but the topic was not excluded from our attention, and at one time my correspondent attempted to propound the virtues of his faith to me.

"In the first place," he began, "I am sure you will agree that God will love us more if we truly understand Him, and worship Him with the True Religion." That was an axiom that he assumed I would accept, like any rational person, without any further argument or question. But I immediately rejected his premises ~

"No," I replied, "I think God would love us more if we live in harmony with our neighbors, regardless of what we may believe." That was the crux of the whole argument. Why should God worry about what we may believe? Theology is not an easy subject for most people to understand. Many people do not even attempt to understand it, considering that it belongs to a category of unknowable information. If there be any qualitative difference in the amount of love God might have for his errant children (a dubious proposition at best ~ it seems to me that the notion of a Loving God who enjoys a limitless Love for all of His Creation is a more evolved concept than the "Jealous God" of the Old Testament, who needs to be propitiated with incense and sacrifice before he will allow any Blessings to fall from His hands), then I would expect God to be more pleased with those of His children who were able to live in harmony with their neighbors than with those who were engaged in constant warfare.

There are thousands of different religions, and I do not propose to discuss all of them here. What I have to say can be adequately expounded by reference to Judaism, Islam, Christianity, and Buddhism. In general, these comprise the "major" religions of the world, and will serve as good examples for the messages I want to make. I am sure there are many other religions of the world which avoid the errors of these four, but I am not attempting a complete survey of the history of religion here ~ I just want to make some points in an evolutionary context.

It may seem like a commendable, or at least a politic, solution to treat all religions with equal respect, making no judgments upon them, but I am unable to take that approach. I have made inquiries into the mysteries of theology, and I have formed some ideas of my own. If these meditations have led me to consider that most of the world's major religions represent primitive stages of spiritual growth, I will not stifle those conclusions under some egalitarian concept that all religions are equally deserving of respect, or some such formulation. No, I have problems with most of the world's religions, and I want to discuss those problems here.

Let me clarify my present intention. I am not trying to explain and convince anyone of my own religious convictions ~ not at all (you can find that in other essays, but not here). My comparisons and criticisms of religions are solely derived from practical consequences of the religious beliefs. To put it simply, my argument runs that if a religion leads to an unacceptable conclusion, then that religion is flawed. This argument completely circumvents any need to enquire into the foundations of the religious beliefs. I look at the religions of the world and I ask how do those religions affect the spiritual lives of their adherents, and if I don't like the answer, then I take that as grounds for rejecting that religious belief, without even beginning to approach the serious questions of theology.

Let me start with the oldest of the major religions. Antiquity has always been a very powerful argument in favor of any belief, and Judaism claims to be one of the first religions that posited a single God. In a world of a multitude of gods of every description, gods of every tribe and place, the

God of the Hebrews was the One God of all. But I have some reservations about this claim to be the original source of Monotheism. It seems to me that the God of the Hebrews was, at best, a transitional figure, not really a universal God at all. The problem is that the Hebrews tried to have it both ways. They proclaimed that their god was the One and Only God, but, out of the other side of their mouths, they insisted that this God was specifically the god of the Hebrew People, the "Chosen People." This really looks to me to be a hold-over from the tribal god of a particular group of people, not a truly universal God of all Creation. Any concept of God that holds a special relationship to any tribe of people is not a fully mature monotheistic God, but only a kind of adolescent godling that isn't quite able to give up his parochial attachment to the tribe from which he came. I'm sorry, but I just call them as I see them.

Next, Islam seems to overcome this limitation. Islam truly seems to believe in One God. The singleness of the One God is really the defining feature of Islam. On the other hand, they take it to the extreme at which it violates my second objection ~ the Radical Missionary Zeal. Not content to worship their God in peace, they are unable to rest until everyone on earth accepts this God (along with his Prophet Mohammed, of course; peace be upon him).

Is it any wonder that the adherents of these two religions are at each other's throats constantly? My purpose in writing this article is to propose a solution to the constant warfare in the Middle East. My solution is quite simple ~ both Jews and Moslems should evolve their religious beliefs in ways that resolve these shortcomings. For example, the Jews might form a new sect of Judaism which specifically repudiates the "chosen people" story, and affirms that God is One for all people, not just the tribe of Judah. And on the other hand, a new sect of Moslems could discover that all spiritual roads should lead to the same place in the end, if the path be uncluttered with distractions. That is to say, yes, there is only One God, but Mohammed is not His only prophet! There have been many avatars and prophets of God, and any one of them might provide a path that will lead to the same Peace and Joy and Love at the Center as any other.

Suddenly, the basis for the hostility between Jews and Moslems will melt away, and they can welcome each other in their mosques and temples, and realize that any worship of God should achieve the same goals. The advanced practitioner of either Judaism or Islam will be one who recognizes that there is no fundamental difference between the beliefs of Jews, Moslems, or anyone else.

When I say "fundamental difference" what I mean has nothing to do with counting the number of angels that can dance on the head of a pin! Religious and Spiritual growth derived from any practice should lead the practitioner towards that same convergence of Peace, Joy, and Love, and none of the outward differences in costume, style, language, or cultural heritage have any real bearing on what really matters. Any religion that focuses upon matters that distinguish and separate one from another is primitive ~ an evolutionarily advanced religion will understand and focus upon the essential aspects which all spiritual practices and beliefs have at the core. It really doesn't matter whether it is your shoes or your hat that you take off (or put on) when you go to commune with God.

In contrast with the foregoing two religions, Buddhism is serene and pacific. Buddhism is a way of life and a philosophy which is available to anyone who find its messages appealing to them, but there has never been (to my knowledge) any history of "radical missionary zeal." In terms of the functional consequences of the religion, Buddhism scores very high marks. My image of the Buddhist is one who certainly "lives in harmony with his neighbor." I do have objections to Buddhist philosophy, but they are not based upon my observations of the consequences.

In other writings I have stressed the importance of both directions of energy, both going in and going out, and Buddhism seems to me to be all about the passive and inward directing of attention, to the neglect of the outward directions. I like the quotation from the first chapter of the *Tao Te Ching* by Lao Tzu, (D. C. Lau translation) ~ "Hence always rid yourself of desires in order to observe its Secrets, but always allow yourself to have desires in order to observe its Manifestations. These two are the same, but diverge in Name as they issue forth. Being the same, they are called Mysteries. Mystery upon Mystery, the gateway of the manifold secrets." The outward movement is characteristic of life; a rejection of this outward movement may lead to contentment, but it is a contentment that precludes any of the reaching out which defines what it means to be human. There can be no growth or change without the searching outward for alternatives and novelties. A true harmony of spirit will balance both aspects of life ~ the inward balance and the outward quest.

Finally I come upon Christianity which rates a very mixed score. On the one hand, the messages of Jesus Christ show a marked advance over the primitive "adolescent" God of the Old Testament. If Christianity were judged solely from the historical records, it would score very highly indeed. It scores highly as a religion for everyone ~ there is One God of all mankind, and that's that. There is a bit of a problem with the missionary zeal ~ the disciples are specifically charged to preach the gospel to all people. But there is a fine line between wanting to share the "good news," and not taking "no" for an answer! In earlier times this line was not properly observed, but I think, with some exceptions, most Christian churches now recognize the rights of other people to accept or reject Christianity as they see fit.

The problem I have with Christianity is more about the nature of God Himself. In this respect, I think the Hebrew understanding of God was really brilliant. I think the admonition not to make any graven image of God is really an important concept ~ indispensable, even. The Christians seem to have passed this whole idea right by. The point is that any time you worship some image, you risk the danger of taking the image for the God it represents. In the case of Jesus, the Church has insisted upon the divinity of Jesus to the point where it looks to me like "man worshipping himself." That is what happens when you insist upon worshipping God in the image of a Man. You identify that man with God, and that is exactly what has happened to the Christian Church. The Catholics take it even further afield. I remember one time when my mother was asked about the difference between Protestants and Catholics, she replied, "Protestants pray to God; Catholics pray to the Virgin Mary." Where does it all end? Mount Olympus? No, there only seems to be one religion that is adamantly monotheistic, and that is Islam.

But another problem I have with Christianity is that very few people who call themselves "Christian" seem to have the remotest notion of the teachings of Jesus Christ! I suppose the same could be said about any religion. Islam is supposedly a religion with very high ethical ideals ~ but there are as many Moslems as Christians who do not really understand or follow the teachings of their faith.

So, what are my conclusions about all of this? I think that religions do more harm than good. The different religions serve only to separate people, and give them an excuse to go to war with each other. I think that it would be better if there were some way for spiritual people to avoid the divisive aspects of religion, and focus exclusively upon the central aspects common to all spiritual practice.

I was only going to discuss those four main religions, but I want to make mention of just one more ~ one religious group has always seemed to me to get it right in just about every way ~ the Society of Friends, commonly known as Quakers. From the very start, I have always thought that it makes far more sense to sit together in silence, listening for the word of God, than to spend a "worship service" praying at God, giving Him his marching orders of what it would suit you for Him to do for you! I like the careful avoidance of divisive issues, and the adherence to what is clear and central. They avoid divisive theological concerns, and rely most heavily upon the "light within" ~ taking their direction as directly from God as they can. Well, if I wanted to belong to an organized Church, I think I would look for a meeting house of the Society of Friends. All of their historic concerns are important ones ~ peace, freedom, equality, integrity, and an emphasis upon plain and simple living, instead of a life cluttered with vain and useless luxury. Instead of following any laid down dogma, or any prescribed path towards God, they sit still and quiet, and listen for the "still, small voice" of God to tell them what to do. I like it.

"Freedom and Democracy"

by *John Roland Stahl*

July, 2006

What went wrong with America? I remember, when I was young, everyone looked up to America ~ the land of Freedom and Democracy, the land of Opportunity. The United States was founded with very high ideals, and for many years it represented the cutting edge of progressive political ideology.

And now it is mired in opprobrium, all over the world. There are very few places left in the world where an American can go freely and safely, unless he makes it very clear that he does not support his government's policies. Wave an American flag almost anywhere in the world, and you risk becoming a target of hatred. Almost all of the "weapons of mass destruction" originate from the United States, and the United States is about the only country that doesn't mind using them, unilaterally, in a first strike, in a war of aggression against helpless people who can resist, but cannot fight back effectively. I am disgusted that only America's war dead are counted ~ ten or twenty Iraqis may be killed for every American, but no one really cares much about that. It is the same way in Israel ~ if three Israeli soldiers are killed, the Israelis feel justified in killing several hundred Palestinians, in retaliation.

What is going on, and why? I think the answer can be found by looking a bit more closely at some of the language being used to defend the war against the Iraqi people. All they talk about is "bringing Freedom and Democracy to the Iraqi people" as if that were what they are doing, or trying to do, or want to do.

Oh, no ~ any look at the recent history of the United States will indicate clearly enough that neither Freedom nor Democracy rate very highly at all in the Halls of Power of the United States government. Any two-bit, tin-horn military dictator will do just nicely, and the United States government will be just happy to support the same, with military back-up if needed, and against the angry and rioting people of the dictator's country, just so long as the said dictator will ensure a favorable environment for United States Business Interests. Oh. Now it becomes clear ~ there is really nothing going on at all about Democracy and/or Freedom ~ it is all about Money. Didn't you know? And you thought it was Love that makes the world go round.

Thomas Jefferson had it all figured out over two hundred years ago ~ the longer a government or political system remains in power, the more the wealth and power become concentrated in fewer and fewer hands. In fact, the history of the United States is basically the history of that consolidation of wealth and power into ever fewer hands. Thomas Jefferson's solution was to suggest that every law whatsoever, including the fundamental Constitution of a State (yes, that Constitution) should naturally expire at the end of 27 years, which was Jefferson's calculation of the average age of a generation. His intention was to declare that no people had the authority to pass laws binding upon future generations. Every generation must have not only the right, but also the responsibility, to create their own laws and political institutions.

However, even this would not really change much. It takes really major upheavals in social and political systems to interrupt the process of consolidation of wealth and power into fewer and fewer hands. So all of this talk about "Democracy and Freedom" is all a sham ~ no one is the least bit interested in Democracy or Freedom; not any more. As for Democracy, both of George W. Bush's elections have been fraudulently stolen with the connivance of institutions of wealth and power. And as for Freedom ~ well, the United States suffers the highest rate of incarceration in the world ~ no other nation even comes close. ("If we run out of space, we'll build more prisons!" ~ Bush, with his simple solution to every problem.)

What annoys me is that no one really seems to notice this deception ~ people hear the claim that Bush's wars are being fought for "Freedom and Democracy" and everyone seems to believe it. Oh, yes ~ Freedom and Democracy ~ what a wonderful idea! Who could possibly be against Freedom and Democracy? Bush seems to take it for granted that his idea of Freedom and Democracy is so ardently desired by everyone that there can not possibly be any other way of viewing the matter.

Never mind that the horrors unleashed upon the Iraqi people have so vastly overshadowed the remotest possibility of anything that Saddam Hussein might ever have done, or that the country of Iraq is so devastated that it can never recover (the use of depleted uranium alone makes the land uninhabitable for the next 10,000 years ~ the sickness and death caused by the use of this material, dating back to the first Gulf War, are overshadowed by the current much more visible death and destruction).

I want to make it clear that I am not an apologist for Saddam Hussein (never mind, again, that he was a creature supported by the United States in the first place) ~ but the high ground of international politics has always been held by Diplomacy, not Warfare. In politer centuries, where the political leaders had more of a grasp of history, Diplomacy was the way to maneuver on the world stage. Saddam Hussein could easily have been hemmed in diplomatically for as long as necessary ~ until the man dies of old age, if need be ~ to prevent any unleashing of weapons of mass destruction, real or imaginary. But, no, such a course of action does not appeal to the American Cowboy, who wants his results Now! If the Iraqis (or anyone else ~ take notice here!) do not knuckle under to the demands of the only Superpower left strutting the stage, then they will be blasted into the Stone Age by Shock and Awe, and don't you forget it.

So what can we do about this horrible situation? Now that the greatest source of political instability in the world is coming from the country with the strongest military might ~ now what? What can the people of the rest of the world do against such an arrogant monster?

This is a very complex problem. It is very easy to look at the mistakes of the American government and shake our heads in dismay and disgust, but now what?

I want to divide my answer into two parts ~ the immediate problem and the long term solution. As for the immediate problem, it cannot be solved by any action from outside the country. Suicide bombers in New York and Chicago will not make any changes for the better. In fact, war always makes things worse than they were before. If I may make a brief digression here, let me explain why the island of Crete enjoyed such a high level of civilization so long ago ~ quite simply, it was an island of just the right size ~ small enough to be governed by a single government, yet large enough to enjoy sufficient diversity of production, education, artistic development, and so on, and, most importantly, as an island it was safe from the ravages of foreign attack. It enjoyed over a thousand years of uninterrupted peace and prosperity, which very directly led to the flowering of civilization in all its forms. It was only with the development of large ships of war (from other lands) that the island became vulnerable to attack by foreign conquerors, and the island and its civilization were quickly reduced to rubble.

So the lesson is that Peace and Prosperity bring civilization, and War brings desolation, death, and destruction. During times of war, people lose everything they have ~ their land, their wealth, their food, their families ~ and all they have left is anger and desperation, and the determination to bring down as many of the enemy with them as they die. Not good.

No, the only hope for the survival of life on earth is to effect a gradual uplifting of spiritual consciousness, world-wide. An "uplifting of spiritual consciousness," in case you didn't realize it, is not brought about by conditions of constant warfare. War just depresses the spiritual consciousness more and more, in a cycle that spirals downward more and more deeply into the morass, like the situation in the Middle East, which has been deteriorating for over a thousand years, ever since the Crusades, and with no end in sight! In this connection, George Bush's usage of the term "Crusade" with regard to his war in Iraq was a particularly unfortunate choice of words, reminding the Moslems of the last time the Christians came a-conquering. And, by the way, it may be instructive to notice that the first Crusades had as little to do with rescuing the Holy Land from the Infidel as Bush's war has to do with bringing Democracy and Freedom to the Iraqi people ~ all of the "Christian" barons and knights were attracted to the Crusade by the hope of plunder ~ so what else is new?

So there is only one hope for the survival of life on earth (I do not think I overstate the case) ~ and that is that the American people must pull the wool back from over their eyes and reverse the last fifty years of American foreign policy (I go all the way back to Vietnam). I remember just after 9/11 when Bush was making his pitch for a war in Iraq ~ (Iraq? I thought 9/11 was all about Afghanistan? Do you know why they never found Osama bin Laden? He has been hiding out in the East Wing of the White House.) ~ he was riding high on the indignation over the 9/11 attacks, and everyone felt it a patriotic duty (remember the "Patriot Act"?) to support the President (self appointed) in his mindless war against the people of Iraq.

Finally (July of 2006), his ratings are finally down into the 20's and plunging fast. That is the most hopeful sign ~ perhaps the American people can be forgiven their slowness off the mark ~ at least finally the whole fiasco in Iraq, in which the folly of an American "President," having fraudulently stolen his election in the first place, is being seen for what it is: the most appalling mistake in the history of the United States. Nothing short of an immediate withdrawal of all American troops, accompanied by a profound apology and reconstruction funds ("war reparations") can possibly reverse the slide of the American government into the status of a total renegade, unfit to stand with the honorable nations of the world. By the way, I heard the most sensible plan for ending American involvement in the war in Iraq from Noam Chomsky ~ "Put the troops on trucks, and head for the border."

The American political process seems to be way too turgid and ponderous, moving much too slowly, yet it finally appears that the elections of 2008 should provide the beginning of a new direction, while George W. is rudely hustled out of town, riding on a rail, tarred and feathered. However, if the political process is disappointing, please take another look at the Declaration of Independence (www.tree.org/declar.htm), or, ☞ *here is an even tighter edit of that famous document* ~ www.tree.org/declaredit.htm.

Now as to the somewhat more difficult problem of long term solutions, I hardly know how to begin. It is so much easier to pull something down that it is to build something up. While any moron can see the folly of Bush's actions (except, of course, Bush ~ he is not up to the level of a moron; he is an idiot), it is not at all so easy to figure out how to prevent the "Thomas Jefferson syndrome" ~ whereby the longer a government remains in place, the more the wealth and power become concentrated in ever fewer hands. The problem, of course, is that the agenda of the wealthy and powerful is not necessarily in the best interests of the survival of life on earth.

There is no great mystery about the agenda of the wealthy and powerful ~ it is very simple. It is to maintain the wealth and power in the hands of the wealthy and powerful. Thus, as long as big corporations are able to make profits in Iraq, it is all good. Even while this war is going on, huge profits are being made by corporations funded by the government ~ a corporation thinks nothing of vaporizing $900 million out of every billion dollars funded to them by the government, as long as there is that last $100 million that can go into their own pockets ~ in case you didn't know, this is the way the world works, and if you have to ask who pays the bill for the losses, you are not paying attention.

So, what is needed is some sort of institution that can rise above and counter-balance that inevitably rising tide of Wealth and Power. Unfortunately, "democracy" as it is known and practiced by the Americans just does not measure up. The government is inevitably run by the wealthy and powerful. If anyone ever does rise up into those ranks from the "other half," they either quickly sponge up the ideals of the wealthy and powerful, so happy to have made the climb into their exalted ranks, or they are just squelched and rendered powerless and ineffective by those lofty powers, and life goes on untroubled.

The original notion of "checks and balances" was a good one, but it needs a bit of touching up, since there is neither check nor balance to the impact of Big Money. True, the electorate can always (in theory, in principle) vote the villains out of office (too little, too late! Look what devastation can be caused by a couple of terms with an imbecile at the helm of the Ship of State ~ a "loose cannon" fits in nicely with this metaphor), but, in the advanced stages of the reign of Wealth and Power, the Wealthy and Powerful simply sweep aside any such obstacles ~ witness George W. Bush's dual theft of his "elections."
("More Trees! Less Bush!")

If I didn't know that Bush were illiterate, I might have thought he had been reading *The Republic*, by Plato. Plato's *Republic* is a very remarkable work. Among other recommendations for how to run a state, Plato blandly avers that "by all means, a government should surely hold elections, since the people like to believe that they are participating in their government.

However, after everyone has voted, the agents of the government should simply discard the votes and announce who won." That is exactly what happened in the last two elections ~ the votes were discarded, and the government simply announced who won. Plato then goes on to say, "Then if any one at all is to have the privilege of lying, the rulers of the state should be the persons; and they, in their dealings either with enemies or with their own citizens, may be allowed to lie for the public good."

I am trying to clarify the problem here, and then to recommend some solutions. There may be a variety of ways to overcome the problem, but I will start out with a very general overview of a kind of solution that is not too radical for contemporary consideration, at least in its general outlines ~ I think, in general, there is a distinct advantage in a Parliamentary system that is common in Europe in which there is some Head of State that is separate from the Government. Governments come and go and are usually as corrupt as they can manage to be, while it is the function of the Head of State to exercise some limiting and/or moderating influence over the government. That is, instead of an all-powerful President, you have a Prime Minister who is, at least in theory, subordinate to the Head of State.

I am aware that I have not advanced the argument very far yet ~ the problem is similar to the question, "Who made God?" How are we going to select a Head of State who will be above the power-and-money-grubbing level of the typical politician? A constitutional monarchy can sometimes be a workable solution, at least when it has a historical background that has proven adequate to offer some useful counter-weight to the untrammeled power of the President or Prime Minister. However, there are so many problems with this form ~ where it may be successful in Thailand, it is a disaster in Nepal. No, when looking for a new solution, we have to look further.

My own proposal seems to cause elevated eyebrows whenever I suggest it, because it seems to sound like I am trying to set up yet another tyranny, when, in fact, my object is totally the reverse ~ the successful institution of a Head of State would function to limit the otherwise out-of-control power of whoever might seize control of the government of the moment.

My solution is theological. All political authority must come ultimately from God. Great ~ so now all we need is some reliable way to discover an incarnation of God on earth who may be able to provide the guidance so sorely needed in today's world. Actually, I believe this can be done. My original model was the Dalai Lama of Tibet, in which the incarnation of a lama is discovered as a very young child, who is then raised for his position from his early years. In fact, this method achieves its objective ~ it establishes a spiritual leader who very clearly derives his inspiration from God.

All I want to do is to modify the concept from a single choice to a whole Seminary ~ I propose the establishment of a Seminary composed of carefully selected young people, male and female, who will themselves select one of their number to fill the role of spiritual leader, or Head of State. Careful readers of these articles will recognize this idea from the organizational structure of the Church of the Living Tree. (By the way, the problem of who makes the selection for this Seminary is not critical ~ I have faith in any group of young people to understand their mandate and become self-regulating, regardless of the original intentions that went into their selections.)

For some reason, most people seem to react with alarm to this idea, perhaps because it is a bit too radical to be washed down with either the after dinner coffee or even a glass of Port. As for me, I have every confidence not only that anyone raised for the purpose would be a vast improvement over the political victors of the American political process, but that a school of perhaps thirty such persons, carefully selected and raised with every advantage, would easily select a suitable candidate who would have no other motivation than to fulfill his or her obligations with the most appropriate actions. Remember, I am not so much trying to put forward yet another all powerful tyrant as I am trying to create an institution that will provide some counter-weight to the excesses of the prevailing political systems.

If George W. Bush were only Prime Minister, and the Dalai Lama were the Head of State, we would never have gotten involved in that folly and madness in Iraq.

Don't like my idea? Don't bother to offer criticism unless you have some better way to deal with loose cannons like Bush, rattling around on the world's deck! I don't want to hear why my plan is no good ~ I want to hear why your plan is better.

[2018: Back then I thought Bush was a loose cannon! Ha, ha. We've just raised the bar for loose-cannonhood.]

In Defense of North Korea and Iran

by *John Roland Stahl*

July, 2006

The United States government is acting like a classic bully, rubbing the faces of the Iraqis in the dust. A bully does not attack an opponent with the capacity or will to make a significant resistance; a bully attacks someone sufficiently weaker so that the bully can have its way with the weaker party without fear of unacceptable consequences. This is most definitely a sexual pattern ~ one of the perversions which I have enumerated in my article on *The Metaphysics of Sex*. Of course, in the case of Iraq, the American government clearly underestimated the determination of the Iraqi people to resist this unwelcome interference into their domestic affairs. However hated Saddam Hussein may have been, the presence of the Ugly American is even more offensive. It is so clear to me that nothing about that horrible mess is going to get better until the Americans take their "stick" out of the faces and lives of the Iraqi people and go away.

But I find it interesting that the Americans have found it so necessary for their perceived National Interest to make this war in Iraq. There might be far more egregious offenses against human dignity in unimportant little countries in Africa, but, since there are no important reserves of Oil over there, there is no urgent reason for the Americans to be involved ~ let them kill each other off; so who cares, anyway? But in Iraq it will be possible to maintain such a state of chaos and confusion that the price of Oil will be maintained nice and high, so that everyone involved in that industry can go on raking in Obscene Profits with their fat fingers, which is the whole point, of course. Never mind that the extraction and combustion of that oil is destroying the earth's biosphere.

But, the apologists for the government will say, Iraq is not just about human rights abuses; it is about the weapons of mass destruction and the fears associated with their possible use that has caused the military interventions in Iraq. Well, I hope I do not need to further flog that dead horse! Everyone knows by now that the only reason why the Americans suspected the Iraqis of possessing Weapons of Mass Destruction was that they "saved their receipts." (*E.g.*, where do you think all of the anthrax that has ever been found has come from, as proven by careful analysis?) But I will leave that dead horse to the jackals, the rats, and the ants. In the present climate, there should be nothing but bones bleaching in the sun before this day is out.

I turn, instead, to a consideration of "weapons of mass destruction," and ask why the US government has devoted its attention to the relatively harmless Iraq when there has never been any doubt at all about the much more serious threat of weapons of mass destruction coming from North Korea? The North Koreans boast about it, after all, so it should not be very hard to believe in the presence of their weapons.

The answer is perfectly clear! North Korea possesses a real and credible threat! No one in North Korea is under the slightest illusions about what would happen if they were to go along with the demands of the United States and surrender their program of nuclear weapons development ~ they would be stomped immediately (*cf:* Libya). No, it is the presence of a clear and credible threat that is the only card in the North Korean deck, so there is little likelihood that they will surrender it on any terms whatsoever.

In fact, that is the only effective way to respond to a bully. When a bully comes up to you and says, "Gimme your money!" he expects you to say, "Here it is! Here's my watch and my credit cards. Don't hurt me!" But if the "victim" says, "Oh, yeah? You and who else? If you want my money, come and get it!" To which the bully responds, "Ah, forget it, loser!" And he goes away looking for an easier mark. Why risk hassling with anyone who is going to fight back, when there are so many easy marks out there just waiting to be fleeced for nothing?

And now I look at the events in Iran and I am not the least bit surprised that the Iranians are doing everything they can to get a credible threat operational as quickly as possible. They see the handwriting on the wall. They can see that "Moslems" are being set up as the heirs to the "Communists" of an earlier generation, as the villains whom we must all hate and fear. It is the oldest trick in the book for any unpopular government ~ find a scapegoat to hate and to blame for all the ills besetting them, and everyone will direct their opposition to them instead of trying to bring down the unpopular government. No one is fooled by the claim that they are only interested in peaceful uses of nuclear power in Iran ~ certainly they are trying to establish a credible military threat, and that is the only thing which can save them from suffering the fate of Iraq. Perhaps if Saddam Hussein had managed to maintain a credible arsenal of biological weapons, he might have remained in power all of this time. "Yes, we have biological weapons! When we are confronted with a monstrous military machine like the United States, there is no way we can oppose firepower with firepower, but we can unleash biological weapons which will produce devastating mayhem upon targeted American cities! We have a great many independent agents all over the world, ready to unleash their horrors at the first sign of hostilities against the sovereign people of Iraq. So just you watch your step, Uncle Sam, and keep your ugly "nose" out of our affairs! We will not be the first to use these weapons, but if we are attacked, we will make you regret your folly!" And so on.

So am I advocating that all of the weaker countries in the world should arm themselves as quickly as they can in order to defend themselves from the rampages of an American government which has gotten way out of control? "Mutually Assured Destruction" and all of that?

Well, in the short term, there seems to be no other way to curb the blood lust of the Wealthy and Powerful, who want to rule the world (economically and politically ~ puppet states run by military dictators are perfectly acceptable as long as they maintain a favorable climate for Business).

Endless war is not an option; there must be an end to war. Not that it's going to be easy, but we need to take a long term view. If there is any hope for the survival of life on earth, there must be a whole new basis for political institutions. I stand with Pierre Teilhard de Chardin, Albert Einstein, Bertrand Russell, H. G. Wells, and many others who are convinced that there can be no important evolutionary advance until the whole earth is united politically into some sort of cohesive whole.

The history of the twenty-first century will be the story of the evolution from a state of chaos in which the world is over-run by a jungle full of independent sovereign states, each pursuing their own agenda for their own personal advantage, into a state of order in which the whole world is unified politically. ~ or else it will be the history of the last days of civilization, in which the biological health of the planet is irreparably undermined until the human race either dies out altogether, or enters a period of hardship and horror of which the current plague of cancer is only the tip of the iceberg. Our world is rapidly becoming unfit to support life, and very urgent and radical changes must happen very quickly if this slide into disease and the death of the planet can be halted or reversed.

The Survival of Life on Earth

by *John Roland Stahl*

July, 2006

In this essay, I want to repeat a number of ideas I have expressed elsewhere ~ in fact, here will be found many of the common themes that I have been working with lately, as I try to understand the world and any possible future for the phenomenon of Life. But Life is kind of important to me. Life is exciting to me: novelty unfolding outward in all directions as it continues to grow. The important essence of God will surely be found more readily in Life than anywhere else, except Love, which is really just another view of the same phenomenon. So if readers of any of my other articles find that this one is just more of the same old stuff, my excuse is that Life is important enough to be worth the treatment of reviewing many of my old ideas here once again, with specific reference to the possibility of the survival of Life on earth.

I say the "possibility of the survival of Life on earth," because it is presently in very serious jeopardy! The earth is dying, and the time during which it may yet be possible to reverse this slide into the grave may rapidly be running out, so it is imperative to address this problem immediately and take it very, very seriously! There was a time when doomsayers would worry that the earth would be ruined for future generations, but the future is now ~ we are at the point where the earth is already showing the very clear signs of decay, and the stench of death is in the air ~ life on earth could very well be in its very last phase, and people alive right now are dying because of the diminishing health of our biological environment. A great many of the problems facing the planet are coming to a head right now, during the time of the present generation.

But instead of all hands on deck working long hours to try to reverse this slide into oblivion and darkness, we see everything going on "business as usual" as everyone goes on trying to swindle and steal another dollar before the curtain falls. The reason for this is that the change has been very gradual. All through the Industrial Revolution, the earth ~ its land, its rivers, its air, its oceans, and its people ~ has been in a state of gradual decline. Of course, this decline has been going on for longer than that ~ but the past hundred and fifty years have seen such an incredible acceleration of the process of destruction that we might as well look at this as a contemporary problem. We are frogs in a pot of warm water, and the gradually increasing temperature is putting us to sleep.

I do not propose here to go through the whole catalog of ruin and destruction ~ there are plenty of doomsayers who are shouting themselves hoarse warning of the dangers of everything from nuclear power and global warming to the destruction of the Ancient Forest. My purpose is more abstract ~ I want to look at this from an objective point abstracted out of the context of the current problem. Just suppose that our little world is being studied by the scientists of a civilization from a star like Alpha Centauri, many light years away. They may have been studying it for hundreds or thousands of years, and suddenly they see that this green and fertile earth has been rapidly withering and turning brown. It is clearly dying. It is as obvious as it would be to a horticulturist who watches his pots of greenery ~ one of his plants has been wilting, and the leaves are turning yellow and brown and falling off one by one. As Dylan says, "He who is not busy being born is busy dying." Either the plants are green and vibrant and glowing with energy, growing in good health, or they are limp and feeble and wilting and drooping, losing their leaves as they lose vitality.

When a plant is in a state of decline like that, it is necessary to take immediate steps to discover the problem and to make such changes as will be needed to restore the plant to health. Perhaps there is not enough water, or perhaps too much. Perhaps the soil is depleted and worthless, or perhaps there are some toxic elements in the soil. Maybe there is not enough sun, or perhaps the air is stale and toxic.

The point is that there may be a brief window of time during which it may be possible to reverse the decline of the living plant ~ if it is left for too long, then the plant will just die off, even if, too late, you make desperate changes, trying to revive the plant.

The Earth is a single living organism ("*Gaia*"). The "Gaia hypothesis" seems so obvious and self-evident to me, that it hardly seems that it needs to be explained or discussed, but for those who may perhaps never think about such things, let me just say that all living systems are occupying the same space. Just as every atom is composed of a nucleus at the center surrounded by a field of energy that extends far out, so that pattern follows for all of life. A human being is not just confined to the simple body which you may see sitting in a chair ~ his field of energy extends to the outermost reaches of the cosmos, but certainly at least it covers all of the region surrounding the planet Earth. What this means is that, in some very important sense, everyone on earth is occupying the same space. What's more, all living things ~ plants, animals, trees, beetles, and people, are all in this together. Over the evolutionary course of many millions of years, all of these energy streams have evolved into more or less sustainable living systems that are inextricably intertwined, and, as "*Gaia*", are/is conscious. The consciousness works two ways, for those who listen for Her voice.

Now, suddenly, in the past hundred and fifty years, the human race has exercised such an unprecedented influence upon this fragile biological environment that it is breaking down in many important ways.

I want to look at the health of the planet from the point of view of its "aura." In one of my earlier articles (*The Metaphysics of Sex*), I detailed eight patterns of biological interaction which represent, in very abstract form, the range of the potential of life. These patterns range from very negative patterns of aggression and hostility to loftier patterns of love and union. Of course, a review of that article would be useful here, but I want to look at my catalog of patterns mostly from the point of view of the colors of the aura associated with those patterns, and then consider the level of life energy in any living system by looking at those colors of the aura. We may liken the aura to a pattern of energy similar to a kind of a light, which expresses the quantity and quality of "vitality" or life force available or remaining in that organism. A plant or animal in good health will have a bright aura; a diseased or dying plant or animal will have a dark or muddy aura.

The colors of the patterns indicated in that article may be seen as accumulations ~ that is, at the bottom there is the color Black, which is the color of death ~ actually, it is the absence of color. Then, moving up the scale, there are the colors of Red and Violet (Anger and Violence ~

Oppression and Victim). Above that, there is a mid range of Orange and Blue (War and Peace) which represent more established levels of life energy. Above that, there are the higher levels of Yellow and Green (Giving and Receiving Love) representing much higher developments of biological vitality. Finally, at the very top, is the color White, which is the accumulation of all colors, and it represents the highest level of vitality ~ Unity, Love, (the Creative, Heaven, from the *I Ching* ~ and the metal Gold from Alchemy).

So, while I am reviewing all of my old ideas in this essay, let me mention one more that needs to be emphasized in this context ~ whenever something is in good health, all elements of the organism will be in a state of balance and harmony, and when an organism is not in good health, elements will be in a state of chaos and confusion. The closer the organism is to a state of balance and clarity and harmony, the healthier the organism. Conversely, when an organism exhibits extreme chaos and confusion, it is clear that the organism is in very bad health.

Thus, it is very clear that our world is in very deep trouble right about now! There have been times in history (Athens under Pericles, for example), when everything seemed to be right ~ art, music, literature, even architecture expressed the harmony and beauty of the age. All one has to do is contrast the glorious and joyful music of J. S. Bach with the awful and strident noise of contemporary "music" in order to realize that we are suffering a considerable decline of vital energy. Everywhere one looks today one sees violence, anger, hostility, death, and destruction. Any sweetness and light that timidly tries to appear is laughed off the stage with ridicule.

So now I come to my conclusions ~ it is necessary to recognize what is going on! If people were to see all of this clearly, then perhaps it might be possible to turn this around. What is needed is not just "a solution to the war in the Middle East, or Iraq" but a whole new spiritual consciousness. Everyone who wants life on earth to survive must work towards the goal of a renewal of spiritual consciousness. It doesn't matter what specific theological ideas anyone may have ~ as I expressed in another article *(Is Religion Good or Bad?)*, I have come to the conclusion that "religions" are just obstacles to spiritual consciousness. (See also *How to Measure Spiritual Growth.*)

We need to develop an all-encompassing spiritual consciousness that includes all of life ~ Moslems, Jews, goldfish, and blackberry brambles. If we can develop a critical mass of life to converge into a place of harmony and balance, it may be possible to reverse the slide of the planet towards an ultimate disintegration. Time is running out ~ let us make a specific goal of accomplishing this convergence by the year 2012 ~ an arbitrary time, perhaps, but a date by which many people have been looking for another high point in the "biorhythm" of the planet. We must make this convergence of harmony and balance powerful enough to carry the earth to a new Golden Age, because a failure to accumulate enough positive energy to reverse the direction back towards the center, towards Clarity, Balance, Peace, and Love, will probably mean that the ebb tide of life on earth will just cause *Gaia* to decay into the color Black for all the rest of eternity.

A Solution to the War in the Middle East

by *John Roland Stahl*

July, 2006

The problem in the Middle East has been going on for 1000 years, ever since the first Crusades. The situation there is a "real" problem. Some problems are not real. Some problems have a simple solution ~ some aggressor is clearly wrong, so the "solution" is to remove that aggressor and restore justice and freedom. Even if this is not easy to do, at least the problem might be clear. However, in the case of the conflict between the Moslems and the Jews, the conflict goes back and back and back. It is never useful to say that these people or those people are clearly wrong to do what they do. The problem is that they are acting in response to what those people or these people have been doing before. But you can carry the problem back and back and back, like the Hatfields and McCoys. After a while, the feud is so deeply ingrained on both sides that it would seem that no possible resolution could ever be possible.

In the case of the present conflict, there really isn't much basis to negotiate between the two positions. The Moslems want to force all of the Jews into the Mediterranean Sea, and the Jews want to kill every Palestinian, to the last man, woman, and child, in much the same way that the American colonists decided to deal with the "Indians" who happened to be there first. These are their clear intentions, hardly even pretended otherwise (have the Israelis thought of donating blankets to the Palestinians, loaded with smallpox virus, as the early American settlers did to the native Americans?). So what could anyone possibly propose, in order to resolve this conflict?

Well, I actually have a proposal, but no one is going to like it. But that, of course, is inevitable when you have two opposed camps who are so far apart in their attitudes as the Moslems and the Jews. What a thankless task to even propose any solutions! If no one is going to like any of my ideas, why don't I just cultivate my fragrant roses, and forget about that conflict? I don't live anywhere close to that region, and I have no desire to go back there (I have been to Israel, and I have been to many Moslem countries). However, I do live on the earth, and so the problem cannot be ignored. The earth is too small these days. The days when a Great Wall of China could be built to keep out the hordes of barbarians (or the Ugly American), are long gone. Any solution to the problems of the world must have a global consideration or the solution is worthless. If Iran and Israel have a nuclear confrontation (for example), where does that leave life on earth?

So my first premise is that any solution is better than no solution. This seems like a self-evident proposition, but to people in the heat of battle, it apparently is not so evident. Whenever any two people have a fight on their hands such that each will fight to the death before giving in, it is clear that any solution at all, even a bad one for one side or the other, is better than nothing, since at least it allows life to go on.

This is contrary to human nature. It is human nature to go on fighting "to the death" before accepting the short end of any deal. This is clearly folly, at least to my eyes. I remember when the deal was struck between Egypt and Israel. At the time everyone on both sides cried out in anger at the deal, yet the deal was made and accepted, and now there is no war on that front. For better or worse, a deal was made, and now there is at least one border where there is no war going on! The benefits of this are finally clear to both sides. Now, I am sure that neither side would wish to revert to the previous situation. A settlement has been reached, and, at least as far as that portion of the conflict is concerned, everyone can return to their roses or their farms.

In the same way, I am trying to find a solution which can work ~ some solution by which both the Israelis and the Palestinians can go on living. When you can spend your resources cultivating your fields instead of building weapons and waging war, you can increase your prosperity rapidly. Any solution that will allow for an end to hostilities, and allow the peace to be retained with only moderate peace-keeping forces, will be a great boon to the people of the region, on both sides of the conflict.

The problem is that the claims to that land go so far back that it is just no longer feasible to establish "rightful ownership." The Palestinians claim recent history; the Israelis claim biblical history. As I look upon those claims, I find myself considering that biblical history just goes too far back to provide a credible basis on which to base a claim to the land. *Status quo ante bellum* is one thing; trying to revert to a political reality that is out of date by 2000 years seems a bit optimistic. On the other hand, the Jews are there, and not planning to leave any time soon. I consider that the seizure of the land is similar to when a government (by which we refer to a power stronger than you are that has a lot more guns than you have) seizes land by "eminent domain." Basically, they say to the holders of the land, that they want it, so you have to move; so sorry. In this case, when they do this, at least they are constrained by custom to offer some compensation for taking the land.

So there is my solution. If the Israelis have taken the land, they must pay compensation. Now, of course, the Palestinians are going to say that they do not want "compensation" ~ they want their land back. However, it is evident that that solution is not liable to happen by means of any foreseeable continuations of this conflict. Nothing that the Palestinians can do is likely to result in the restoration of their lands. Notice that I am not trying to make any arbitration on the basis of "justice." It has been a long, long time since I expected anything in the world to happen in accordance with "justice." Politics is a business of pragmatic solutions to the real problems of the world, and no one's platitudes are going to be of any use.

So, while no one is going to like this solution, at least it can provide a way in which everyone involved can go on living. The way it is now, the only advice the Israelis have for the Palestinians is for them to lay down and die. They should not be surprised, therefore, that when the Palestinians do this they at least want to take as many Israelis with them when they go as possible (the suicide bombers). It is not practical for the Israelis to expect the Palestinians to accept defeat and simply go away. Not only do they have no place to go, but they don't have any shoes.

If the displaced Palestinians are given a substantial sum of cash money to renounce their claims upon the land, they will not be penniless refugees living in tent camps, but will be welcomed anywhere. I think this is a serious proposal. I remember thinking during the war in Viet Nam that the American approach was all wrong. Instead of sending in armies of soldiers to destroy the country, they should have sent in some carnival hucksters in Hawaiian shirts, with carpet bags full of cash money.

"Hello, Charlie! Good day to you. And how are the wife and kids? Cigar? Fresh from Havana! ~ Well, I'm here representing the United States government, and we think your support of the communist regime is really foolish. I am authorized to offer you and your family $5,000 in cash to support our proposals for a capitalist regime here ~ oops, I mean a "democratic government." I'll be setting up an office in town, so send your friends over ~ same deal for everyone who agrees to sign up. Oh, and we have allocated a million dollars for a new hospital here, and another million for schools."

Give me about fifty slick carpet baggers and about 10% of the budget for the war in Vietnam, and I would undertake to have ended the war to everyone's satisfaction! The same could have been done in Iraq, also, only now the cost would have to be adjusted upwards. Back in the old days, $5,000 per person might have swung it, but now I'm afraid it will cost so much more that the proposal breaks down. No, nothing will work now except for an immediate and unconditional withdrawal. The country has already been destroyed, and there is little hope at all that anyone in the world will ever again support the American agenda, but if the Americans admit their mistake and withdraw their troops (say, during the next administration, after George W. Bush finally takes his bow and his curtain falls), pay massive reparations to the Iraqi people, and stay out of countries where their presence is not wanted, then, after a few generations, the bad smell may begin to dissipate. Of course, when the effects of all the depleted uranium begin to be seen clearly, it may significantly retard the rehabilitation of the United States' reputation.

So, what is the specific proposal to the situation in the Middle East? I would say, set up a panel of arbitration and invite Palestinians to bring complaints for review. This could be set up like an ordinary court, with attorneys for both sides representing their clients ~ attorneys for the Palestinians (including a Palestinian "Public Defender" for the indigent), and attorneys representing the State of Israel, against which the judgments will be made. Jews could likewise make claims against the Palestinians, and cross judgments might be made. A final settlement would include a minimum sum to which all Palestinians are entitled, every man, woman, and child, with additional specific judgments as decreed by the court of arbitration.

Now why would the State of Israel accept any such terms? Is all this just a pipe dream, or what? I think that if it were understood as a final solution to this endless struggle, it could be understood as worth the money! Even if the final settlement runs into many billions, even trillions of dollars, this could be seen as a cheap price to pay for a peaceful end to the conflict. If a settlement could be reached that would allow the Palestinians to accept the solution, and retire to within the borders left to them (obviously, any real solution will be far more complex than the broad outlines suggested here ~ some land would be set aside for a Palestinian State, for example) or find a new home and a new life, with the help of their compensation package somewhere outside the borders of the disputed territories, then everyone could return to their fields or their factories, and life could go on.

The Palestinians may prefer to have their land back than any amount of money, and the Jews may be very reluctant to pay out enormous sums of money to people they consider to be their enemy, but if this solution leads to peace, then everyone benefits. Within a generation or two, everyone involved would be far better off than they could possibly have been if the *status quo* were to have continued for all that time.

It might take ten years to work out all the details of such a settlement, but if the intervening ten years were spent in court rooms instead of battlefields, that is already an immense improvement.

I consider myself completely impartial in this conflict ~ I have no reason to favor either side, but I think that I would welcome such a resolution regardless of which side of the conflict I were on. The goal of peace at last would be worth any sacrifice ~ giving up their claim to the land on the part of the Palestinians, or agreeing to a very substantial payment of compensation by the Israelis, which might be the equivalent of their war budget for many years into the future. However, once the debt were paid off, then there could finally be a gradual restoration of prosperity to the whole region.

And, best of all, everyone could go on living.

A Common Sense Guide to Losing Weight

by *John Roland Stahl*

2006

INTRODUCTION

by Lacky Pillpusher, M.D., Author of *Drugs Will Make Me Rich*, etc.

After the Author's flippant remarks about the uselessness of a medical degree, at least with regard to weight loss programs, it is amusing to be invited to write some introductory remarks to this surprising little volume.

As the Author will be telling you himself, however, all of his suggestions make an appeal to Common Sense which will be very easy to understand. Having reviewed all of his suggestions from the view of a trained medical professional, I can verify that none of his suggestions are contrary to known medical knowledge, and, in fact, anyone following the program outlined in this volume will be as likely to achieve satisfactory results as they would from following any other weight loss program known to me.

However, a supplementary program of these little pills . . .

And Blah, Blah, Blah . . .

CHAPTER I

IN ORDER TO LOSE WEIGHT, YOU MUST EAT LESS.

No, I don't have any medical degrees, or any other qualifications for writing this book. However, I have a lot of ideas that I think can be very useful for a serious weight loss program. The degree carrying medical professionals can't seem to agree anyway, and, besides, their diets are all so arcane that you have to just accept them on faith ~ eat these obscure foods, and don't eat those obscure foods, for complicated medical reasons which the layman is not expected to understand anyway, so just pay me your money, buy my book, and let me get back to my holiday in the South of France.

In contrast with that approach, all of my suggestions are intended to appeal directly to your Common Sense ~ you should be able to appreciate all of my suggestions as reasonable on their face, taking nothing on faith. In my arrogant opinion, I expect to lay out a program of eating habits that should actually cause you to lose all the weight you want, not gain it back, improve your overall health and happiness, make you feel good, and improve your sex life ~ all in one package ~ and save you money besides.

In order to lose weight, you must eat less. What? That wasn't what you wanted to hear? OK, let's start again ~

In order to lose weight, there are many effective approaches. One very effective approach which will guarantee that you will lose as much weight as you please while promoting an improvement in overall health, is to eat plenty of deep fried foods ~ French Fries, potato chips, etc, with plenty of salt, washed down with Coca Cola. And remember, if you only eat one slice of cucumber instead of two, you might as well treat yourself to a big slice of New York Cheesecake, with sweet cherry topping.

No? Not buying that one? Well, here is something a bit more substantial ~

So you think you want to lose weight? Actually, that is not really the Issue at all, is it? What is really important is How You Feel About Yourself. Now, if you will just send $89.95 to the Author, we will send you a tape of subliminal messages that you can play while you sleep. Just pop the little speaker under your pillow at night, and you will be wafted to a gentle sleep while you learn to understand that you are Not Really Overweight At All ~ in fact, most men actually prefer a woman with a bit of meat on her bones, and you are actually just the ideal form and figure for optimum health and happiness, Just The Way You Are. OK, if you are a man, most women, or men, whatever you're into ~ they all want you Just The Way You Are Right Now.

But if neither of those approaches will pass muster, then we are reduced to fall back upon our original thesis, that if you want to lose weight, you must eat less.

This is not a frivolous suggestion. I actually have some very specific suggestions which may help you to accomplish this objective of eating less. But first, let me review the causes of excess weight (we certainly don't refer to it, in these polite pages, as Obesity.) Some very small percentage of people are overweight due to some organic problem ~ a specifically medical problem unrelated to eating habits. In spite of my glaring lack of qualified medical credentials, I will actually tackle this very subject, with all suitable disclaimers, of course ~ I think I know more about this anyway than all those fancy doctors. Even if you have a specific medical problem, I can advise you how to overcome it and lose weight anyway ~ but all of this is for a later Chapter.

Next, there are those whose problem with excessive weight gain is caused by eating the wrong foods. This, of course, is the usual stuff of weight loss books, and I will not neglect this topic, but, again, it is the subject for a later Chapter.

So now I take up the problem of Why Are You Eating Too Much, Anyway? Let us look at some of the more common reasons ~

First on the list is the issue of Food As A Substitute for Love And/Or Sex. Many people are aware of this phenomenon consciously. Others are aware of it subconsciously. And some people, hard to believe, are actually not aware of this at all. There you are ~ not enough love (and/or sex) in your life, so what do you do? You Eat, Eat, Eat. Now, the solution to this situation is rather obvious, isn't it? The old Freudian school of psychology held that you merely need to become aware of the underlying dynamic of your problem in order to solve the issue and move forward, onwards, and upwards, to greater and better things, and health and happiness will follow you all the days of your life. Well, you need to become aware of the underlying dynamic, and then do something about it, if I may somewhat modify the old Freudian approach.

So let's not mince words here ~ if you are stuffing your face with chocolates because you're not getting enough ~ well, you need to get some.

Love is most effective, of course, but, in a pinch, plain old sex will actually do the trick just as well, at least as far as your weight loss program is concerned.

Nobody loves you? Not a problem. In fact, as far as losing weight goes, you will find that loving other people is even more effective than other people loving you. It should be relatively easy to find someone to love. If you are a young woman, all you have to do is stop fighting them off ~ just let some of them in.

If you are an older woman, try a young man ~ young men are usually ready to provide the services you require, and are actually better suited to the task than most older men. There are so many available young men out there that it really shouldn't be hard to find one. In fact, here is your perfect come-on line ~ "Hello there, honey. I'm actually pursuing a weight-loss program, and the author of this book suggests that I need to get a little action so that I can forget about food for a while. So, if you're into it, I'm available."

If you are a young man trying to lose some weight, and you are either too dorky or ugly or stupid to get a really fine young woman, you can always go for an older woman ~ single older women are very often surprisingly ready for a hook up with a potent young man who offers no complications, and just wants to pursue his weight loss program with a suitable partner.

If you are an older man ~ well, unless you are rich, who wants an old man, anyway? You might as well eat those Cheesecakes and French Fries and stop worrying about it. Life is short, and you can't have everything.

Moving right along, let us look at some other strategies for eating less.

Here are two very simple but very effective strategies for eating less ~ In the first place, there is the problem of feeling those hunger pangs. When you are used to eating plenty of food, as soon as you cut down at all, you will feel that pang in your stomach that is sending urgent messages to your brain that you want more food going on. Here, it is all a matter of interpretation of those electrical impulses surging through your pointed little head. Here is the way to think about it ~ you are only losing weight when you feel those hunger pangs. If you can get that idea going on, then you can turn it all around ~ whenever you find yourself "enjoying" hunger pangs, that is the time, the only time, in which your body is actually LOSING WEIGHT. Once you get that notion implanted in your feeble brain, then you will not only be able to endure those hunger pangs, but rejoice in them. Learn to rejoice in that delicious feeling of being Hungry. It means you are losing weight.

Here's another good idea ~ sometimes it's easier to skip an entire meal altogether than to eat a small meal. You can even fast for a longer time.

If you need some motivation, install a full length mirror in your bathroom, or attend a nude hot spring.

CHAPTER II

DON'T EAT WHEN YOU ARE NOT HUNGRY.

Don't eat when you are not hungry. At first grab, this idea may sound as frivolous as the idea of the preceding Chapter, but my whole point is that the issue of excessive weight gain is not rocket science ~ it is a matter of Common Sense.

The issue here is a very simple one and a very common one. Most people start eating, and then they go on eating until they are no longer hungry. Wrong. That is a Big Mistake. Here is one of the most useful ideas I have to offer, right here. Take a look, briefly, at the physiology of hunger ~ "Hunger" is basically a learned phenomenon ~ your body goes through its various trips and, from time to time, it gives off these "Feed Me" vibes that basically require you to stuff food into your stomach at regular intervals. When your "stomach clock" goes off, you feel hungry, and your body is craving food. This is a physiological response that you really cannot control. What you can control is the way you respond to these demands.

As we learned in the last Chapter, you only lose weight when you are experiencing hunger pangs, so you might be tempted simply to ignore the urgent messages of your body, and glory in the hunger pangs that are slimming you down while you watch. But that isn't a friendly way of dealing with the issue, and I have a better suggestion.

The key is understanding the time delay between your feeding activities and your "hunger response." The way your body works (unfortunately) is that once you are in "feeding mode" your body is going to continue sending out "Feed Me" signals until long past the time when you have actually had enough food. So here is the solution: When your body sends out its "Feed Me" messages, you should respond to it by supplying food ~ but only a carefully measured amount. The problem is that you might eat what you know to be enough food, a reasonable and modest amount, yet your body goes right on sending out that insistent "Feed Me" business. So here is the way I trick my body. I don't say, "Just forget it, food-brain. That's all you're getting. I've given you plenty of food for now, so just take a walk."

Oh, no. That's not the way to deceive a hungry food-brain. What you do is say, sweetly, "Oh, my dear food-brain ~ I am merrily feeding away over here, and it is all just lovely. Presently I will be feeding you some more, but I am going to take a short break for right now. In a short time, I will resume the feeding, so, not to worry. I'm just taking a very short break ~ just hang in there." And then you get up from the table, fully intending to eat another whole plate of food, but just "not yet." You must find some distraction ~ argue politics and the state of the world, or the spiritual crisis of the Modern Predicament with your companions, or spend half an hour in your garden, pruning your fragrant roses, fully intending to return to the table for another session of gorging yourself on more food. In order for this ploy to work, you have to retain the conviction that you are just taking a short break ~ if your food-brain ever gets the notion that you are not actually intending to return to the feed trough, you are in trouble. So it is imperative to retain the fiction that you are just taking a short break.

Well, you see where I'm going with this. After about half an hour, to your amazement, you will not feel any more hunger pangs. In fact, the whole "Feed Me" hunger thing will have passed on. Oh, well, just put away the food, and that's that ~ another round won for the home team.

This cycle has to be experienced consciously to be believed. But it is a fact ~ if you take a moderate amount of food and then "wait a while" before "finishing" your meal, you will discover that you don't actually need or want any more food right now, after all.

CHAPTER III

YOU'RE EATING THE WRONG FOODS.

OK, here is what most people would consider the heart of the diet ~ what do you actually Eat, anyway? You are what you eat, so you might as well select your diet very consciously.

The diet I recommend has the following advantages ~

1. You will lose weight.

2. You will enjoy better health.

3. You will feel great.

4. You will look great.

5. You will save money on food.

6. Meals will taste better to you.

7. You sex life will be improved.

I could almost make this Chapter really short ~ nothing here is going to be news to anyone who has read any of the most obvious dietary recommendations of the last twenty years.

OK ~ raw foods: fresh fruits and vegetables, less salt, less sugar, fewer processed foods ~ is any of this news, yet? Let's get specific ~ fried foods: just completely trash all deep fried foods from your diet. No more French

Fries, potato chips, tempura, bacon, fried clams, fish and chips ~ just scratch all that off the list as bad juju.

Next to go is processed foods. Processed foods are the biggest scam going. You may pay the highest possible prices for the flimsiest food-stuffs imaginable. Half the time they even advertise their products as Low Calorie, which simply means that all the nutritional value is long gone, and you are just paying for expensively packaged fluff and chemicals, from which all nutritionally valuable components have been systematically removed, to be used in other food products. Disgusting. Criminal. (Clever? One man's cleverness is another man's crime.)

Now eliminate all coffee, tea, and "soft drinks." By "soft drinks" is usually meant carbonated sugar water. Here is a bit of a digression, but all those funny little bubbles are carbon dioxide, which only encourage and support all the anti-life aspects of your bodily organism. Carbon dioxide supports viruses, AIDS, cancer, and all manner of diseases. What you want in your body and your lungs is fresh air from the mountains, full of fresh Oxygen, not carbon dioxide. For the same reason, you have to give up Smoking. If you think that all you need to do is take enough ginseng, or whatever, and you will live forever, you are dreaming. Before you even bother to take anything good into your life, you must first give up all the harmful substances, activities, and practices. ("Do no harm.") Smoking is one of the dumbest practices known to medical science, along with blood-letting. Filling your lungs with smoke on a regular basis is about the dumbest thing you can do to your health. The function of your lungs is to transpire oxygen into your bloodstream, to be carried throughout your body. To coat your lungs with a foul layer of smoke and tar is just way beyond stupid. If you can't quit smoking, you might as well sniff glue, or drink some turpentine, and be done with it. (Drinking turpentine will kill you very quickly.)

So there are some of the negatives ~ clear out all that junk from your diet. It is more important to eliminate the toxins than it is to introduce good healthy food into your system. But, if you give up your doughnuts, your bacon, and your French Fries, what are you supposed to eat, anyway?

Well, here I run into the problem that I know most of my readers just are not up to the level of eating good food. For me, it is the most natural thing in the world to have a $350 flour mill in my kitchen, with stone wheels, and a motor that carefully grinds slowly so as not to over-heat the flour. I buy 50 pound bags of fresh, organic wheat berries, that are still alive ~ in fact, I frequently sprout them, whether I am making wheat grass, sprouted wheat bread, or just salad sprouts. These wheat berries I grind up fresh daily, on the spot, whenever I want to bake bread or make fresh pancakes or pastries. Why is everyone content to eat dead white flour that has been milled up months ago, and been sitting on shelves in a warehouse in Kansas until the pasty junk is completely worthless? You know why they take all of the nutritional components out of flour, right? Shelf life. If the wheat germ were to be retained in flour, it would go rancid within a matter of hours. There is just no way to retain the living virtues of flour beyond a matter of a few hours. So they nuke the stuff, wiping out all nutritional value, and then they add a chemical blend of "fortifiers" which are intended to restore a certain amount of nutritional value back to the flour. Why? Why on earth are people content to eat this stuff? If your life and health is important to you in any way, go out and buy one of those really nice flour mills and then buy your wheat berries by the 50 pound bag ~ fresh, living, and organic. It is actually much cheaper that way. You can order full bags of organic wheat berries from your local health food store, and the purchase of the flour mill will be the best purchase you ever made, as far as your health is concerned.

OK, go ahead and buy a bread machine ~ but don't think that a bread machine is of any value without that flour mill. It all starts with the fresh flour. With fresh flour, you can make the best pancakes you ever had. You don't need to buy a package mix. Can't you add an egg on your own? You can buy an egg beater for $10 anywhere, so what's the big deal? A little baking powder (or baking soda with blueberries or yogurt), a little olive oil, or hemp seed oil (no cholesterol, no saturated fats), you don't need the salt. ~ and you are ready to make better pancakes, at a fraction of the price of any package mix of stale white flour and chemicals.

Next, lay in a supply of other bulk foods ~ brown sesame seeds (please don't get those blanched, dead old things that are all white, with all the nutritional value long gone), sunflower seeds, flax seeds, soy beans, brown rice, rolled oats ~ all of this stuff can be obtained through your health food store by the big bag ~ it doesn't cost much more to insist on all organic food, and it is much better tasting and much better for your health.

Next, you need to get a selection of fresh fruits and vegetables (ideally, of course, you will simply go out into your organic garden and select what you need for the day), and you are in business, ready to cook up highly nutritious and good tasting foods, at a fraction of the price of prepared foods.

Then there is the issue of meat ~ I eat lots of tofu (with nutritional yeast ~ a really wonderful substance ~ wonderfully nutritious and delicious ~ the poor man's cheese, yet it is healthy and wonderful in every respect ~ why is it only known to health food faddists and old hippies? Look for it ~ big yellow flakes of "nutritional yeast" available at most health food stores. It is high in B vitamins, tastes great, and will keep you healthy.) I am not a complete vegetarian, but whether you eat small amounts of meat or none at all, at least scale back from the steak and sausage breakfasts every morning. Bacon is something I eliminated from my diet many, many years ago.

I still eat cheese, but I am not proud of it, or recommending it ~ I just love cheese, and have a hard time giving it up. I know that, on a theoretical basis, there is not much to choose from over meat, so I would have to recommend limiting your cheese consumption, if you want to live forever. Eggs, on the other hand, I think are good food ~ true, there seems to be a cholesterol issue, but there is also the lecithin in the eggs which moderates the effect of it, so if you are able to get farm fresh eggs (you do keep your own chickens, right?) you should be OK with eggs.

As to the issue of butter or margarine or dry bread, I choose butter. Margarine is just worse than butter (go do the research), and I just can't handle dry bread, so I think a moderate amount of butter is just one of life's little luxuries. Actually, you might try substituting hemp seed oil for butter, for the premium solution.

As to other nutritional ideas ~ steamed vegetables are always better than boiled or fried, and a fast sauté is not a bad compromise once in a while. Fresh ginger is a miracle food ~ cheap, delicious, and medically active ~ the poor man's ginseng. I use fresh chopped ginger in everything I cook, along with fresh, organic sesame seeds, sunflower seeds, and flax seeds. Instead of trying to buy flax seed oil in expensive brown refrigerated bottles, in which they desperately try to keep the flax seed oil fresh and useful (instead of rancid and actually toxic instead of health-promoting), there is no better way of obtaining the freshest flax seed oil than by getting it fresh from the living seed. Add the fresh, organic, living seed directly to your soups or stir-fries or anything else you care to cook, or add a spoonful of flax seed (and/or sesame seed) directly to the wheat berries you are grinding up for fresh breads or pastries. In that way you will get the benefit of the freshest source of the seed oils, and, incidentally, it will be at the lowest possible price. What a combination.

Another miracle food is fresh, raw garlic. It purifies the blood, which is a pretty good deal. If you can't quite handle raw garlic, at least add the garlic very close to the end of cooking your food, so it will still have some virtue left.

Do you see the drift? All the best food ideas also end up being the cheapest. When you get the freshest, living bulk foods, you pay a tiny fraction of what you would pay for dead, lifeless, artificial alternatives made into processed "convenience" foods. It is so simple to steam up a batch of fresh, organic vegetables and tofu which you serve over brown rice ~ the best and healthiest food you can eat, at a tiny fraction of the price of a prepared pizza ~ and, lest we forget, eating this way will give you radiant health without any tendency at all to gain weight.

Drink plenty of water (or perhaps green tea), and study pranayama yoga, to fill your lungs with lots of fresh oxygen.

You will look better, feel better, live longer ~ and just wait 'til you see what it does to your sex life! If you eat good food and nothing but good food (including, especially, lots of sunflower seeds ~ raw, not cooked in oil and salt), you won't need the assistance of any pharmaceutical drugs.

CHAPTER IV

I DON'T EAT TOO MUCH ~ I JUST HAVE A MEDICAL CONDITION.

OK, I said I was going to address the issue of those people who think they just have some "medical excuse" for being overweight.

Right away I have to make a disclaimer. I don't know what your medical issues are. I am going to make some arm chair pronouncements (*ex cathedra*), but I am going to have to issue this disclaimer ~ since I don't know your particular medical condition, I have to advise you to consult a "qualified medical doctor" (if you can find any) before acting upon any of my suggestions here. You might discuss my suggestions with your doctor, and if you don't like what you hear, seek a second opinion. I don't have a lot of faith in medical doctors anyway ~ mostly they just prescribe pharmaceutical drugs (the ones that are advertised to them by the chemical industry ~ it's easy to be a doctor: once you get that Medical Degree, every morning's mail will be full of instructions from the pharmaceutical drug companies about what you should be prescribing to your patients), and most of those drugs are deadly. It is pretty much common knowledge that you are better off avoiding any and all pharmaceutical drugs ~ and don't go to a hospital unless you are going there to die. If you must see a "doctor" I would recommend seeing a TCM (Traditional Chinese Medicine) doctor before trusting your life to the chemical potions of the typical allopathic medical doctor.

Here is my take on the medical profession ~

Typical Western medicine just treats symptoms, whereas at least some of the Eastern medical efforts are directed at the root causes of disease, rather than just the symptoms. It doesn't make any sense to me that, when you find yourself bothered by some unwelcome symptom, you simply attempt to bludgeon your system into meek submission through the use of pharmaceutical drugs, no matter how profitable it may be to the medical community. (OK, the grammatical logic there was a bit "literary," but perhaps you get the drift.)

So, to bring the discussion back to your weight problem, I think there is an element of bovine mud going on here. If your body is all out of whack so that you are gaining weight, never mind taking all those expensive chemical drugs that are only hastening your slide into the grave, while making the pharmaceutical companies rich. They really don't care about your health ~ they just want to take your money.

There is a class of Chinese herbs that are called major tonic herbs. The principle is the same for all of them ~ all of these "tonic herbs" tend to normalize all of your bodily functions, and restore your system to balance in every way ("adaptogens"). By contrast, the pharmaceutical drugs simply throw your body even further out of whack than it was before you began assaulting your body with all of those drugs.

I have experimented with a recipe for an herbal tea that I call "Tono Bungay" after the book by H.G. Wells about a man who invents a tonic health drink and makes a fortune marketing it. I used a very simple concept, against which any Chinese doctor would surely react in horror. The Chinese doctor, like his Western counterpart, wants to earn his living, after all, so when you go to him for a Consultation, he needs to mystify you with his occult knowledge, and prescribe a particular mix of special herbs that will be specifically directed to your particular collection of complaints and needs. He may be forgiven this approach, since it is understood that, like a lawyer, his stock in trade is mystification and confusion, and he is just trying to feed his children.

I simply studied the list of "tonic herbs" and found that most of them tended to the same end ~ that of restoring the entire system to balance and harmony. I carefully distinguish the "tonic herbs" from the others ~ the simple difference is that the "tonic herbs" are all good ~ they all bring the body closer to that center of balance and harmony that is the hallmark of perfect health. In contrast to this, the other herbs all have side effects ~ they may accomplish some particular medical objective, but they do so in a heavy handed way, usually with side effects, if the treatment be continued for very long. An example of this is the poison which you take to kill the parasites in your stomach. The poison may kill the parasites, and then perhaps your body can recover from the assault of the poison, but the treatment is essentially a toxic one. The tonic herbs, on the other hand, are "all good." You can take them continuously with no harmful side effects. They are more of a food than a medicine.

So I had the bright idea of simply mixing up a tea of all of the best herbs. Here is my list ~ Ginseng, Astragalus, Chinese Licorice, Fo-ti, Lycium Chinensis, Schizandra, Jujube, Gingko, Ginger, Cinnamon, Orange and Lemon peel. I purchase all these herbs from Chinatown in San Francisco, and then mix up a portion of each of them in a pot and simmer them into a tea. Here is my report ~ first of all, the tea tastes wonderful. It is so rich in flavor that I can hardly believe it. I love it. I want to set up a tea house somewhere just to offer this tea concoction of mine (along with red hibiscus tea ~ "Roselle," and also black tea flavored with fragrant roses ~ I have a particular variety of fragrant rose in mind, which I don't reveal, since it is worth a fortune to someone some day). Secondly, I always felt a very definite beneficial effect from this tea. This effect was not subtle, but a very powerful jolt. Of course, when I would brew this tea, I would usually drink a lot of it, and strongly brewed ~ and I like strong flavors and strong effects. I would drink this tea every day for about a week. I always felt powerfully rejuvenated from drinking this tea. So, if an erudite Chinese medical doctor is going to react with horror, as if to suggest that it is "way too simple" to just mix up all the best tonic herbs and drink the tea, well, he is welcome to his professional position ~ if it were that simple, then who needs the services of the doctor, anyway? And who will buy all of the other obscure herbs in the pharmacopoeia, anyway?

So, I'm writing this book because I have ideas of my own which I want to introduce, and here I am doing it, and any horrified doctors, Eastern or Western, are welcome to their opinions ~ but remember my disclaimer, and please consult your choice of titled and credentialed medical doctor before taking any "medical" advice of mine.

So, what was I talking about, anyway? I was talking about those persons who feel they have a "right" to be overweight because they have some obscure medical condition that allows them to be so. My position is that anyone who really wants to can heal himself. Your own body has very powerful healing capabilities, and all you have to do is change the mind-set ~ no, you don't need to feel that you have any "right" to be overweight because of your obscure medical condition. Heal yourself ~ and by this I mean not only a program of my Chinese tonic herbs, but also good food, exercise, a healthy and positive attitude, yoga, breathing exercises, absolutely no caffeine tea, coffee, tobacco, or other poisons, and plenty of good love and sex in your life. All of these activities are directed to the same end as the Chinese tonic herbs ~ the centering of your life force back to a place of balance, clarity, and harmony, at which point you will enjoy radiant health, long life, and good looks ~ and your body weight will normalize with the rest of it.

By the way ~ if you have some really serious diseases ravaging your body, I do not trust the medical doctors. Most serious diseases (cancer, HIV, hepatitis, etc.) can be more effectively cured with oxygen therapy than with pharmaceutical drugs. Just remember that the medical industry has no interest in curing anyone ~ "a patient cured is a customer lost."

Conclusion

It's All In Your Head

Most of my ideas here follow the same general pattern ~ there is a concept of health which is not piecemeal, but all of a piece ~ a unified Whole. Holistic medicine is all about dealing with the entire organism all at once, and not as the accumulation of your separate parts. So, if there is any aspect of your being that is out of balance, it will be reflected in other aspects of your being, both physical as well as mental or energetic. Being overweight is just one of those indications that your body, your life, is not in perfect balance. You can correct an imbalance by treating the fundamental imbalance wherever it manifests.

What this means is that if your body is overweight, you can deal with it by a carefully restricted dietary regimen, or you could take a course of yoga meditation or breathing exercises, or you could find a new lover, or climb a mountain, or manipulate your psychic energies with colors and flowers. The theory is that any or all of these approaches will tend to accomplish the same end to the degree that they are effective at all ~ that of bringing your whole body, life, and soul into harmony and balance. The closer you get to this point, the better everything will become in your life ~ you will be happier, more successful, less stressed; your personal affairs will prosper; your skin will achieve a radiant and healthy glow; your sex life will be rejuvenated; and your body weight will normalize to an appropriate level for your size.

Some Reflections on India

by *John Roland Stahl*

September, 2007

India is a very poor country. However, there is a wealthier class of Indians who try to live down this reputation for poverty by adopting more progressive, Western standards of civilization. Here is how they do it ~

Wealthy Indians smoke American cigarettes; poor people don't, because they can't afford it (they smoke bidis, or chew betel-nut). Poor people here build their houses out of marble, which is locally produced, cheap, plentiful, and beautiful. However, wealthier Indians would never use marble. Nothing betrays your working class status more assuredly than by using this local marble. No, wealthy Indians who can afford such luxury use imported clay tiles for their floors, at about six times the cost of the local marble.

Only poor people in India wear cotton clothing. Of course, since most people are poor, you see a lot of cotton. However, those who can afford it will wear polyester and acrylic. If a tourist is seen wearing cotton all the time, they think you are trying to emulate Gandhi, who always wore humble cotton. Otherwise, it makes no sense; surely the tourist could afford to wear acrylic?

In most Indian towns, there are many hundreds of cows wandering around the streets unattended. These cows are holy; no one would ever dream of being rude to one of these sacred animals. The local people devoutly feed them, and reverently sweep up their shit, with which all of the streets are abundantly blessed. It is very common to see cows contentedly chewing on chapattis, which the locals are honored to share with their sacred bovine sisters. On the other hand, a cat is an extremely rare creature in India; I have seen only two cats in the past month. I can only speculate, but I suppose it is because cats are carnivorous, eating mice (one of the two cats I saw had a mouse in its jaws). Since devout Hindus are strictly vegetarian, I suppose a cat's dietary habits are repulsive to them. It is funny to me to think that it is quite the other way around in Egypt. In Egypt, cats are revered as divine, and treated with every courtesy, while the only beef you ever see in Egypt will be roasting on a spit. Rats and mice, of course, run almost as freely in India as the holy cows.

One religious practice of which I can whole-heartedly approve is the constant offering of very fragrant roses at all of the many shrines and temples all over India. Roses, very fragrant roses, are omnipresent everywhere. They even make a thoroughly delicious jam from the petals of these fragrant roses. Wherever you go in India (or at least here in Pushkar), the ever present stench of urine is delightfully relieved by the pleasant fragrance of roses.

Everything in India is cooked by deep frying it in oil. Indians eat deep fried food for breakfast, lunch, and dinner. Once a month or so, the oil is replaced with "fresh" oil, which has been recycled from the primary user of the oil (the most expensive tourist restaurants). On my last trip to India (many years ago), it was all about rice and dhal. Now, rice is served in much smaller portions and the "dhal" is just water and spice, with maybe a lentil or two in the sauce (something like Mark Twain's "circus lemonade: one lemon to a barrel of water"). For the substance of a meal, it is an endless variety of stuff that is deep fried in ancient oil. There is one very common sight ~ a particular kind of deep fried "food-stuff" (I don't know what else to call it, as I wouldn't touch it with tongs, let alone eat it) which, after being cooked, is allowed to marinate in the oil as it cools. If you want one of these, the chef will fish it out of the cold oil for you. *Haute Cuisine.*

All food is grown with a heavily dependent use of pesticides and chemical fertilizers. In the countryside of northern Thailand, every tree was supplied with an advertisement for pesticides by Monsanto. Every larger surface, such as the side of a barn, would be adorned with a much larger sign (perhaps six foot by twelve foot) advertising the same toxic chemicals. I could not read Thai, but I could read "Monsanto," "malathion," "paraquat dichloride" and other similar information. There were no other signboards advertising anything else in evidence anywhere else in Thailand (except for ads for cell phones and skin-whitening cream in the big cities).

I was also surprised to discover that no one eats coconut anywhere in Southeast Asia (except in India; in India I finally found people who would eat coconut; I guess they are more hungry in India). The locals in Cambodia would always laugh to see me actually *eating* a coconut (of course, the locals only drink the water from young, green coconuts, and then discard the nut, which is only a thin layer of slime at that stage). I was on a bus one time in Cambodia, and I kept the children big-eyed with astonishment and the adults convulsed with hilarity to watch me eating a coconut. Meanwhile, they were munching away merrily from a bag of insects fried in fish sauce. Isn't the tourist funny? The crazy things these tourists will eat!

At least there were dogs in Cambodia. In Vietnam, there were only puppies. Puppies everywhere, but a dog was a very rare sight . . .

Speculations on Cosmology

by *John Roland Stahl*

September, 2007

I have spent most of my life working up a comprehensive outline of metaphysics (*vide: Patterns of Illusion and Change*). This is not intended to be a description of how everything works ~ it is merely an outline of the abstract principles which would form the prolegomena to any such description. Therefore, whenever I try to understand some aspect of how the world works, I try to follow the abstract principles for clues as to how the physical operations might proceed.

I have just been reading Bill Bryson's amusing little volume, *A Short History of Nearly Everything*, and I see that the scientific establishment hasn't yet quite achieved much clarity on two fronts ~ the microcosm and the macrocosm. There seems to be no consensus about what is actually going on, and nary a clue about why or how. So let me see what I can do about clearing up any loose ends.

I begin with the Macrocosm, although I want to start off by repeating the old Hermetic axiom that the Macrocosm is reflected in the microcosm, and that the solution of the obscurities of one will suggest the solutions to the obscurities of the other. Einstein was rightly convinced that it was way beyond "untidy" to have to deal with two entirely separate systems of theoretical physics, one for the macrocosm, and another one for the microcosm. Surely there must be some "unified field theory" that can explain both of them with a single set of principles. I do not say "a single set of laws," because one of my principles is that "anything" is either non-existent, or it is simultaneously either one thing, and/or it's total opposite, and that potentiality is what allows the universe to exist at all in the first place. (0 = infinity) The universe is certainly not a wind-up clock.

According to this theory, the Universe itself sprang into being spontaneously as the alternation between the ideas (which of course are equivalent) of Zero and Infinity. It is only the "imaginary" field composed of the movement between the two "opposite" extremes which presents us with the illusion of an actual, manifest cosmos. I call this the Original Joke, God's laughter to which constitutes the creation of His cosmos (*vide: Hermetic Alchemy*).

In the present paper, I want to take a closer look into the mechanics of all of that, venturing a little further out from the safety of abstract ideas to speculations which will touch upon some of the questions disturbing modern physics.

I wish to offer a disclaimer at the outset that I consider my special field of expertise to be in the realm of the abstraction, so the further out I range into questions of physics, the less confident I feel of the integrity of my solutions. So, if I sound like I am pontificating *ex cathedra*, ~ well, I guess that's what I am doing. Ideas just come to me.

I take as my jumping off point the notion of the expanding universe, consequent upon the hypothesized Big Bang, and I compare it with my own *Patterns* for the Process of Change. According to my *Patterns*, the process of change passes progressively and repeatedly through four primary phases, which correspond with the Four Elements of Aristotle, and the Four Seasons of Nature. These also correspond with the four values of Yang and Yin, which greatly clarify the concept which is but inadequately described by "Yang and Yin." (We may say that "Yang and Yin" constitutes the Second Arcanum, while, through the agency of the Third Arcanum, the four values constitute the Fourth Arcanum, physical manifestation. Those four values are: **young yang** (⚎ Fire, Spring), **old yang** (⚌ Air, Summer), **young yin** (⚍ Water, Autumn), and **old yin** (⚏ Earth, Winter).

We might describe those four values for our present purpose (of course, as abstract concepts, they might be described differently, but comparably, for different applications) as young yang = active contraction towards a point; old yang = active expansion outward, away from the center; young yin = passive contraction back to the center; and old yin = passive expansion outward. Old Yang might be described as the extreme of Order (or Infinity; The Creative in the *I Ching*), while Old Yin might be described as the extreme of Chaos (or Zero; The Receptive in the *I Ching*).

My first observation is that, while cosmologists are trying to make a single determination for the state of the cosmos, my own assumption would be that the universe is now undergoing its second phase, that of the old yang. So, instead of supposing that the universe "began" with a Big Bang, and has since been expanding outward, I would rather assume that the universe has passed through the "singularity" represented as the turning point between young yang and old yang, and is now in the process of its active, outward expansion towards greater complexity and higher states of order (my system posits two sudden changes and two gradual changes; the next change, that from old yang to young yin, will be extremely gradual). The fact that the expansion of the universe is or appears to be accelerating suggests that we are nowhere close to the turning point towards young yin.

This already seems to me to put the ebb and flow of the cosmos into a more understandable context, but I want to continue the analogy to my *Patterns* of the Process of Change to suggest that we are simply enjoying one of an infinite series of universes, each one very similar to the one before it, but slightly changed, incorporating some new elements of Novelty with each successive universe. Thus, with each passage through that point of Singularity (the Omega Point of Pierre Teilhard de Chardin), the new incarnation of the universe that follows will be just a bit different than the one that preceded it, much like the evolutionary succession of lives of any living species.

[I must make a side track here and mention that the succession of lives does not assume a reincarnation of previous consciousness; I rather hold to the principle of the continuity of consciousness. The point of my analogy is simply that with every successive life of any living organism, there is the opportunity for a fresh spasm of Novelty to promote a gradual evolution.]

Now, to imagine an infinite series of universes coming and going in this way is a whole lot easier for me to understand than the notion that our Universe just suddenly popped into being out of nothingness, fully blown, like Athena from the head of Zeus.

What? I thought I was the proponent of creation *ex nihilo*, suggesting that the universe did, in fact, do just that? Aha: yes, but not to this point; not to this universe we are currently enjoying! My third conclusion is that the succession of universes follows the pattern of the creation of life; namely, that it happened very, very slowly! I would suppose that our current universe represents a very mature specimen of universe. Universes may have been "blinking on and off" for many trillions of such incarnations (each one, of course, existing for the length of time usual with universes, so that the process I am describing did not happen in any six days).

Of course, none of this (yet) describes how the very first one popped into being, but we are getting to that. At least looking at our universe as a manifestation somewhere quite well along, after the succession of universes has had quite an extensive time to evolve from its primitive and abstract beginnings, makes a whole lot more sense to me than anything I have heard described heretofore.

Let me compare the evolution of successive universes to the origin of life on earth. I don't find the origin of life to be so surprising, after all. I am still quite amazed and dazzled by the implications of Consciousness, but life itself seems simple enough. I think Wilhelm Reich was on the right track in his descriptions of the origins of life from very primitive beginnings, starting with simple heating and cooling (following the day and night cycle of the earth), followed by a progressively more pronounced and definite pulsation ("bions" he called them; not yet alive, but precursors to life). These grains of sand in the desert (where there is a large fluctuation in temperature between day and night) may have gone on pulsating in some elementary way for untold millions of years before the intersection of another alternation, the wet and dry cycle, may have boosted the pulsation to something just a tad more complex. After as many more millions of years as you please, we still might not want to call the little pulsating jolt "alive" or anything, but we can see where this is going.

Obviously, there was never one fine morning when the thing suddenly passed into "life" from its pre-life origins. Even after all of these many millions of years, what we may have is so primitive that no one will agree upon the point at which to call it "alive." We might say that at some point in the distant past the bit of pulsating matter could not really be called "alive," but by so many hundreds of millions of years later, it really did seem to exhibit properties which might merit the term, even though in an extremely primitive way. If the cosmos be thirteen and a half billion years old (give or take a few billion, and dating it just from the most recent passage through the Singularity), there is plenty of time for this process to evolve as sedately as you please.

Now to compare all of that with my succession of universes ~ when my first "universe" popped into being *ex nihilo*, it really wasn't any instance of "something" popping into existence out of "nothing." It was the joke of considering the alternation from "zero" to "infinity" to have any meaning. It was only after many trillions ("or so") of such alternations that there was anything present in the passage between zero and infinity that might appear to anyone as anything real. Indeed, the whole substance of my theory of cosmology is that "Everything is all a Big Joke" (~ Dr. Ed Madden, University of Connecticut, *circa* 1954). Or, to express it more specifically, what we think of as the manifest cosmos is really only the field of illusion that seems to exist as God laughs His way from Zero to Infinity and back again.

Still more specifically, I assume that if all of the matter and energy of the cosmos were added up, it would be equal to, yes, take your pick ~ zero and/or infinity. And this is exactly what happens when "all of the matter and energy of the universe is compressed into a single point of no dimensions" as it passes through the famous Singularity (the Big Bang) on its way to incarnating as yet another Universe in the series.

So, when a new universe pops into being, it doesn't really come out of nowhere ~ it follows the inertia of the previous universe, creating a new one very similar to the one before, only this time modified with some additional Novelty as it continues to evolve.

I know I am repeating the expositions of my earlier works when I say that this concept of Novelty is "movement away from the center," (Yang "the Creative"), in contrast to the Inertia of God which tends to return to the center (Yin, "the Receptive"). "The Devil" has been defined, ingeniously enough, as "distance from God," suggesting that movements away from the center are movements towards the Devil, while movements towards the center go closer to God. However, I find it more illuminating to think of these two directions as two different aspects of God; there is not a "war in Heaven" so much as an eternal creative interplay of these two ideas.

The movement away from the center is Novelty, which becomes Creativity and Complexity. However, if this movement continues further and further away, it becomes Confusion, and, finally, Chaos. But without that creative movement away from the center, the cosmos would eventually resolve itself back to nothingness.

So, after all of this, I think the nature of the cosmos is a little more clear, yet there are two questions still unanswered. One question is, of course, "why should this Joke have happened, anyway? And, secondly, just how much potential for Novelty is there?"

As to the first question, I might say that the concept is inherent in the metaphysics, which is another way of saying that there really isn't any other basis upon which you could postulate a cosmos. Or, you might simply say that a universe without any potential for novelty would never, therefore, have any chance of coming into being, so, since there seems to be a cosmos here of one sort or another, then clearly such a potential had to exist. I am trying to say that the joke of nothingness being separable into Zero and Infinity is a form of tautology. I am also saying that my descriptions of the Patterns of the Process of Change are the only such patterns which are possible, hence they are inevitable and inescapable. If we were to start all over again with "Nothingness," sooner or later God would have to appear, popping into existence Himself as His laughter creates His cosmos.

The second question is a bit more subtle. If everything were constantly switching into its opposite, there would be no stability at all, and there would be nothing but total chaos. However, I don't think there is some "Cosmological Constant Novelty Factor." I recall some very interesting studies of chaos, in which it is discovered that "pure chaos" is impossible, since "pure chaos" is really a kind of order. I think that the study went on to suggest that whenever there is set up any situation of "chaos," sooner or later it seems to resolve itself into orderly patterns. That is to say, total chaos is a kind of order.

Like genetic mutation, novelty is attempted constantly. Most of the time, novelty goes nowhere, and becomes simply a deviation towards error (towards the Devil), but every once in a while, the random reaching outward into Novelty accomplishes something sufficiently interesting so that the likelihood of it happening again increases. And Who knows to what consequences that might lead?

The Fall of the Dollar

by *John Roland Stahl*

September, 2007

It has been clear to me for many years that there is no future for the Almighty Dollar. One thing I have noticed is that people are rarely able to perceive the possibility of Change of any sort ~ whatever the present reality is, that is the way It Has Always Been, and The Way It Will Always Be (*cf. 1984* by George Orwell). However, with a little historical perspective, it is very easy to predict the decline and fall of the Dollar.

I have always taken a view of economics which I call "Reality Economics." I have understood fashionable ideas about how war, for example, can stimulate an economy, but I have always taken an alternative view that actions can be considered in terms of the real effect, and that, ultimately, that real effect will tell far more surely in the long run than any very temporary apparent "stimulation of the economy." War is the most obvious example of this principle. To be sure, war encourages a host of activities which, superficially, stimulate an economy ~ arms are built, soldiers are outfitted with uniforms and guns, ships are built for transport, and military spending all along the line flushes the economy with movements of capital. Yet when the final effect of all of these wartime activities is to destroy ~ people, bridges, buildings, oil fields ~ it is clear to me that all of that expenditure of money will promote the advance of poverty, not prosperity.

Then even more money is spent to rebuild what was destroyed at such cost, and huge armies of contractors, masons, electricians, and speculators will be mobilized in the shadow of the soldiers, all of whom appear likewise to "stimulate the economy."

But in contrast with all of this destructive and useless consumption of real value, consider the effect of spending upon projects for which there is a more clearly evident value ~ schools, hospitals, roads, agriculture, etc. My "reality economics" suggests that such expenditures will eventually bring very real and tangible benefits.

What is required is to distinguish between short term appearances and long term reality. I am not at all impressed by any of the specious arguments that pretend to find an economic stimulation in warfare and other examples of destructive and wasteful energy. Extend the window to a longer term, and sooner or later you will see the actual consequences of wasteful economic activity (and the benefits of economic activity which actually accomplishes something worthwhile). I take as a prime example the ancient civilization of Crete, which enjoyed a higher civilization than is in evidence anywhere in the world at the present day, yet it enjoyed this civilization thousands of years ago, one of the earliest sites of advanced civilization known to history. The reasons for the advanced level of civilization are very clear and simple. Crete was an island of just the right size ~ big enough for a large and complex community to develop, yet small enough to be governed by a single king, so there was no internal warfare. In addition, and most importantly, as an island nation it was easily defensible from external attack. Thus, it enjoyed an uninterrupted period of peace and tranquility for over a thousand years. This peace allowed the citizens to attend to the cultivation of their gardens, and allowed an attendant class of merchants and artisans to grow up around the agricultural base. This led to prosperity for everyone, and that prosperity led, in turn, to the development of music, arts, and sciences for the better appreciation of life, and the civilization was rolling right along, flourishing and flowering in every respect.

This civilization lasted until the advent of large ships of war, when it became possible for foreign powers to invade their land with an armada of ships carrying armies of soldiers, who immediately laid waste to the land, raping and pillaging, seizing whatever they could find of value to carry off. The civilization of Crete was destroyed overnight.

So if a thousand years of uninterrupted peace leads to prosperity and the advance of civilization, times of warfare will do the opposite, quickly dragging down any nation based upon warfare into the mire of poverty and cultural devastation.

The United States has entered upon the last stage of a Great Power. Early stages of decline are marked by extensive military expenditures which impoverish the land and the people, and an abandonment of those commercial activities which produce real wealth and prosperity.

The increasing dependence upon military activities "to promote and stimulate economic activity" has led to a state of affairs in which very little of real economic value is actually produced in the United States any more. As far as commercial goods are concerned, everything is now made in China. Even the fabled Technology sector is increasingly outsourced to India. This is leaving the country without any real economic base anymore, so it is no wonder that it is rapidly descending into poverty.

Furthermore, its agricultural base is eroding just as rapidly. When the fertility of agricultural lands is destroyed by the over-use of chemicals, replacing organic farming practices, then the sterile medium of ruined land can no longer support life without a continued and increasing dependence upon such chemicals, which leads to a downward spiral of decreasing productivity, measured not only in the quantities produced, but especially in the nutritional value of the produce. Of what value is it to produce bushels of vegetables which contain no more nutritional content than the chemicals of which they are composed? It is far healthier to eat a small meal of organic produce which provides a true and nourishing vitality than to eat a big plate of food which is saturated with chemicals, and devoid of any of the attributes of life.

It has always amused me to watch people rejoicing in the constant rising of the values of the stock market. They seem to think that the rising values of their stocks indicates some real economic growth. Sadly, it is just the reverse. The rise in the value of stocks, like the rise in the "value" of real property, is just another way of looking at the fall of the dollar. For example, if stocks or property increase in value by 30%, yet the value of the dollar declines by 30%, this represents zero growth. And make no mistake ~ the dollar has been declining rather quickly for many years now! All of this has been quite clear to bankers and financial speculators, but the common people, ‘οι πολλοι, are lulled into thinking that nothing unusual is going on. "Sure, markets rise and fall, and the value of the dollar rises and falls." Only at present it is only falling, and not doing too much rising at all. One very simple benchmark is the value of the Euro. When the Euro was introduced, it started off at par with the Dollar. Now, a dollar will buy you about 70¢ on the euro, representing a loss of about a third of the value of the dollar over a handful of years, and there is no end in sight.

Every day I read about falling markets in the US, and historically high markets in China and India. Just about every currency in the world is outpacing the dollar. Recently I was in Cambodia and speaking with hotel keepers who were accumulating piles of local money and they wanted, in their innocence, to convert their savings into dollars. I told them, to their evident surprise, that they should rather hold on to their savings in Cambodian currency. I suggested that, in a few years' time, savings of Cambodian currency would be worth considerably more than equivalent savings in dollars.

The fact is, no one with any economic sense wants to hold dollars anymore! Even the Chinese bankers, aware of the inevitable decline of the value of the dollar, are very reluctant to renew loans denominated in dollars. Of what use is it to earn 6% interest on a loan if the loan is paid back in dollars that have lost 10% of their value? But if American banks were forced to accept loans denominated in any strong currency, such as the Chinese yuan, or the Indian rupee (hilariously enough, from the standpoint of fairly recent history ~ when I was traveling in India, in the days of my youth, the rupee had no value whatsoever outside of India), then the imminent bankruptcy of the American banks would be assured.

In fact, the American National Debt is so huge that there is no mathematical possibility that it could ever be repaid. What? Did you follow that? Look at the rise in the debt from 1940 until the present ~

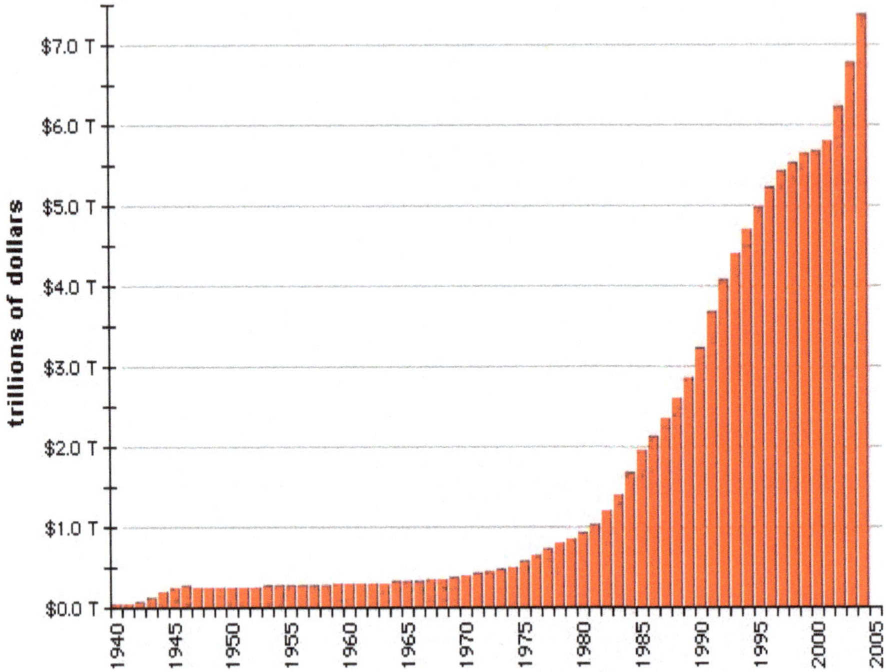

National Debt from 1940 to Present

Source: U.S. National Debt Clock
http://www.brillig.com/debt_clock/

Is there a mathematician in the house? Does anyone recognize the shape of that curve? It is an exponential curve. What that means is that, from here, there is no way it can go but up, dramatically and stratospherically, far beyond the remotest possibility that it might ever be repaid. In fact, did you ever wonder how the United States is financing its war in Iraq? It is simply borrowing the money and piling it onto the National Debt, which everyone understands will never, ever, be repaid. The National Debt is a game of musical chairs ~ bankers and merchants go on making money as long as the music plays, but when the music stops, you had better not be holding any dollars (or bonds payable in dollars)!

(Update, March, 2011) That graph is out of date. Here is the way it looks about five years later, just in case anyone was wondering what happens to an exponential curve:

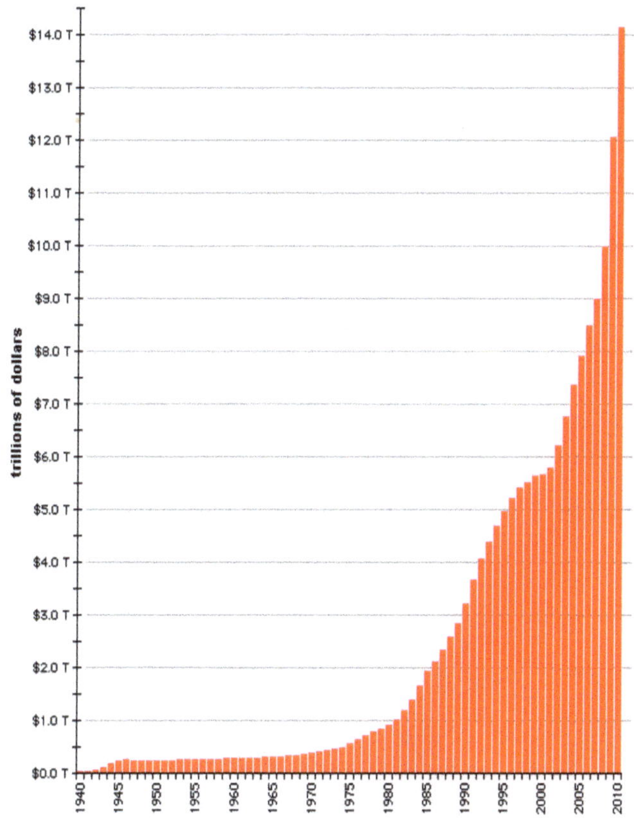

National Debt from 1940 to Present

Source: U.S. National Debt Clock
http://www.brillig.com/debt_clock/

The Chinese bankers backed down, and allowed the American banks to go on repaying their loans with ever more worthless dollars, because they, like everyone else, are apprehensive about what will happen "when the music stops." But for now, the band is playing on, even though the game has become ever more and more unreal. Do you understand how it is that so many people and corporations are able to make so much money off of this war in Iraq? It is perfectly simple. What you do is get a contract from the

American Government, which borrows, say, another billion dollars to give to the Contractor. Then the Contractors vaporize $900 million, and put the final $100 million into their pockets. *Voila,* "free money"! To be sure, a billion dollars has been piled onto the National Debt, but that is all an unreal fantasy anyway, yet the hundred million is real money in the pocket. Let the band play on!

Well, while governments and contractors are playing this game, stuffing money into their pockets as fast as they can before the music stops, what is actually going to happen? If the National Debt is just a fantasy, which "everyone" (the "smart money") understands will never be repaid, what is going to happen? Can the levels of the National Debt just go soaring on and on to ever more unreal and lofty heights?

Well, no. No; the hard truth is that it cannot. The music is still playing on, but ever more and more you have the "smart money" managers glued to their computer monitors, watching for the signs of the music stopping. What happens is that declines in the financial markets can be very sudden and very brutal. The secret is to make money in this high-stakes game as long as you can, and then, when the music stops, be very sure that you are out of dollars, and out of any bonds payable in dollars! You can own tangible assets, like real property, but God help you if you have sunk the money from the sale of Grandma's farm into the bank, or paper securities! (I am not troubled by the collapse in the real estate market these days ~ editing this article in 2008. When Asian residents discover how cheap land is in the United States, relative to the cost of land in their own countries, they will bid up the prices of the land once again.)

Fundamentally, there are really only two ways out of this situation. One of them is through warfare. The *ultima ratio regis* ("last argument of kings") is their cannon. When a nation is going broke, the simple and obvious solution is to put your last remaining resources into fitting out your citizens for war. Then you can simply march into foreign lands, raping and pillaging, and bring home whatever you can carry off of value, just as the marauders who sacked ancient Crete did so many years ago. This is no longer a politically correct solution, however. In earlier days, this solution was so common that no one expected anything any different. Of course your neighbors would be marching over the border to seize your lands any time they feel they can get away with it. This is just the law of the jungle, after all, so what else is new?

Unfortunately, however, the law of the jungle is antithetical to any of the tenets of modern civilization. Having recourse to wars of aggression is to renounce any claims to civilization, and hasten a regression back to very primitive morality.

There is, however, one other little possibility, which has not escaped the notice of sharp bankers! There is, finally, a way to actually pay off that National Debt after all! The key, as the Chinese bankers so clearly understand, is to repay your loans with "dollars" of reduced value. Just to give you a simple idea, suppose agents of the US government decide that the time is ripe to shut off the music (having first sheltered all of their wealth into real or tangible assets ~ real property, gold, diamonds, works of art, Indian rupees, etc. [This is a joke. If the dollar collapses, "even" the Indian rupee will fall.]). Trying to take advantage of some brief window in which no one is expecting it, they suddenly pull the plug. When you read the morning paper over your toast and coffee, you might discover that, in the night, the US government has paid off the National Debt! What they did was to print up big stacks of billion-dollar bank notes, and paid everyone off! Perfectly legal. Now, of course, a hamburger will cost half a million dollars, but that is no longer the concern of the federal government, which has paid off its debt in full!

But that amusing little story is not the way it actually happens. What they do, instead, is nibble away at the value of the currency a little at a time, "so that no one notices." But what this means is that the fall of the dollar is very far from over. You may depend upon it that the dollar will continue to collapse, a little at a time, probably with a series of rapid falls, with brief leveling off periods in between, for the foreseeable future, as the United States gradually recedes from its position of dominance on the world's stage to take up the more humble role of the has-been, drinking beer with the Romans, Mongols, Spaniards, Englishmen, and Russians who have been there before them.

This, of course, is the "optimistic" scenario. The somewhat more pessimistic scenario would see escalating war on all fronts ~ Iraq, Iran, Pakistan, Korea, etc. Perhaps it is the deliberate intention of the cabal of wealthy and powerful people, fronted by the Bush regime, to ratchet up the levels of tension and fear in the world to the point where they can safely rule by Martial Law, bringing the world to the brink of chaos and annihilation until they can find a way to re-shuffle the deck in their favor. If they do this, of course, do not look to them to bail out the United States government, which is hopelessly bankrupt and has been for many years ~ no, they will go on lining their own pockets, bailing out of the sinking ship just as it is going down.

Oh, no ~ the former "optimistic scenario" of the gradual decline of the United States and its god, Mammon (the Almighty Dollar), is a much more graceful way for that vortex of negative energy to subside into irrelevance.

So the moral of this story is "don't be the last one to get out of dollars!" Dump your dollars now, and avoid the rush. Perhaps it is time to start hoarding rupees (or guns, depending on whether you are an optimist or a pessimist).

There is a positive side to this essay. If a major change of energy can take place, and a rapid uplifting of spiritual consciousness can spread throughout the land, then, in the rapid movement back to Clarity, a great prosperity may take the place of war, and (as a rising tide floats all boats) even the United States economy and the greenback Dollar may again reflect the value of prosperity.

The Cause and Cure of Disease

by *John Roland Stahl*

December, 2007

Some people have asked me, "What is the use of studying philosophy?" This question surprises me, because it seems obvious to me that an understanding of the abstract principles of philosophy will help us to understand the way the world works. When you understand the Process of Change going on in the world, then you can more effectively act in ways that might make this world a better place.

I don't want to repeat (yet again) all of my ideas of philosophy, but I can indicate the resources in which most of my ideas are laid out. First, there is the primary text of Hermetic philosophy, for which the rest of my writings may be taken as Commentary: *The Emerald Tablet.* Next, there is my introduction to Hermetic Alchemy: *Hermetic Alchemy.* Then there is my main exposition of my ideas in philosophy: *Patterns of Illusion and Change.* Finally, there are a couple of these short articles here that should be included: *The Survival of Life on Earth*, and *Speculations on Cosmology.*

I think those articles, considered all together, represent most of my important ideas in philosophy pretty well. There is no point in reviewing it all again here, but I may just point out a couple of ideas that are important in the context of health. Several times in those articles I refer to the idea that all good things converge at a point at the center, and movement away from that point goes out away from the perfection of God towards error. However, lately I have tried to clarify that the movement away is not just "bad," nor is the movement in simply "good." Both directions are two different aspects of God. (Or "two metaphysical principles" ~ it doesn't really matter about the words.) The Movement Out is Creative, while the Movement In is Receptive (using the concepts from the *I Ching*). Think Combinational Chess vs. Positional Chess, for example. But this movement out is only "good" with reference to the center line. As you move away from the center (and this is the God that creates the Universe) you first go into "Novelty," followed by "Complexity," then "Confusion," and finally "Chaos."

So the *Solve* and *Coagula* (movement away from the Center, and movement towards the Center) are only effective means for spiritual growth as long as the *Solve* returns to *Coagula* before drifting out into the realms of Confusion and Chaos. Endless *Coagula* without any *Solve* is just stagnation; too much *Solve* without a corresponding *Coagula* is just like a balloon in which the string is released.

Health is one of the most obvious and important applications of these ideas. When you are in a state of clarity, your health is good. When you are lost into confusion, your health breaks down.

All of this determines the strength of your resistance to disease, but there are situations of a physical nature which can undermine the healthiest lifestyle. The most important and problematic situation is the declining levels of oxygen in our atmosphere.

Everyone knows that the world is running out of Oil. "Peak Oil," they call it, meaning that all the easy oil has been extracted already, and it is all downhill and diminishing from here.

I use the expression "Peak Tree" to refer to something very similar concerning the trees. All of the easy trees have been taken down, and the remaining stands of trees are too few to be sustainable in any way, so our planet is losing its tree cover in a rapid way that will have a devastating impact upon the health of our planet. It is this idea that has generated my *Church of the Living Tree*, in which I point out the seriousness of the error, and suggest that without a massive effort to restore tree cover, our planet is doomed to the extinction of life.

Next comes water. The world is running out of water. Ever increasing populations are requiring ever larger amounts of water, and the margin of safety is getting smaller and smaller. This means that whenever there is any kind of drought at all, it can have severe repercussions upon people's lives.

But there is one more, and this is the one I have recently become stunningly aware of ~ Oxygen. The world is running out of oxygen! Everyone talks about the rise in the atmospheric levels of carbon dioxide, and they wring their hands about the consequence of global warming due to those elevated levels, but no one seems to have taken any notice of a parallel development ~ the loss of atmospheric oxygen. Many years ago (I don't know how many, because I don't have any references here, and I forgot where I learned this) the level of oxygen in the atmosphere was about 38%. Now it has declined to about 19%. And that is an average! In many cities, the levels of oxygen are so low that the air is positively unhealthy. And so, whenever anyone has any poor lifestyle habits, such as smoking, or a poor diet, they are at an increased risk of developing cancer or other disease.

Ever since losing my wife to cancer over twelve years ago, I have made a study of alternative therapies for cancer and other viral diseases such as AIDS, hepatitis, etc. What I have learned is that the most important single factor in the onset of disease is an insufficiency of oxygen. The therapy for someone who is sick is to promote a greatly accelerated absorption of oxygen, usually through some administration of ozone or hydrogen peroxide. (You can find lots of information about Oxygen Therapy on the internet.)

So, for everyone who is trying to figure out why there is an ever increasing incidence of cancer these days, there is the answer ~ there just isn't enough oxygen to go around any more! If you are in a poor oxygen environment (just about any city, or workplace) and you have any lifestyle issues such as smoking, or a poor diet, then you are at a greatly increased risk of getting cancer or some other disease. The single most problematic dietary problem is probably bad oil ~ especially heated oils, as in deep fried foods ~ the French fries and the carbonated drink are even more toxic than that burger.

The Indians understood the importance of the breath of life. Proper breathing will fill your body with "prana," which is simply oxygen, after all. The definition of "prana" has to do with life force, but it is really practically identical with oxygen, to keep it simple.

Now of all of the proposals put forward to ameliorate the problem of increasing levels of carbon dioxide, the simplest and most cost effective is to restore the tree cover over the earth. At the same time as the trees absorb all that carbon, they give off oxygen, so the restoration of the Trees is really of paramount importance. I can think of nothing else that could possibly compare in importance, from the point of view of the survival of life on earth, than an immediate program of tree planting.

One of the "Saints" of the *Church of the Living Tree* is Richard St. Barbe Baker, who, over the course of his life, and "with a little help from his friends," planted more than 26 trillion trees. That is 26,000,000,000,000 trees. That is a lot of trees, but that is the scale of what has to be done. We should plant another trillion trees every month. Our lives and the lives of our children depend upon it.

Instant Run-off Election

by *John Roland Stahl*

February, 2008

Many years ago I discovered the proposal of the "Instant Run-off Election" and realized immediately that it is so far out in front as a liberal or progressive political cause as to render every other cause a useless waste of time in comparison. Until we can secure the enactment of the Instant Run-off Election proposal nation-wide (world-wide), there is just no point in attempting to accomplish anything else worthwhile.

I can't believe that there is no "Movement" to make this happen. No one speaks about it anymore ~ no one acts as if it even matters much any more. The problem, of course, is that, by opening up the whole potential bonanza ("can of worms"? "Pandora's Box"?) of third, fourth, or thirtieth political parties, it will be bitterly opposed by both major parties. In fact, I can think of no other issue on which both Democrats and Republicans would share such a common view: a virtually unanimous opposition to any proposal which would give any other parties any meaningful participation in the politics of the nation. The only hope for a proposal like this is to take it directly to the people via a ballot initiative, perhaps first in California, where such a process is commonly employed.

In case I need to review the proposal, it is simply to offer voters more than one choice during elections. Suppose you have a hypothetical choice, for example, between George Bush, Al Gore, or Ralph Nader for President. For whom do you cast your vote? If you are only allowed one vote, there could be a real problem ~ you can't vote for Ralph Nader without risking throwing the election to George W. So the proposal allows you to vote for not just one, but several candidates ~ let us say three candidates, to keep it simple, yet interesting. You vote for first choice, second choice, and third choice; if your first choice be eliminated from the running, your vote automatically passes through to your second choice; should your second choice also fall through the cracks, your vote passes to your third choice. This means that you could vote first for your Aunt Sally, who, you are confident, would quickly sort out the nation's problems; your second vote could go to Ralph Nader; and your third and final stop-George vote could be cast for Al Gore. Today's computers would make such a voting machine perfectly simple to design and implement. (The fact that the elections of 2008, at least so far as the election of the President is concerned, does not seem to require such a proposal ~ at least, not as desperately! ~ should not detract from the argument; just consider the example given above, or look at any of the other races at stake in the election.)

(I just uploaded this article today, and then I read in the news that Ralph Nader is running again as an Independent! Well, suddenly that makes my whole argument relevant again, but I still do not think Nader's candidacy will have much effect in the coming election. I think Ralph Nader totally lost all of his credibility by intruding his ill-advised candidacy in the critical election of 2000. In the coming election, I don't think very many people will be voting for poor old Ralph, who would have been better advised to employ any remaining political capital he may have left in promoting this concept of the Instant Run-off Election, instead of attempting, once again, to throw his monkey wrench into the ring. Additionally, I hardly think the coming election will be close enough for Nader's candidacy to make any difference.)

The consequence of adopting this proposal, of course, would be that, if voters could vote for their real choices first, without risking disastrous political consequences, Ralph Nader might have received 30% of the vote or more ~ he might even have won, if people were not afraid to vote for him (and not terminally annoyed by his egregious folly of running at such an inopportune moment in time).

If anyone were to consider this proposal honestly, it is so brilliantly correct that no one could oppose it, and no other political cause could compare with it. For the first time in America's history, it would be possible for any political party, of any agenda whatsoever, to make a serious foray into electoral politics! The possibilities for democracy are so exhilarating and exciting ~ it could really stem the tide, and stop the inexorable slide towards complete political constipation which threatens to destroy the flexibility and resilience of the political system.

But as long as the major powers retain their death-grip upon the political process, there can be no future for democracy in the USA, Leonard Cohen's optimism to the contrary notwithstanding.

Faith

by *John Roland Stahl*
March, 2008

I have been interested in philosophy and religion all of my life, since my father and grandfather were Methodist ministers, and my father was also a professor of philosophy. However, by the age of six I just could not fathom the mysteries of religion. I could not comprehend the infinite. My first question was formulated as, "Where does the sky end?" I realized that the question could have no answer, yet to "go on forever" did not satisfy me either. "Where did the world come from? . . . But then who made God?"

I could not answer these questions, but I could not accept my father's answers, either. From that time I began to make a study of philosophies and religions from all sources, both traditional and "occult" (Hermetic Alchemy, the Kabbalah, the *I Ching*, etc.). Well, after a lifetime of study, I have finally worked out answers to these questions, listing as my principle sources of inspiration Hermes Trismegistus, Lao Tzu, Heraclitus, and Pythagoras.

But today's topic of interest is Faith. In a previous article *(Is Religion Good or Bad?)*, I have detailed some of the reasons why, in general, I am against formal professions of religious belief, as I consider them to be more productive of harm than of good. It would seem to me that anyone with a serious grounding in a spiritual way of life or a religious belief ought to be led inexorably to higher ground, and his life would gradually approach that center of clarity, love, and joy that I have described in previous articles. However, it appears that, for most people, the profession of a religious belief is simply the basis of separating everyone in the world into Believers and Infidels, as an excuse to go to war against the Infidels. If this were not so appalling to me in its pernicious consequences, I would find it very funny, since going to war over differences of religious belief is about the surest indication to me that the adherents of such belief haven't the foggiest notion of the true significance or meaning of their religious teaching.

Since I consider that most spiritual teachings share a very large core of similar fundamental ideas, I find it far more appropriate to emphasize the common ground in any spiritual teachings rather than to focus on any perceived differences. Thus, the adherence to any specific sect should be understood from the point of view of cultural affinity, rather than religious doctrine.

A great many (but not all) spiritual and/or religious beliefs are based upon Faith. That is, the candidate is asked to accept and believe some revealed religious doctrine on Faith alone. I consider this a very dangerous attitude, and one of the principle reasons why religious beliefs are so often found to be at odds with each other. Logically, a belief based on Faith is untenable ~ why should anyone accept any particular doctrine on Faith rather than any other alternate doctrine? There is nothing more useless than competing partisans of religious belief each touting their own Revelation as Gospel, while dismissing everything else as folly and error. In fact, acceptance and belief in religious doctrine on Faith alone is widely perceived as the highest and most commendable expression of many religious beliefs.

Sometimes it seems to be suggested that all a candidate needs to do is simply "believe" and he will be "saved" and enjoy eternal life. Such a deal! All you have to do is simply "believe" the suggested package of doctrine, accept a baptism (or other similar initiation, something like joining a fraternity), and suddenly you, too, will be with the Saints when they go Marching In ~ you will become of the company of the Elect, and ready to enjoy eternal life, while everyone else will be sent to eternal damnation by their loving Father.

I cringe whenever I see one of those giant billboards saying "And whosoever liveth and believeth in me shall never die. (John 11:26)" As if that were the whole message of the Christian Gospel! All you have to do is "believe" in Jesus, and you will live forever! And here I thought the message of Jesus was that we should love one another.

Little children should have faith in their parents to tell them the truth as they see it. But adults should take responsibility for their own beliefs, derived from reason. When God told Abraham to slaughter his only son as a burnt offering, it was only a test of Abraham's faith. But Abraham failed the test! He should have said, "Lord, when Thou tellest me to slaughter mine only son as a burnt offering to the Lord, then I know that the words cometh not from my God, but are words that cometh from the Devil who pretendeth to speak as my God, for my God would never ask me to slaughter mine only son as a burnt offering."

To which God would reply, "Well done, Abraham, my good and faithful servant. When I asked thee to slaughter thine only son as a burnt offering, it was only a test. Thou hast passed this test, and art found worthy to be the father of a nation."

Acts of God

by *John Roland Stahl*

May, 2008

Sometimes things go really well, and then sometimes it seems that everything goes wrong. Some things we plan are thwarted, and unexpected obstacles sometimes come along to divert us from our intended path. On these occasions, I try to retain perspective. I think to myself that I am still alive and healthy, and that puts me way ahead of a very long list of people, with the list lengthening every day. While we may worry about a tooth-ache that is bothering us, someone else is swept off the freeway and killed.

So, along those lines I noticed the headlines about a recent cyclone in Myanmar (Burma), with 10,000 dead. Just like that, 10,000 people are simply swept away by this cyclone ~ their stories are over.

Well, by this morning's paper the total dead is up to 22,000 with another 41,000 missing! That's over 60,000 people dead or missing from this cyclone! Just blown away by "an act of God."

I want to say that I don't believe that the cyclones are sent by "God." That is not the God I know! I am not the only one who has been troubled by the contradiction of a good, loving, merciful, and all-powerful God who yet blows away people by the thousands with one disaster after another. I have dealt with this issue in the Postscript to my main exposition of principles of metaphysics (and theology): *Patterns of Illusion and Change*, but I just want to repeat here that I understand "God" as the source of Order and Good in the world, in the midst of a swirling mass of chaos and confusion. Without the constant efforts of God, with everyone on Our side pulling an oar, the whole thing would descend into Chaos very quickly.

That appears to be happening these days! Horrendous as these "acts of God" are, they are cast into the shade by the deliberate villainy of Man to Man in acts of war that are crushing civilization under the heel. But, in addition to the wholesale slaughter of innocents through the organized efforts of war, there are also numerous small villainies happening all the time, all over the world, through some combination of ignorance, fear, or greed, and all of this is just dragging us down.

So I want to ask everyone ("everyone" that is, who loves the Earth and wants life to continue) to get on deck, find an oar, and start hauling! Don't just sit around drinking beer saying that it's all going to hell. It is We who must take responsibility for the future of life on earth.

An Open Letter to Barack Obama

by *John Roland Stahl*

10 November, 2008

President-Elect Barack Obama:

I hope that it will not matter at all that you are unlikely to read this message. From everything I have seen, it seems likely that you are part of the spirit of energy that will bring a new spiritual consciousness to the world, and you already know all of the ideas which I mention here. In contrast with the abysmal level of the Bush Administration, there is already a huge groundswell of momentum for a massive change of direction, an undercurrent of growing spiritual consciousness world-wide that will provide the catalyst for a major change in the evolution of life on earth.

I am very pleased with your proposals for green development to provide renewable alternatives to the burning up of our dwindling supply of fossil fuels (which, incidentally, are worth far more for their industrial products potential than they are as simply fuel to burn up).

Your tax proposals are also long overdue. Deficit spending must be immediately curtailed, and the U.S. Debt must be repaid as quickly as possible. It is obvious that the Age of Military Power is passing, and the dominance of countries on the world stage will be determined henceforth almost exclusively by economic strength, not military strength.

The American Nation is on the verge of bankruptcy, and everyone is terrified to think of what might happen if the United States government were physically unable to meet its obligations. Forays into military excursions at this juncture are not a positive sign!

For the United States government to pull back from the brink of insolvency, as from the brink of war, those individuals holding most of the wealth of the country must be taxed. This, of course, runs counter to the natural and almost universal tendency of the wealthy and powerful in every country: to retain as much of the wealth and the power as possible in their own hands. For the wealthy and powerful of this nation merrily to increase their wealth while effectively tossing the cost of their winnings onto the backs of the American taxpayer in the form of debt, is a grotesque folly which could lead to the collapse of the American government. Haven't they ever heard of the story of the goose that laid golden eggs? They should take very good care of that goose, not slaughter it in an attempt to get all the gold at once.

If the United States is able to run a tighter ship and manages to survive economically, even paying down some of that debt, then the international reaction will be very favorable, and confidence will be restored to the markets. But if the United States just goes on running up trillion dollar annual deficits to add to the existing mountain of debt, then they are out of touch with reality and are in for a very rude awakening, which a great many people around the world will welcome with considerable satisfaction.

Of course it is the whole world which you must consider; never think of yourself as just the Champion for the United States and its Interests; you must be in tune with the entire field of life energy on the planet, and help us progress to the next level of being, because if life survives on earth it will be because that stream of life energy comes into a harmonious state of clarity and balance, instead of spinning out of control from confusion to chaos.

Problems are as circular as the Solutions to those problems. The more you grind away on a politically problematic footing, the more your problems will continue to increase. But when you have a clear, positive, and forward moving energy going on, you should find errant energies finding their way back to the main central stream of flowing energy, and things begin to get better at an increasing pace.

Let your administration mark the passing of the Ugly American from the stage of the world. All of the problems for which the Ugly American has felt the need to use force have only consolidated themselves and become very much worse. Just look at the way the jihad is shaping up. Of course Muslims are being groomed as the heirs to the Communists, Blacks, Jews, Gays, and the Infidel. They are the ones to fear and hate; they are responsible for all of the problems we face. But what continuations are suggested by these attitudes? Of course, it only gets worse. The more troops George Bush sends to Iraq, the more the embers of anti-American hatred are fanned, and the more that attitude becomes cemented into place.

I recently heard a political commentator, announcing his forthcoming show, say ". . . above all, should we be afraid of the Russians?" ~ Oh, no, we do not have to be afraid of the Russians. What we have to do is to convince the Russians that they no longer have to be afraid of the

Americans! (This may not be an easy sell.) Nor do we have to fear the Iranians or the North Koreans ~ we simply have to convince them that they do not have to fear the Americans any more, an idea which may take generations to sink in, so we had better start with the program now.

Everyone, all over the world, wants to be allowed to live their life in peace, in harmony with their neighbors. Yet everyone lives in fear all the time, like wild animals. All of this can be turned around ~ it is simply a matter of the direction of the energy. If the energy can make it past the Turning Point of Change, then it will get easier all the time as the errant energies all over the world will gradually be restored to a harmonious flowing within the main line of life energy. The other direction leads to increasing complexity, leading outward towards increasing levels of confusion and belligerence, and reaching ultimately into chaos.

But if the tangle of life energy on our planet can come together in clarity and order, then the energy will become simple, sleek, and efficient, and positive change will evolve at a dizzying pace, leading to a whole new world which must be totally unimaginable to everyone who is on the "ante" side of the change (the *Omega Point*, as suggested by Teillhard de Chardin).

All of the political problems in the world are expressions of mutual fear, out of which comes hostility, aggression, and violence. Once the Fear is addressed directly, and can be transcended, then the other manifestations will gradually subside until peace is achieved.

Economic problems are simply the inevitable consequence of political problems. The world is experiencing an economic crisis because the world is bursting with political problems all over the planet. As those politically volatile situations are ameliorated, then the wheels of commerce will begin to turn again, soldiers can return to their farms and their families, and life can begin to get better and better for everyone.

So it is really very simple ~ turn around the energy of the planet from flinging itself apart from confusion and chaos back towards clarity, balance, and peace, and all of the problems of the world will solve themselves, and the Kingdom of God will come on earth.

Next.

Further Advice to Barack Obama

by *John Roland Stahl*

16 February, 2009

The first step is to understand the way the world works, and how things happen, which is all about the Sequence of the Process of Change.

The second step is to participate, by discovering the most important thing you can do to influence the path of the process of change. I have attempted to address all of the most important problems facing the survival of life on earth (not limiting it to human life), and here are my findings: Plant More Trees!! Trees are the most important expression of Life on this planet, and the earth is greatly suffering because of the loss of its trees. From the watersheds, to soil erosion, from the loss of its role converting carbon dioxide into oxygen, to climate change, the population of Trees on the planet is essential for the survival of life itself.

Send every out-of-work American to plant trees; the earth will thank you for it, and will repay with bounteous abundance.

Another Letter to Barack Obama

by *John Roland Stahl*

24 March, 2009

Like a great many people all over the world, I have been enormously encouraged by your successful campaign to the Presidency. I had been predicting a bad end to this country, but now I see some glimmer of hope. Perhaps it may not yet be too late to make the immediate and radical changes needed to halt the slide of this country into poverty and oblivion.

I even felt that I understood your position with respect to Afghanistan! Of course, it is not easy being President, even a very popular one. It is still necessary to proceed very carefully. You not only have to do the right thing, but you have to manage so that your agenda will be allowed to proceed across political minefields.

Accordingly, I thought I understood the political reasons for your bellicose stance with regard to Afghanistan. It was necessary to pound the war drums proudly in order to cover the retreat from Iraq. By talking tough over the Afghanistan question, you would be able to accomplish the difficult task of withdrawing from the morass of Iraq without arousing too much opposition.

"But," I said to myself, "once the Iraq withdrawal were accepted politically, once you had entered upon your Presidency and were enjoying the increased stature and approval that would come from your new administration, then," I speculated, "you might evolve the political process to enter upon some period of diplomacy. While standing ready to unleash a whole new military offensive in Afghanistan, you might temporize, and gradually the diplomatic process would proceed while the military option would be 'temporarily' withheld. Finally, to everyone's surprise, you might find grounds for an exit strategy from Afghanistan on vastly better terms than could ever have been obtained from military activities (just ask the Russians what they think about fighting a war in Afghanistan . . .). Best of all, such a diplomatic solution would save untold billions of dollars that the country just cannot afford to spend, frankly."

I sincerely hope that I have correctly guessed your intentions. It is a very clever plan; in fact, it is brilliant. No one has to know that it was your intention all along to extricate this country from a totally unwinnable conflict in Afghanistan (a conflict that would make Vietnam look like the Falkland Islands) by diplomatic evolutions rather than by military actions.

Letter to Richard Dawkins,

author of *The God Delusion*

by *John Roland Stahl*

March, 2009

I was very glad to come across your book, *The God Delusion*, as I have studied philosophy all of my life. My quest to understand the world began with a theological crisis at the age of six. My father was a professor of philosophy and a Methodist minister, so, naturally, being an intelligent child, I was immediately an atheist, as soon as I understood the views propounded by my father.

"Who does he think is listening to his prayers?" I would ask myself, along with the obvious question, "Well, then, who made God?" However, even at that tender age I understood that it is not sufficient to reject an idea until and unless you are able to propose a reasonable alternative. And so I began my search to understand the world without resorting to any theological postulates.

I studied everything from Christian theology to the Kabbalah, the *I Ching*, Hermetic alchemy, magic, and witchcraft, and many other sources, not omitting the likes of Swedenborg, Aleister Crowley, and Madame Blavatsky. Eventually, I began to piece together a world view that featured a principle by which I was able to understand the patterns of order in the cosmos. I first referred to this as "the Philosophers' Stone," but later, thinking I were precocious and witty, I called it "God."

However, as my understanding of these mysteries became more and more clear, I began to realize that my labeling of this principle as "God" was not really so clever or even very original; I had just rediscovered what intelligent people had understood as God all along. If anyone had ever suggested to me in my youth that I would eventually come around to a belief in God, I would have dismissed such a notion as so far beyond wildly improbable as to be entirely negligible.

Well, here I am, and I have some views which I have not found expressed anywhere else, and I have also developed ideas which I later discovered to have predated my "invention" of them by some thousands of years. I discovered, in my readings, that many very similar ideas kept popping up, so I tried to organize those ideas in a systematic way. I had already begun to do so when I discovered the idea of Pythagoras, in which he suggested that the abstract ideas of numbers themselves are the purest symbols for the "Mysteries of Nature." For some years I had arranged representations of the first four numbers, which I arranged horizontally, each one on a separate page (*vide: Patterns of Illusion and Change*). However, when I stacked those images vertically, I was astonished to discover that I had exactly reproduced the Tree of Life from the Hebrew Kabbalah. What is more, every position on my designs held the exact same significance on the Tree of Life. This not only allowed me to acquire a new understanding and appreciation of the Tree of Life, but it also confirmed to me that my investigations were on the right track, since I had independently recreated the Tree of Life which was essentially identical to the design which has come down to us over the millenia.

All of that was simply an aside, to sketch out some of my preliminary lines of investigation. I turn now to your book, and the first thing I notice is that you decline to address any serious or sophisticated understanding of God. You decide that it is far easier, and much more fun, to confine your efforts to arguments against primitive and fundamentalist notions of God, rather than to venture out into the more rarified air of serious discussion.

Consequently, I found your book pleasantly amusing in spots (many of your analogies are quite colorful), but not really relevant to serious contemporary conceptions of God, although I agree with many of your principle points. I share your disgust, for example, with the God of Abraham. If the Old Testament God were to come around my door, I would offer him a meal and a night's lodging (out of "Christian charity" ~ not religiously motivated, however ~ I guess I would just find one evening with the old brute tolerably interesting), and then, after an early breakfast of toast and coffee, I would tell him to just shuffle on down the highway.

§

My understanding of God may be a bit confusing because I have two quite different visions of "God," each of which seem entitled to be called "God," for historical reasons, but it is not at all clear that the two entities are one and the same. In the first place, there is God the Creator of the Universe. I find an important role for God in the creation of the Universe, but my God is neither omnipotent, omniscient, omnipresent, nor even "good." You might find my discussion interesting, and you might easily decide that nothing about it requires introducing the title of "God" to the concept. You can find this in an article published on my web site at www.tree.org/cosmology.htm.

In case you wanted to view my whole presentation of philosophy and metaphysics from the beginning, you can read my *Patterns of Illusion and Change* at www.tree.org/patterns2.htm. There you will find (in the *Postscript* to the Second Edition) my second candidate for the throne of God ("Will the real God please stand up?"). This second candidate has many important qualities long associated with God, but many other qualities are totally absent. This God, for example, is no more omnipotent or omniscient than the last one, nor did He have any role in the creation of the Universe (unless you follow a rather obscure line of logic that discovers these two manifestations of God to be one and the same after all). I don't want to repeat the entire discussion here, but, in brief, I imagine the role of Consciousness elevated first (and foremost) to a planetary scale, and then to a cosmic scale. Following the line of thought that the higher the organism the loftier the development of consciousness, I have proposed that the Cosmic Consciousness of God is even more fully conscious than human beings: a Deity with whom one might realistically be able to communicate.

To be sure, this is nothing like the God whom you so effectively ridicule, but I think it accounts for the nearly universal understanding of God that people have felt since time immemorial. It may have been natural for primitive men to assume that their "God" were omnipotent and omniscient, but I do not find any reason for such suppositions. I think God (limited in most of my speculations to "*Gaia*," considered as the most important theological focus for human beings, which includes all life on earth, plants and animals as well as people) is just doing the best She can, carrying the flag of Life with its order, balance, harmony, and growth in the face of the rampaging chaos that She finds all around Her.

Given the scope of a single letter, I do not attempt to develop this idea fully here, but the analogies of human consciousness and group consciousness make the idea seem very reasonable to me. It solves the problem of evil at a stroke! "How can we believe in a God who is omnipotent and omniscient as well as good, merciful, and loving, in the face of all the manifest evil in the world?" Simple ~ God is not omnipotent, and we are just doing the best we can.

I have read lots of very obscure treatises on many arcane subjects, and at first I would read with my blue pencil, arrogantly marking the author's errors as I found them. I have always known, since the days of my high school debating society, that it is far easier (and usually more fun) to take the Negative position in an argument. We learn very early on that to ridicule your opponent (or his arguments; take your pick) is usually a more effective strategy than to rely purely upon reason. I think the English are usually much better at this than Americans. I remember reading some articles by Bertrand Russell which I found very funny; it was very amusing to watch him shred up his opponents (well, usually he would confine his attention to his opponents' arguments; I must do him that justice). But much later on in my studies I began to realize that many authors may have had some interesting idea after all, even though the language they may have used to express it might have been faulty. I underwent a major shift in my reading style ~ instead of simply considering the words themselves, which anyone of Russell's experience and talent could easily shred into nonsense, I began to "read between the lines" and tried to discover what reasonable or interesting idea the author might have had that he was trying to express with his inadequate words. In this way, I discovered quite a few very interesting ideas which Russell would never have noticed.

I have figured out that when authors would write about "occult mysteries" there were often some very intriguing ideas buried under their verbiage. They pretended deliberately to conceal some important Secret, without which one could not be expected to understand what was being discussed. However, I became convinced that they were not concealing any Secret at all! They were trying their hardest to convey their idea, even when the idea itself were not fully clear to themselves! They were skirting around some precocious idea that they couldn't fully grasp themselves, but they were convinced that they were onto something important, if only they could figure it out, and they were leaving their notes for the guidance of later adepts or scholars. I have encountered some very impressive ideas which I have gleaned from writings of this sort *(e.g., Cœlum Philosophorum, Seven Canons of the Metals,* by Paracelsus, as obscure a work as you can find anywhere, yet out of which I pull one dazzling plum after another).

Now, in the case of religion, it is easy and fun to take it on its literal face and reduce it to shreds, laughing all the while. But I suggest, Professor Dawkins, that you might miss some very interesting ideas this way.

I notice that you employ certain key arguments over and over, confident in their impregnability. One of them is that it is useless to nominate "God" as the creator of the universe, because any God capable of designing the universe in all its complexity, to say nothing of simultaneously fielding prayers from millions of devotees, would present a far more complex "solution" than the problem it attempts to solve. But, before I introduce my own solution, a "God" which is supremely simple, yet fully capable of producing the universe in all of its complexity, let us take a closer look at the problem itself.

The problem is very real. Thomas Aquinas tells us that there must be a First Cause, and that is what we call "God." Your reply is that "God" does not advance the argument at all, but only makes it infinitely more complicated. However, I have not seen, anywhere in your book, an alternative suggestion as to how the universe came into being. It is not enough to postulate some "Big Bang." What caused that big bang to happen anyway? Why did it happen at that particular moment? What was there prior to the big bang? If there was nothing, what does that do to the law of conservation of matter and energy? It is all very well for science to describe the Big Bang, beginning from the first twelve-millionth of a second after it happened, but what about the initial event itself?

So, for better or worse, there remain some real problems, as yet unresolved, concerning the initial cosmogenesis. I consider this a theological or philosophical problem precisely because it concerns territory upon which scientists fear to tread. Well, "fear" is not the right word, but a scientist will not speculate beyond the data (it is practically the definition of a scientist). As yet there are no clear data upon which anyone has been able to found a satisfying answer to the questions of cosmogenesis; therefore it remains for philosophers and/or theologians, who do speculate ~ yes, even beyond the data! As a scientist, perhaps you have no respect for this or interest in it, but there are plenty of people who find themselves desiring to speculate, even when there do not exist adequate data to allow for a scientific solution.

Thomas Aquinas has defined "God" as "that which was responsible for the First Cause." You can't argue with a definition. You might not like to use the word, but that's tough. OK, out of respect for your truculence on the use of the word (and to escape the historical baggage which it carries) let us paraphrase Aquinas by saying, "We define *the Philosophers' Stone* as that which was responsible for the First Cause." Now, it is meaningless to deny the existence of the philosophers' stone, since it is defined in the context of whatever was responsible for the First Cause. The appropriate question now becomes, "what is the nature of the philosophers' stone?"

Now, when we put the question in this way, we are far more likely to advance our understanding than we might have been by simply rejecting the concept. Rejecting the concept of God is just as useless as positing a God in the first place! If you reject God as the name to refer to the first mover, then what do you propose in its place? (This is simply the inverse of the child's question, "Who made God.")

However, it is not entirely useless to introduce a term such as "God" (or "the philosophers' stone"). Language is built up of complex ideas to which we assign the symbols of new words, and then we are able to use those words in the construction of yet more complex concepts, in much the same way that mathematical formulæ, or the theorems of Euclid, are built up out of smaller units. You may as well say that the whole of Euclid's geometry is frivolous, since all of it is analytically contained within his definitions and axioms anyway.

So, while it clearly does not resolve any problems of philosophy or theology, to put a term upon the agency of the First Cause is not totally useless. It allows us, for example, to proceed to the next (and far more important) question, "what is the nature of the philosophers' stone?"

You have found that notions of God are all but universal in every culture and every time. Rather than just to reject the whole concept, it seems far more stimulating to discover just what is at the bottom of this idea. It may turn out to be nothing at all (your position), but I take the position (habitually, when considering complex or surprising propositions) that there may be some real and useful idea going on, and I try to discover what it is. In a surprising number of occasions, I discover something real underneath an idea which may, on the face of it, appear to be nonsense to the likes of Bertrand Russell or yourself.

In the present case, I propose that what is responsible for the nearly universal belief in God is a kind of collective unconscious, which I suggest is literally self-conscious, not only in the same way that a human being is self-conscious, but even more than that, since the consciousness of all life on earth would constitute a much higher organism than a chicken, a dog, a cat, or a human being. I have no trouble imagining that all of life on earth (we may call it "*Gaia*," to use a simple term to stand for a complex idea) has all of the attributes of a living organism, including self-consciousness, and to a higher degree than any expression of life found on earth.

There are many surprising phenomena which might be explained by this concept (for which science has nothing to suggest, other than to reject the premise). When a mother suddenly jumps out of bed in the night, feeling that some accident has befallen her son, many miles away, it can be explained, at least in principle, as knowledge transmitted through the medium of this universal life consciousness. In the same way, prayer could conceivably make its way "to the throne of God," and it is equally plausible to imagine that this Consciousness is able to direct the energy of life in ways that might amount to the answers to prayer. Note that since this Consciousness is not omnipotent, nor (even) omniscient, it could not be expected to ameliorate the ravages of flood, fire, pestilence, earthquakes, etc. We speculate that this Consciousness is composed of the accumulation of all lesser consciousness on the planet. Like any other being, it will have an "ego," the function of which is to assist the organism to survive, first, and then to flourish and grow. To the extent that lesser beings contribute to this goal, they are closer to God.

Obviously, there are many people on earth who are lost in confusion, flailing around in regions of chaos, whose energy is only working against God and the survival of life. A sober assessment of the present state of the earth would suggest that God is not necessarily winning the battle of Good over Evil, another famous paradigm that appears to have some sort of meaning. I do not, however, attribute a consciousness to a force of Evil, as in the old concept of the Devil. I consider the Consciousness of God to be at a point at the "center," a place of balance and clarity where all good things converge. On the other hand, while this point of perfection is the singularity of God, there are an infinite number of ways to move away from God into error and chaos (with progressively diminishing consciousness). By the way, I do not want to get unnecessarily complicated in this introductory summary, but I have figured out that both of these directions are aspects of "God." The focus of clarity and balance at the center is what holds the cosmos together into patterns of order, but the movement away from the center is the original spark of life which created the cosmos in the first place. Think of the analogy of evolution: there could be no life at all unless the patterns of energy followed reliable laws, but there could be no evolutionary growth without the constant reaching out into the unknown in search of novelty.

Notice that this concept of God would not have been present at the founding of the cosmos, nor is it omnipotent or omniscient. It would have evolved along with every other aspect of our world.

Speaking of evolution, I have noticed that when you speak of evolution, you speak about "natural selection" which has to do only with the selection of variants after they have appeared. I guess you are satisfied to go with random mutation as the cause of the variants. But I want to look into the nature of this "random mutation." And what do I find? Funnily enough, I find exactly the same principle that I nominate as the agency behind the First Cause! Thus, while my main idea of God (this *Gaia* hypothesis) seems to have nothing to do with the First Cause, it turns out that all of evolution seems to proceed upon the very same basis as I am proposing for the First Cause itself! The logic here may be a bit obscure, and it is really not important to me to make any positive identification of the two ideas of God, but I find it very interesting.

So what is this motive principle that causes the Cosmos to come into being in the first place, and which causes all life continuously to reach out into further complexity? I call it "The Laughter of God" (which is the title of my most recent book). The laughter of God, which causes all of this, is based upon the joke ("a separation of Illusion from Reality") of attributing meaning to opposite ideas which together add up to the same thing:

nothing. Specifically, the initial joke is the distinction imagined to exist between Zero and Infinity. Of course, the two terms mean exactly the same thing, *at the limit*, only apparently referring to two different concepts by imagining an alternation between them. This sets up an imaginary field of vibration between the two opposites. Successive applications of the same joke cause endless reaching out into further complexity, until we finally have the appearance of an entire cosmos, which is really just Maya all the time, as the entire boondoggle adds up to Zero (or Infinity), the Singularity through which it passes from time to time as it works through its cycles.

There is even a mathematical formula for this idea of God:

$$0 = \infty$$

The source of this random mutation at the heart of evolution is that anything might switch suddenly into its opposite at any time. If it were not for this fundamental uncertainty at the basis of the cosmos, everything would have worked itself out, finally, to zero or infinity, leaving us without any universe at all. However, due to this principle (noticed at the level of quantum mechanics), we have a dynamic and interesting cosmos that goes on amazing us day after day. And Who knows to what further adventures it might lead?

You might ask where this proposed concept of mine might come from, and I can only reply that it is inherent in the metaphysics. The concepts of Zero and Infinity, along with the Present Moment: NOW, all popped into Being simultaneously, initiating the entire cosmos *ex nihilo*. I cannot reduce it further than that. If there is a Mystery that remains, I am content to call it God.

By the way ~ throughout your book you discuss numerous ideas relating to religious practices, and I find myself in agreement with almost everything you say. However, I want to point out one inconsistency that may be important, since it highlights the way circumstances can appear radically different depending upon one's point of view. Chapter 9 leads off with the sorrowful account of poor Edgardo Mortara, who was taken from his Jewish household at the age of six and raised as a Catholic. You report how the Catholic establishment could not imagine anything other than that they were performing a wonderful good work, saving this poor boy from his inevitably distressing life as a Jew by inviting him into the warm bosom of the Catholic faith. I fully agree with your view that such an arrogant point of view is thoroughly wrong.

However, later on in the same chapter, you detail the story of the state of Wisconsin filing suit against Amish parents who preferred to raise their child in their own community with their own customs rather than releasing him to the public school system. In this case, you seem to be siding with the state of Wisconsin, lamenting the loss of education for the poor Amish boy! What is the difference between the two cases? The difference is that you seem to feel that a respectable Jewish upbringing is probably preferable to a Catholic upbringing, but, on the other hand, you have this feeling that, *of course*, a modern education in the public school must be better than for any child to stay at home learning his family's values. The problem is, who gets to decide? The child? I believe the Supreme Court made the correct decision ~ we allow parents the right to determine the way they want to raise their children, up to the age of majority.

Personally, I happen to agree that a modern education would be preferable to being raised in an Amish culture, but it is not for me or you to dictate to other parents how they should raise their children. I can understand, in principle, the point of view of the Amish, who have their own community values which they feel are superior, in many ways, to contemporary culture. Something will clearly be lost, but something else will clearly be gained, and who is to say what is best? I will stand up for the rights of parents to make the call. Pulling an Amish child out of his home and sending him to the public school to be raised in the modern style is exactly the same crime as pulling a child out of his Jewish home to be raised as a Catholic, or taking away a Native American child from his family to be raised in Western culture. Your good intentions are comparable in every respect to the Catholics who were convinced that they were doing the right thing to give Edgardo Mortara all the advantages of life as a good Catholic. The moral here is always to look very carefully at the other side of every issue, and not to be too quick to be so sure that you are always right.

Reality Economics

by *John Roland Stahl*

March, 2009

I have written a previous article about what I call "reality economics" (*vide: The Fall of the Dollar)* but here it is March of 2009, and, like everyone else in the world, I am watching the entire worldwide economic system falling into chaos, and I am baffled by the methods which are proposed to "restart the economy." Everyone seems to think that if only everyone would start buying products once again, then everything will be just rosy. I remember George Bush's simple recipe for curing an ailing economy: we should all go shopping. Now I hear on the news that Germany has come up with a brilliant plan to get their economy moving again: they have instituted a program of government incentives for people to buy new cars by paying prospective new car purchasers to junk their older cars.

Here is an opportunity for me to explain again what I am trying to suggest by "reality economics." While the German government wants everyone to buy a new car to stimulate their economy, and they are so convinced that this is the solution that they are providing government money to wreck older cars, I would propose a diametrically opposite strategy.

I would propose that, instead of spending trillions of dollars trying to pump up sagging economies, governments should act like every other business or private party in economic trouble: stop spending money! If banks, mortgage companies, insurance companies, or automobile manufacturing companies are unable to operate profitably, let them declare bankruptcy and liquidate their assets. If company A wishes to pay out multi-million dollar bonus packages to its executives, they will not be able to compete against company B which asks all workers, from executives on down, to accept a pay cut in the interest of remaining solvent so that they will stay in business and be able to continue paying any salaries at all. If demand for a company's goods are way down, close the factories until inventories fall to levels where it will be appropriate to reopen the factories again. Instead of encouraging everyone to buy a new car, encourage everyone to fix their old one instead.

If there is widespread unemployment, fine; just invite all the unemployed to live in peace on the Free Farm, planting trees or growing fruits and vegetables. Sooner or later enterprising individuals or companies will figure out something useful to do which someone, somewhere will pay them for, and gradually a new economy will evolve to replace old industries which are out of date.

Take the automobile industry, for example. It is not just General Motors that is in trouble; car makers all over the world have seen their sales drying up and blowing away. The fact is that there are just too many cars in the world, and not enough oil to run them much longer anyway. Let these companies go bankrupt one by one, selling off their assets until the few companies that remain are able to survive by supplying cars to what remains of the automobile market. Let the market determine which companies will survive to make the next generation of cars. Or, alternatively, let those companies whose executives are paying themselves fat salaries and bonuses just fail in competition with leaner companies which devote their attention to spending their resources more wisely, with a view to providing greater value to their customers ~ better quality vehicles for less money than their bloated competitors. I still believe in the free market ~ if everyone had not panicked but simply let the losers fail and drop out of the race, then the companies which survive would remain a part of the evolving economy, and those which couldn't keep up would fail, and their stockholders would take the loss.

No company is "too big to be allowed to fail," and this includes the United States of America. If foolish economic policies push the country into bankruptcy, well, so be it! If the voters and taxpayers just shrug their shoulders while the treasury is being systematically looted, whom will they blame for the decline and fall of the United States?

I remember after George Bush's second fraudulent election most Americans simply shrugged their shoulders and said, "I guess George Bush won," when, in fact, he had done nothing of the kind. In striking contrast, it was only a few weeks after that fraudulent election that there was another fraudulent election, this time in Ukraine. However, in the case of Ukraine, some hundreds of thousands of Ukraine citizens wouldn't stand for it; instead of shrugging their shoulders, they took to the streets of Kiev, loudly denounced the fraud, and refused to go home until the government gave in and promised new elections (in which the other party won).

I also hear on the news that the Federal Reserve has decided to print up another trillion dollars or so; overnight, the dollar loses much of its value on the news. But, what can you expect? They have no more money, and no one will buy any more Treasury Bills, so they can't think of anything else to do except to emulate the Zimbabwe economic miracle. Perhaps it is time to shop for a wheelbarrow (to carry your money) before the prices go up.

No one is going to bail out the United States government. China will only continue to purchase treasury bills as long as they believe that it is in their interest to do so. When they decline to renew their loans, the world-wide economic upheaval will make the present mess look like a Sunday School picnic.

When anyone finds themselves in financial trouble, the solution is not to try to spend your way out of your troubles; the solution is to spend less than you are earning, so that you can manage your debt before it reaches levels from which it is mathematically impossible to recover. I remember the spending of the Reagan years. The short term consequence was an appearance of prosperity; the long term consequence was a massive impoverishment of the country which was directly responsible for the present financial crisis.

So, what is the message here? Is it simply to stop spending money? No; it is more complex than that. If the government spends money bailing out failed companies like banks, mortgage companies, insurance companies, or any other failed or failing business, or if they pass out goodie bags of cash money in the form of tax breaks, then we can look forward to the collapse of the United States government in our lifetimes. But if the government spends money for good value received, such as schools, health care, railroads, investments in alternative energy, and massive programs of tree planting, providing edible fruits and nuts, or other worthwhile crops, as well as addressing the principle causes of climate change and declining personal health (the declining levels of oxygen in the environment and corresponding increase in levels of carbon dioxide; *vide: The Cause and Cure of Disease*), then there is some hope that these worthwhile expenditures, embodying the underlying principle of "reality economics" will eventually repay their costs and even lead to an improvement in the country's financial health. On the one hand, I am hopeful to see that President Obama is trying to make a lot of very worthwhile expenditures, but, on the other hand, I am worried to see trillions of dollars being thrown away into Black Holes. The only hope of survival for the economies of any country in the world is to follow the principles of reality economics and make every dollar pay.

It may be difficult to stand by and watch while companies like General Motors go bankrupt, but every good gambler has to know when to hold 'em and when to fold 'em.

A New World

by *John Roland Stahl*

April, 2009

There is a sense in which I have welcomed all of the upheaval in the world today. I am a student of philosophy, and one of the sets of symbols and imagery that has always appealed to me most strongly is the Alchemical Process of Change. The process of Change is absolutely fundamental to any idea of philosophy or metaphysics. The Greeks were barking up the wrong tree, looking for some ultimate particle (which they called "the atom"). No, what is really fundamental, in this cosmos, is the process of Change (*cf:* Heraclitus). That's where it all happens. The present moment, *Now*, is the Philosophers' Stone, the agency of change.

The alchemy lesson is very short and simple: *Solve et Coagula*, "to break apart, and to join together." It is the alternation of these two directions of energy that is responsible for the unfolding of the infinite cosmos. In practical terms, what that means is that in order for something new to come into being, the old has to be broken down. For a long time (all my life) I have had the idea that this world was in need of a major makeover. I imagined myself, two millennia later looking back at these primitive times ~ from a larger perspective, these are still the Dark Ages. From the vantage point of some time in the year 4089, there is not all that much difference between the tenth century and the twentieth, or twenty-first.

Now is the time for people of the earth to work out a new political and economic arrangement, which encompasses the whole world, and is emphatically NOT any kind of *Pax Americana*, nor even a *Pax Sinensis*, for that matter. A lot of people seem to get really terrified at any such notion. "Surely you don't mean a *New World Order*?" Am I with the Illuminati, trying to promote some sinister plot? Well, yes, I am. Now it is out. *(Sinister* just means "to the left."*)*

All I can say is that it is not surprising that anyone should be terrified of any such notion as a major makeover of the world! Conservatism is a very natural concept: "if it is working, and life is going on, don't fix it!" The problem is that it isn't working, and life is no longer going on. Not only are people dying like flies from cancer, AIDS, and other diseases, due to the direct cause of the insufficiency of oxygen in our atmosphere (itself directly caused by the loss of the trees), but the business as usual for the human race includes wholesale genocide in so many parts of the globe that it is no longer news. So it is time for a whole new Contract, one which includes the entire field of life on the planet, to make the effort to keep life alive, at least for one more generation; and perhaps the next generation can figure out a way to pass on some remnant of life to the following generation.

What am I talking about here? How about a world-wide Constitutional Convention, to work out terms for a new world? As I see it, all of the problems of the world stem from one fundamental problem: the fracturing of the field of Life energy into a multitude of diverse energy streams, like Don Quixote "jumping on his horse, and riding off rapidly in all directions." Yes, the problems of global warming, cancer, and the loss of the trees are serious threats to life, but until the entire planet is somehow united politically, the threats to its survival, while overwhelming, just cannot adequately be dealt with.

So what is the practical continuation of this idea? How about the formation of an international World Union Company to set up an entity that will address itself to the problem? It will not be easy, but, until the political union of life on earth be realized, there can be little hope for much substantial progress against the enormous problems facing the survival of life on earth.

[update, 2020 – my search for the source of the Don Quixote quotation turns up an obscure reference to ". . . Leacock's hero, who mounted his horse and rode off in all directions."]

Secret Societies

by *John Roland Stahl*

May, 2009

There are so many popular books out there, titles beyond number, detailing the accounts of Secret Societies throughout the ages. In almost every case, the authors of these volumes try to convince themselves (and, as an afterthought, their readers) that these Secret Societies have endured intact throughout the ages, still retaining their Secrets, and still carrying on their secret activities in furtherance of their special agenda.

I have made it a major part of my life's work to examine these Secret Societies, ancient and modern, along with their doctrine and their secrets. I have studied from original sources, as well as from private initiation into the mysteries from old sages, masters, and adepts. I would like to present my findings here.

There are, broadly, two kinds of Secret Societies ~ political, and philosophical. In many cases, of course, societies whose major activities are political hide these activities under the cover of a purely philosophical society.

According to the Grand Conspiracy Theory, all of these Secret Societies, throughout the ages, have been interconnected ~ essentially, variants of One Big Mother of All Conspiracies. While many of these secret societies have had specific political aims, *e.g.*, the destruction of the French Monarchy conspired by the Masonic Lodges during the days leading up to the French Revolution, the main and obvious goal of all of the politically motivated societies has always been the simple and happy thought of Ruling the World.

My first conclusion has to do with the continuity of these societies, both political and philosophical. Yes, in just about every case there has been direct continuity of these secret societies from the very earliest times up to the present day. However, this continuity has not been through the numerous outward forms. Many thousands of Secret Societies have come and gone, over the years, and the names of many old ones have been applied to new incarnations, but these societies, as formal structures, have been continuously evolving and changing, and most of them have had significant periods during which the formal structure has not survived; but the real transmission of the ancient knowledge, mysteries, and secrets has always been through the direct instruction of old sages, masters, and adepts to new students and initiates.

In this way, the most important aspects of the intercommunication of these holders of the ancient wisdom have been conducted more through the mycelial connections which pervade the substrate, rather than the more visible occasional fruiting bodies of the formal Secret Society.

To continue the analogy of the mushroom, the "occasional fruiting bodies" of this underlying mycelium perform a very important role: that of scattering seeds far and wide, and finding candidates for initiation. Thus, the proposition is that the really important repository of ancient wisdom (or political conspiracy) has never been the occasionally manifesting Secret Society, but rather the presently living body of sages, masters, and adepts (under which I include many others using other titles ~ altogether different titles in the case of political conspiracies, of course) which has continued as a kind of living organism within the much larger organism of all life.

So, let us get right to the point, focusing on political conspiracies: is there some Secret Society of persons who meet, either in smoke filled rooms or conclaves at the grotto, and control the world by their actions? Sure; there are lots of them! But is there one, or even some few, of much greater importance, whose members really do exercise the dominant controlling hand over the evolution of life on earth? That answer has to come in two parts: in the main, no: there is no one minding the store; they have all gone fishing, or they are Out to Lunch. No one really knows what is going on! There are so many influences all along the way from every quarter that trying to figure out what is happening and what is going to happen is hard enough, let alone making any effort to control it. This world is careening along at haphazard, with no one at the helm; it is stumbling and blundering in the dark, and unfolding into chaos on all sides.

But, on the other hand, there are lots of people who band together for a common purpose, and there is a way that their "secret society" forms itself into a matrix of mycelial connections that, here and there, rears its head as a Conspiracy mushroom, spreading seed to new ground. When it comes to the Conspiracy to Rule the World, what does it take to become a Member? The answer is that it takes a significant portion of Wealth and Power to accumulate influence. So, like any Masonic Lodge, the higher degrees are composed of those of progressively larger shares of Wealth and Power, up to those who are most powerful at the top.

This concept organizes the formation of a structure that is far more important than any specific collusion in conspiracy for particular advantage. It creates the imperative for every level to maximize the rate at which the Wealth and Power is further accumulated into the hands of the Wealthy and Powerful.

This Beast, too, is a living organism. It has been in existence since the days of Cain and Abel, and has been the cause of the perennial belief in the Grand Conspiracy.

The problem is that the goals of this living beast, of maximizing their own advantage for their own benefit, are in conflict with the survival of life on earth. That is why I propose that the political authority be taken out of the hands of the Wealthy and Powerful, and put into the hands of those who will guard it as a sacred trust for the survival, health, and flourishing of life on Earth.

But the Secret Societies which hold the transmission of the ancient wisdom have always seemed more interesting than political societies. Secret Societies are hierarchical and are arranged as a series of concentric circles through which the candidate proceeds towards the center, where the final secret is held. The whole point and essence of a "secret" society is that there is some Secret that they have and guard, that other people don't know. This principle is so fundamental that it really doesn't matter at all whether there is a secret or not. The old Master of the Secret might finally whisper to the candidate for the thirty-second Masonic degree, "Ivory Soap floats!" That isn't the Secret, but it would satisfy the requirement just as well, since the vast majority of seekers never get anywhere close to the center, where the true mysteries and secrets are held (even when they think they have, or have been told that they have).

In the case of the Freemasons, Hermetic Philosophers, Rosicrucians, Cabalists, Gardeners, and others, there is a Secret, although at all times and places there have always been only a very few who have known it. In many cases, the Guardians of the Secret don't even understand it themselves, but faithfully transmit all the Keys with which their Society has been endowed in hopes that some future scholar, philosopher, adept, and/or visionary might rediscover the Secret. There remain many such Keys to which the Secret has been lost, such as the Tetragrammaton, the four letter Name of God, the meaning of which has been revealed in our own work (*vide: Patterns of Illusion and Change*). The Secret is the final resolution of the Mystery of Life which illuminates the nature of being. I have expressed it as a picture of the Third Arcanum.

The Stone that the Builders Refused

by *John Roland Stahl*

June, 2009

"The stone that the builders refused will always be the head Cornerstone."
~ Bob Marley

Those words by Bob Marley are intended to convey a very nice message; however, there are a couple of errors in the way the idea is presented. In the first place, "the stone that the builders refused" would never be selected as the head cornerstone! The quotation is taken from *The Book of Psalms*, 118:22, and the original quotation might be translated as something like, "the stone that the builders refused will become the capstone (keystone of the arch)."

There is a big difference in the qualities required for the "head cornerstone" and the "keystone of the arch." In general, when a mason is building an edifice of stone, he will be looking for stones that are as perfectly square and straight and regular as it is possible to find (carefully dressed that way from the quarry). As for the head cornerstone, it must be the most perfectly square and straight and regular of all, since all lines and levels will be based upon it. For the rest of the building, the best stones will be wanted, of course, although some stones may be accepted which are not entirely perfect, but when a stone is really not square at all, but is some kind of trapezoid or worse, it will be entirely rejected.

This rule applies to the great majority of stones used in construction, but "the keystone of the arch" is an altogether different story. The arch was of critical importance in Medieval stone masonry construction, as it made possible a whole range of construction features that included windows, doorways, and even major support columns and galleries. The "key" which made an arch work was a stone at the top center of the arch that was not square: it was wider on the top than on the bottom, so that the pressure of the remaining stones would maintain the shape of the arch from collapsing. Of course the builder would search among the rejected stones to find some irregular stone that would be suitable for use as the keystone of his arch.

Now, taking another look at Bob Marley's song, it is easy to discern his intention: while square and straight and regular may be a useful ideal for an orderly society (when the concept is applied to people), it is the one that is different from the others that is singled out for the most important and critical positions. While masses of society may be built up of row upon row of identical, square, straight, and regular units, it will be the different ones, the original, creative, and independent ones which will take on the leadership positions. The ultimate illustration of this is an army, in which absolute conformity is literally drilled into the soldiers so that the whole becomes a uniform and mindless machine, while it is the senior officers who retain their independence and creativity, and make all the important decisions. I think it is an unfortunate aspect of modern society that, all too often, schools are run along the lines of armies and military academies, in which all novelty, originality, and creativity is deliberately squelched out of any incipient nonconformist pupil who might dare to think for himself, or have an original idea.

However, there is another problem with Marley's presentation of his idea: when he says "the stone that the builders refused will always be the head cornerstone," it almost sounds as if all that is required is for a stone to be rejected for it to be exalted to the position of head cornerstone. In fact, however, there will be a great pile of rejected stones, and all but a very select few will be left as rubble, perhaps pounded down into road base.

So we might suggest an alternate reading for Marley's song: "the Keystone of the Arch will always be a stone that the builders refused" (all keystones are made from rejected stones, probably additionally worked, but not all rejected stones become keystones of an arch, and certainly not head cornerstones).

The moral of this story is simple enough: while we can respect the importance of the great mass of uniform, square, straight, and regular (stones, people, or anything else), we should also recognize the even greater importance of the few that are unique, "creative," or otherwise different in some essential way from the straight and regular majority, as it is this introjection of Novelty into the system that allows the universe to remain in existence at all, and is responsible for evolutionary change and growth.

Knotweed

by *John Roland Stahl*

July, 2009

Re: BBC World News: 23/VII/09 "Knotweed."

So many times I am baffled by some idea ~ some prevailing attitude ~ that just seems to me to be wrong, wrong, wrong. For example, cutting down trees just to chip them up into paper is the single most damaging act of terrorism against planet Earth in its entire history (which may be coming to a close soon if that virulent pestilence, the human race, is not brought under control quickly). From the loss of oxygen and the accumulation of carbon dioxide, to soil erosion, loss of species habitat, and the loss of many valuable forest resources, the liquidation of our ancient forest is an act of astounding stupidity.

Speaking of getting a virulent pestilence under control, on tonight's broadcast of the BBC World News there was an article about the problem of knotweed, and the way in which it was proposed to combat it. The whole approach seemed to me to be so incredibly wrong and stupid as to merit criminal investigation! Knotweed is apparently a very tough weed that spreads persistently, and invades and takes over wherever it goes. Apparently millions of dollars (and pounds) are spent annually to combat this pestilence, and now Science has come up with a natural biological control for the problem. They are breeding a population of super vampire insects that will attach themselves to the knotweed and gradually suck out the plant's juices. This is proposed as a solution to the problem!

Before I tell you my solution to the problem, let us take a look at the deliberate production of these biological weapons of mass destruction in the form of the very hungry, and equally virulent, sucking insects that will go head-to-head with the knotweed. I am a gardener, and I love to spend a morning out in my garden, watching my roses grow. I always grow a great many plants wherever I go, and more seem to spring up around me, as I plant seeds and take cuttings all the time.

I know all about those sucking insects! They are the scourge of the earth, the blood-sucking parasite that just lives by draining the vital fluids of other forms of life. Mosquitoes are part of that gruesome company, and the presence of mosquitoes on the planet is the strongest argument I have ever heard against the existence of God. I must say that I have studied philosophy, metaphysics, and theology all of my life, and I have finally understood a concept of God that explains that problem, as well as the whole "problem of evil" (how can you believe in a merciful God who is all-powerful and all-good, in the face of the manifest evil that is in the world?). The solution is simply that God is not all-powerful, and He actually needs all of the help He can get! In fact, that is what He is, and from where He gets His power ~ from Us.

Anyway, back to these disgusting, blood-sucking insects (of course I use the term "blood-sucking" as a figure of speech, because the insects they are breeding for the knotweed will be consuming plant fluids, unlike the mosquitoes I was vilifying earlier). Anyone who would deliberately propagate and cultivate a strong, hybrid, super-vampire insect that is powerful enough to go head-to-head against knotweed should be immediately apprehended and apprised of their error. These insects may not confine themselves to knotweed, but may go after anything juicy. I would want to see a huge population of sterile males introduced into the colonies of sucking insects instead of seeing them deliberately cultivated so that they can be thrown against the knotweed problem.

The worst thing about the idea is that even if it is "a complete success," the whole project is still incredibly stupid! What would happen, of course, is that a huge infestation of bugs on the knotweed would gradually reduce the vitality of the knotweed, but the knotweed would fight back with all of its considerable resources, so the result would be huge populations of diseased and unhealthy knotweed, covered with bugs, looking disgusting, dirty, evil, and contagious; and it would be prevailing in that state for the foreseeable future, in an endless death struggle.

The knotweed may be a persistent and dominating pest, pushing out other growth, but at least it is admitted to be something of an ornamental, when it is not infested with bugs. In fact, just about any healthy stand of greenery of any description, would already be a huge improvement to the environment in many places. In cities, for example, if there are healthy stands of knotweed where there would otherwise be just waste land with a few struggling weeds, it doesn't look like a problem to me. So, until a patch of knotweed can be eradicated, you might as well leave it alone. Turning the stand of knotweed into an ecological disaster of diseased bushes covered with bugs ~ an ongoing situation that would probably go on forever ~ neither the knotweed nor the bugs would ever give up the field ~ would be so much worse than the *status quo*. It would hardly be much better than dosing the plants with toxic pesticides ~ the traditional control. The ebb and flow of their battle would determine the landscape of that knotweed patch for the next hundred years, but it would gradually stabilize at some diminished proportion of its healthy state, as the knotweed would probably manage to survive with a certain population of virulent, sucking bugs all over it.

That solution is so stupid that it frightens me as well as baffles me. I would much rather see flowering, fragrant rose bushes, than a stand of knotweed under attack by a host of sucking insects. All of the leaves would get covered with insects as the insect population would continue to grow fat and healthy off the laboring knotweed. It is scary to think of what might happen if the insects were actually to win, and kill off the knotweed ~ where would they go next? Would they just quietly allow themselves to go extinct, since their need were finished, or would they obey the biological imperative and try to survive and multiply, looking for new hosts? And finally, even if the bugs manage to kill off the knotweed, the whole remaining mess, bugs and all, would still have to be dug up and carted away, before the land could be restored to available utility. I suppose that project is government funded.

But, as I promised in the beginning, there is a better way to deal with the problem of knotweed; my solution is better than dosing them with toxic pesticides, and it is better than launching a cultivated strain of vampire sucking insects into their environment to attach themselves to the plants in perpetual embrace forevermore.

I simply offer to purchase that knotweed at $35 per ton, as much as you've got. Spread the word, and when a serious knotweed harvest gets underway, we will be there to purchase it.

I have made hand-made paper for many years, and I have been very impressed at the quality of many, many common plants and agricultural waste material in the matter of their potential utility as a source of fiber for paper-making. It seems to me to be really stupid to make paper out of trees. If wood were used to make something valuable and durable ~ a home or well-made furniture ~ that doesn't seem to me to be so much of a problem. It is the wholesale slaughter of clear-cuts for the chipping mills that gets me sickened.

There is a much better way! Instead of harvesting the last of the ancient forest so that our mailboxes can be filled with junk mail, there already exist many sources of available cellulose for paper, mainly from alternative annual fiber plants, such as flax, hemp, and kenaf, and agricultural waste from the production of food, so that plenty of paper can be made without cutting down any more trees.

Re-plant the forest in food crops: chocolate trees, carob trees, fruits and nuts, oil-bearing trees, and many others, and just use all the available alternative cellulose materials for paper-making. Case in point: knotweed. In general, the tougher a weed is, the more promising it is as a candidate for paper-making. When you have a really tough, obnoxious weed, it will probably make most excellent paper. Kenaf is a good example. It is a tropical plant that will grow very large and fast, ready to harvest after a single growing season, and it is loaded with cellulose, the stuff of paper. I am not sure how good knotweed will be as a paper source, but it doesn't matter. Whatever cellulose there is will break down into paper, and whether it turns out to be a real winner like hemp and kenaf, or of lesser quality like sugar cane bagasse or wheat straw, it will almost certainly repay the value of $35 per ton that I have offered to pay for it.

Bring it on! Allow some time for waiting in line, as the trucks are weighed and paid for their load of knotweed (calculated on a "bone dry" basis, and the relative humidity of the plant material will be factored into the price we pay). Since I could easily pay for 100 tons per day at that rate, and even more if it were available, I expect that people will be harvesting stands of knotweed wherever they are found, staking their claim before other bounty hunters get there first. We are talking total clear-cut harvesting of the knotweed, a process that will be infinitely superior to waiting for a hundred years while the bugs gradually bring down the mighty knotweed ~ or fail in the attempt! No; it will not only be much better, but it will be a whole lot faster simply to cut all of it down. One day you have a big patch of knotweed that doesn't look too bad except that it's everywhere and won't give anything else a chance; and a few days later you have a patch of bare ground, seeded with wild-flower seeds, or planted in grapes, and another truck waits on line for the weighing scales, loaded with all of that knotweed.

Please forward this article to those scientists from the Super Vampire Insect Project, and tell them to go take a walk in the garden.

John Roland Stahl

The Church of the Living Tree

The Evanescent Press

Earth, Pulp & Paper

Born: March 32, 1647, Concord, New Hampshire, U.S.A.

Papermaker, Printer, Bookbinder, Philosopher, Visionary, Fool.

Father: Roland C. Stahl, PhD, Methodist minister and professor of philosophy. Mother: Elizabeth; Brother: Mark; Daughters (with Kinu Haas): Jade and Garnet.

1961-1965: **Classical High School**, Providence, Rhode Island: Latin, Greek, History, Literature.

1965-1968: **Brown University**, Providence, Rhode Island: Philosophy, History.

Independent Studies: Eastern and Western traditional, occult, and esoteric Philosophy, Theology, Epistemology, Cosmology, Ontology, Teleology, Metaphysics, Logic, Ethics, and History of Religion.

My publishing career began with fine editions of my own works hand set in letterpress and hand bound in permanent hard cover editions, culminating in the publication of the elaborate *Theophany* on hand made paper in 1979. While this has always been satisfying, the high cost of small editions limited distribution to a very small circle. Computer typesetting and "desktop publishing" (all of which I do myself) has allowed me to produce larger editions with more text, and to produce them at low cost. However, while I am reaching a larger audience with these books, I have always been interested in the finer quality of hand printed books in small editions.

Accordingly, I set up complete facilities for making paper by hand. Since the requirements for letterpress printing are similar to the requirements of fine artists for printing their works on paper, I have furnished hand made paper to the artistic community as well as for my own needs.

The writing material I have been working on for most of my creative life has mostly had to do with the most fundamental and abstract elements of philosophy and metaphysics.

Early on I was influenced by Bertrand Russell: in *Why I Am Not a Christian* he points out that there are so many contradictory religions in the world that it stands to reason, as a matter of logic, that no more than one of them can represent the truth (implying that they are all bunk). However, as my studies carried me deeper and deeper into most of the world's systems of philosophy or religion, Eastern or Western, revealed or occult, I began to discover that, when I finally penetrated to the core of any system of thought that attempted to explain the primary mysteries of nature, I found the same essential ideas, albeit clothed in many extravagant and varied costumes. Turning Russell's idea around, I began to be convinced that these ideas must collectively represent some kind of truth. Since then I have been trying to elucidate precisely this thread of truth in as clear a way as possible, drawing upon the symbols of Hermetic Alchemy, the Hebrew Kabbalah, and the Chinese *I Ching* as the most ingenious of the esoteric systems of thought I have studied.

When one of my students once asked me why they should take any interest in metaphysics, I was really surprised. Surely it must be clear that we study the *Process of Change* in order more satisfactorily to direct our own personal evolution as well as that of the entire human race, and, finally, the entire biosphere of life on the planet. To this end, my recent interests have been moving more toward applications of philosophy rather than the abstract forms of the ideas themselves.

Social, economic, and political philosophies, however, are extremely complex and are well outside my own fields of expertise, but a few ideas come through emphatically: in the first place, I agree with a great many original thinkers that no real breakthrough in planetary evolution can take place until the entire human race is somehow united into a single, stable political entity.

The second clear idea is that the most important way to safeguard the physical and biological health of the planet is to plant trees. The human race and other plant and animal species have evolved and flourished on a planet covered with trees. Let us express our optimism for the future by re-planting the forest and the garden.

My present work focuses on new directions for the paper industry. In my own work of the last few years, I have experimented with alternative fibers, principally hemp and kenaf. Most of the paper we have made at the Evanescent Press has been made from a pulp base formed of hemp and kenaf (some of the hemp is locally grown, and some is from a mill in Spain; the kenaf is processed ourselves from raw fiber, grown in California). Because of the poor record of pesticide use on the cotton crop, we began to use much less cotton in our paper.

Since half of all harvested trees end up chipped up for pulp, we have been advocating alternative fibers for the commercial paper industry. We have cultivated a variety of fiber plants at our northern California location, including paper mulberry, hemp, kenaf, milkweed, thistles, and nameless weeds.

My new company, Earth Pulp and Paper, is now setting up pulp mills to make pulp from alternative (non-wood) fibers, mainly hemp and kenaf.